D1548532

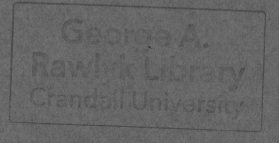

The ethical standards of the British House of Commons depend almost entirely on the personal ethics of its individual members. Parliament expects that its members, as holders of a public trust, will be "honourable members" in both name and deed. Maureen Mancuso examines the current state of British legislative ethics and raises important questions about whether the ethical standards of an institution should depend entirely on the personal ethics of individual MPs.

Based on extensive personal interviews with more than one hundred MPs, Mancuso is the first to take a systematic approach to the investigation of British legislative ethics. She identifies a significant divergence in ethical attitudes and divides MPs into four types: the Puritans, who stake out the moral high ground; the Servants, who conform to the traditional ideal of the MP as public-spirited constituency advocate; the Muddlers, who are not bothered by personal conflicts of interest; and the Entrepreneurs, who use their position to achieve an end not explicitly prohibited. She explores the implications of this unexpectedly diverse ethical ecosystem, along with various possibilities for reform.

All those interested in British Parliament and parliamentarians will find this book, with its unique insights into Westminster, essential reading.

MAUREEN MANCUSO is associate professor of political studies, University of Guelph.

The Ethical World
of British MPs

MAUREEN MANCUSO

McGill-Queen's University Press
Montreal & Kingston • London • Buffalo

Legal deposit first quarter 1995
Bibliothèque nationale du Québec

Printed in Canada on acid-free paper

This book has been published with the help of a grant
from the Social Science Federation of Canada, using
funds provided by the Social Sciences and Humanities
Research Council of Canada. Publication has also
been supported by the University of Guelph.

McGill-Queen's University Press is grateful to the
Canada Council for support of its publishing program.

Canadian Cataloguing in Publication Data

Mancuso, Maureen
    The ethical world of British MPs
    Includes bibliographical references and index.
    ISBN 0-7735-1261-6
    1. Great Britain. Parliament. House of Commons –
Ethics. 2. Legislators – Great Britain – Professional
ethics. I. Title.
JN677.M35 1995   398.410766   C94-900910-5

Typeset in New Baskerville 10/12
by Caractéra production graphique, Quebec City

For Kevin

Contents

Acknowledgments

There are many people without whose help this book could not have been produced. First, I must thank the one hundred members of parliament who gave so generously of their time to participate in the survey. Without their cooperation this project would not have been possible. I also am indebted at Westminster to the security guards at the St Stephen's entrance and the Central Lobby attendants who expedited my entry into the House and assisted in identifying my targeted sample MPs.

R. S. Lankester, A.J. Hastings, and Roger B. Sands, the former and present registrars of members' interests, gave me their time, copies of the register and numerous reports of the Select Committee on Members' Interests, as well as updates and information about the committee's operations. Austin Mitchell, MP, gladly served as a test pilot for a number of drafts of the research instrument and helped perfect the wording of the questions. He also provided the necessary current details about parliamentary salaries and allowances.

This book would be less than it is without the conscientious oversight of David Butler, Nuffield College. From the beginning he has enthusiastically supported this research, sharing with me his voluminous knowledge of Parliament and parliamentarians. Even from across the Atlantic I constantly benefited from his well-placed guidance and comments.

At Nuffield College, Byron Shafer and David Miller provided both encouragement and assistance by way of commenting on chapter drafts. Mark Philp at Oriel College was helpful about the theoretical discussion of legislative ethics; his comments and suggestions were much appreciated. Brenda O'Neill of the University of British Columbia provided much-needed assistance with all facets of SPSS^x programming and interpretation.

Michael M. Atkinson of McMaster University, friend and chief critic, gave unselfishly of his time – proofreading the entire manuscript, sorting out my statistical nightmares, and advising on the presentation of the data.

This book is dedicated to Kevin Porter, my personal editor-in-chief, who has patiently endured the entire process. His insight, perspective, support, and technological expertise have sharpened both the content and the presentation of my research. His contributions and encouragement far outweighed my exasperation with having to relocate virtually every comma in the manuscript.

Donald Akenson and Philip Cercone at McGill-Queen's University Press encouraged me to prepare this manuscript for publication. I would also like to thank Rosemary Shipton for her professional and effective editing of the text.

This book has been published with the help of a grant from the Humanities and Social Science Federation of Canada. The University of Guelph also assisted with publication. I must thank the British Council for their generous financial assistance and support. I am grateful to the Canadian Parliamentary Internship Programme for the opportunity to pursue my doctoral studies in Great Britain. Thanks also to the editors of *Parliamentary Affairs*, in which selected material from this book has appeared in different form.

The Ethical World of British MPs

Introduction

> Right now in this place, there are not high hopes for ethical standards. It is unstructured. No one tells you what is expected of you. There is no guidance. You are pretty much left on your own.
>
> A member of parliament

The ethical standards of the British House of Commons, as an institution, depend almost entirely on the personal ethical determination of its individual members. The same cannot be said of many other legislatures: the United States Congress, for example, has constructed a substantial regulatory edifice – composed of statutory restrictions, codes, and bureaucratic watchdogs – to govern, direct, and shape the behaviour of its legislators, as well as to enforce its own ethical self-image. While this more formal system does not guarantee a more elevated political morality, it does provide its membership with a host of tangible rules, prohibitions, and guidelines. To a greater or lesser extent, other legislatures have followed suit, codifying and specifying their ethical expectations.

In the House of Commons, however, only a few broad normative generalizations express Parliament's ethical self-conception, and the paucity of formal structures make it difficult to examine in any detailed or accurate way the interactions and mechanisms that govern the ethical behaviour of MPs. Individual members are given wide latitude in interpreting for themselves which types of activities are appropriate and which are inappropriate. Each MP is ultimately expected to make such decisions based on the dictates of his or her own conscience. A guiding body of specific rules, restrictions, 'official' interpretations, and precedents is notably absent. Instead, MPs must build and maintain personal ethical standards to govern their behaviour.

The primacy of individual attitudes in shaping institutional behaviour means that an understanding of these attitudes is fundamental to a comprehensive view of Parliament. The perceptions, judgments, and preconceptions that shape the ethical decisions of MPs are the foundation of British legislative ethics. Unfortunately, almost nothing is known about the substance of these attitudes. MPs are exhorted to avoid "activities inconsistent with the standards the House is entitled to expect from its members,"[1] but as the opening quotation indicates, there remains a great deal of uncertainty over what those standards and expectations encompass.

The image of the honourable member permeates the institutional structure of Parliament, its internal procedures, and even its rhetorical conventions, which dictate that MPs refer to one another through the formulaic epithet "the Honourable Member from ..." To impugn or challenge another member's honour remains the gravest of insults. Election to Parliament is assumed to confer heightened ethical insight into public affairs. Thus Parliament presumes that deviation from the standards of honour will be entirely attributable to the rare and unfortunate election of a scoundrel who perverts his honourable calling. In a field of "honourable gentlemen," such an individual would be easily identifiable. Yet this simplified, black-or-white moral world may have little correspondence with the reality of conflicting interests and motivations of contemporary members of parliament.

Thus several disturbing possibilities exist: members' behaviour may be less consistent with these nebulous standards than expected; some or even many members may be unclear as to the actual content of the standards; or the standards that are in fact prevalent in the House may be quite different from formal requirements. If it is true that MPs are not sufficiently informed of what is expected of them, their real attitudes may vary widely from the "honourable member" ideal promulgated by the traditions and etiquette of the House.

Further, despite a resurgence of scholarly interest in the political attitudes of the parliamentary elite, the extent to which the ethical perceptions of MPs are aligned and integrated remains unknown.[2] Parliament implicitly assumes the existence of a broad ethical consensus among its members, but this assumption has not been verified empirically. Measurement of the perceptions and views of individual members may indicate that, as Searing found to be the case with respect to the "rules of the game,"[3] this important ethical consensus is a hopeful illusion.

The implications of ethical dissensus are far-reaching. Should there be a multiplicity of competing ethical standards operative in the House, rather than a single common standard, then much of Parliament's ethical strategy is dependent on a false axiom. If different members cannot be expected to resolve similar ethical quandaries in the same way, then, in the absence of coercive regulatory mechanisms that do not rely on this expectation, Parliament's means of controlling its own ethical atmosphere is severely weakened. Individual conduct considered "unparliamentary" can flourish and eventually become institutionally accepted. This ethical deterioration leaves the House vulnerable to progressively legitimized abuse, misconduct, and corruption.

The importance of MPs' attitudes is heightened by the extensive intermingling of public and private roles and resources in Britain, where "grey zones" of behaviour are frequent facts of life.[4] A good example of such intermingling has been the problems of a number of select committee chairmen, notably Michael Mates, who, while chair of the Defence Committee, served as a paid consultant to a lobby company specializing in helping defence manufacturers secure contracts. His entanglements and those of his colleagues have come under scrutiny by both the media and the House Select Committee on Members' Interests.

A more complete understanding of the ethical underpinnings of Parliament is especially important in the current climate of increased attention to ethical matters. Legislatures worldwide have in the last decade been preoccupied with ethical introspection and reform: studies have been undertaken and, in many instances, reform packages introduced. Yet the "Mother of Parliaments," reluctant to probe its own norms and procedures, risks being left behind by its offspring as a source of inspiration and a model for emulation. During this same period, Britain has undergone significant sociopolitical and economic change. Parliament's system of ethical management, premised on the concept of *noblesse oblige*, may have been overtaken by the ascendance of a neoconservative ideology that encourages fewer restraints on self-interest at all levels of society.

At the same time, other cultural forces have been at work from the opposite direction. Researchers have pointed to an ongoing value shift in western industrialized states.[5] The transition to a post-materialist society embodies a growing desire for participation and inclusion in the political process. A materialist electorate may have tolerated or ignored ethical irregularities as long as they did not significantly impede the provision of basic services. Post-materialist voters, however, tend to focus more closely on process rather than result. Increased attention to ethical issues is one byproduct of this shift.

This concern, however, cannot focus on anything more substantial than supposition, tradition, and the occasional leak or scandal. What is missing is empirical information about how MPs make their ethical decisions, decisions that are the fundamental building blocks of British legislative ethics.

This book is an attempt to supply the missing data. Based on interviews with one hundred randomly selected members of parliament, it explores, both theoretically and empirically, the attitudes of

MPs towards political corruption and legislative ethics. By systematic analysis of the MPs' perceptions on general and specific ethical issues, a description of the overall ethical disposition of the House will be constructed. The variations in these perceptions, especially the readily apparent and wide division over what does and does not constitute corruption, will be broken down and examined by means of an attitudinal typology of MPs. The differences of opinion and attitude depicted in this typology will be assessed in order to understand their origins, their strength and persistence, and their consequences.

Chapter 1 discusses the theory and operation of legislative ethics in Britain. The existing, largely informal framework that governs the ethical behaviour of MPs is summarized. The reliance of the system on the discretion and honour of individual MPs is noted and examined. This overview leads to the identification of two major interconnected problems that challenge the system. Parliament must ensure that the large amount of discretion it grants to its members is exercised wisely and in accordance with institutional goals. Yet this effort is confounded by the multiple roles MPs are required to play, as competing legislative, representative, and private interests come into conflict and circumscribe the autonomy of members.

In Chapter 2 the research methodology is discussed and explained, and the information gathered in the interviews is categorized. Based on their observed tolerances for a number of potentially corrupt acts, the MPs in the sample are divided into a fourfold, two-dimensional typology of ethical attitudes. This chapter explains how the typology was constructed and introduces the four types of MPs – Puritans, Servants, Muddlers, and Entrepreneurs.

Chapters 3 through 6 explore in detail the attitudes, perceptions, and characteristics of each of the four types of MPs. Included is a general perceptual profile, and a background and personal profile, which outlines the various political, spatial, and socioeconomic traits and factors found to be significantly associated with MPs' attitudes. These chapters will also reveal the MPs' reflections on a number of ethical issues, such as the Register of Members' Interests, outside employment, lobbying, and sanctions and discipline. Finally, the comments of the MPs will be used to pinpoint the ethical strategies they employ in the parliamentary environment.

Chapter 7 synthesizes the profiles of the four types and examines how they can be expected to interact in the context of ethical reform. Types that would favour or oppose particular efforts are identified and the possibility of shifting alliances between groups of MPs with different goals and perceptions is examined. At the same time, these interactions provide a blueprint for the ethical ecology of the House.

The conclusions arrived at in this book will provide a picture of what is and what is not ethical in the minds of British legislators. Specifically, the research will indicate what the political elite believes constitutes a corrupt act; the factors that shape and determine MPs' attitudes towards corruption; the degree of consensus among the elite; and the factors to which existing subcultures can be traced. This book has relevance not only for social scientists but for policy-makers as well. An empirical record of the attitudes and perceptions of MPs is an essential tool for the assessment of the effectiveness of existing ethical guidelines, and in the creation of new mechanisms to ensure the ethical conduct of legislators.

CHAPTER ONE

British Legislative Ethics

Members of parliament routinely confront potential ethical conflicts as they conduct the business of elected office. As candidates they are required to help raise party funds. As employers they hire staff and administer the operations of at least one and perhaps two offices. As public officials, they take responsibility for the perquisites associated with their position, such as franking mail and claiming travel allowances. As voting legislators they must reconcile their personal inclinations with the dictates of their party. As parliamentarians they are approached to accept the hospitality of foreign governments and of business and other organized interests. Few guidelines, written or unwritten, exist to help MPs resolve ethical dilemmas. Instead, they are forced to rely on a personal standard of right and wrong.[1]

But what are these personal standards? In the mind of the British MP, what constitutes corruption? These are questions rarely asked, and even more rarely answered. Given Britain's propensity for secrecy, the public knows very little about the ethical standards of parliamentarians. And because there are few statutes governing the ethical conduct of MPs, informal rules, norms, and conventions are critical in shaping the attitudes of MPs towards political corruption.

Most parliamentary norms and conventions[2] are procedural in nature and few, other than parliamentary privilege, pertain to the ethical conduct of members. Except for the revelations contained in published diaries of former parliamentarians such as Richard Crossman or Barbara Castle, and the remarks made during House debate at the height of the Poulson scandal,[3] MPs' perceptions of legislative propriety remain largely unknown. The only way to determine the content of these informal rules is to ask the MPs themselves. The core of this book consists of a questionnaire, administered to one hundred randomly selected MPs, designed to determine both how MPs evaluate allegedly corrupt acts, and to what extent, if any, MPs subscribe to a common set of ethical standards. This book asks the crucial and heretofore unanswered question, "What are the ethical standards of MPs?" and seeks to answer this question by examining the attitudes of the MPs themselves.

Questions of ethics, morality, or corruption have received little political or scholarly attention in Great Britain. Yet the headlines of leading newspapers have continued to reveal allegations of fraud, deception, dishonesty, profiteering, security breaches, and sex scandals. Such allegations have implicated local officials, a number of MPs, ministers, the deputy chairman of the Conservative Party, and even former Prime Minister Thatcher.[4] It has thus become increasingly difficult to describe the British Parliament as free of the taint of scandal.

In the literature on political corruption, the study of legislative ethics is a relatively new endeavour. In the past, attention to the subject has been sporadic, arising in response to particular allegations or scandals and declining after individual cases have been resolved. Thus, while there has been a certain amount of reactive interest in morality in government, journalists, interest groups, academics, the public, and legislators themselves have not considered in depth the ethical framework of the legislature. Concern for the standards against which legislative conduct should be judged, for the punishment of those who violate these standards, for the wisdom and efficacy of codes of conduct, even for the fundamental definition and scope of ethics within the legislative process, has been notably absent from the political debate.[5] Such concern need not be based on the presumption that corruption is widespread. On the contrary, it is probable that in Britain the majority of MPs share a principled commitment to high standards of conduct in the execution of their official duties. But lapses in judgment do occur, scandals break out, and media attention focuses preferentially on misdeeds, often to the exclusion of positive accomplishments. Thus, the tendency has been for discussions of legislative ethics to be cast in an accusatory and adversarial spirit.[6] Such discussions have placed even conscientious legislators on the defensive. Accurate exposés serve a useful function in directing public attention to specific abuses, but they are no substitute for the systematic study of elite attitudes.

The traditional case study approach to corruption in Britain has been encouraged and perpetuated to some extent by the parliamentary system itself. Parliamentary practice has fostered the idea that informal norms of conduct, not codified rules, constitute the best safeguard against acts of political malfeasance. While ministers, civil servants, and local councillors are obliged to adhere to a code of conduct, MPs still are without one. Instead, their behaviour is guided by an outdated set of statutes that primarily address the act of bribery.

Unfortunately, there is more to political corruption than patently criminal acts. There is, in particular, an extensive grey zone of activities not expressly prohibited by law, but nonetheless unseemly and suspect. And while scandal normally settles on a few individuals, blame for corruption cannot be placed entirely on the wayward. Parliament is open to certain systemic vulnerabilities in the area of legislative ethics. Without a code of conduct to guide them in these areas, MPs are left with the responsibility of monitoring one another's behaviour and applying their own standards. The parliamentary system places the responsibility for identifying and punishing corrupt behaviour firmly in the hands of MPs.

Since the early 1980s there has emerged, notably from the United States, a broader and more sustained discussion about the ethical responsibilities of elected representatives.[7] The scope of ethical inquiry has been enlarged to include not only individual corruption, conflict of interest, and the use of office for personal financial gain, but also an entire range of legislative activities and decisions that establish the ethical tone of everyday legislative life. These include access to and abuse of privileged information, administration of the perquisites of office, submission of parliamentary questions, staff allocations, and exercise of autonomous legislative judgment. It is to these broader questions of legislative ethics that we now turn.

LEGISLATIVE ETHICS

When a private citizen is elected as an MP, he assumes a second identity, one composed of a structure of special obligations that are often more demanding and restrictive than the general moral obligations of private life.[8] According to Stuart Hampshire, there is a moral threshold crossed by those who undertake to represent in a public role the will and interests of others.[9] Legislators may be held to standards that, if enforced against ordinary citizens, would violate their privacy. For example, legislators are often required to disclose more information about their financial affairs than is demanded of their fellow citizens. Publicity about a wide range of activities that would otherwise be private is justified on the grounds that legislators enjoy considerable discretion in exercising their political power.[10] In order to maintain legitimacy, the wielders of this power must be held to some form of ethical standard.[11]

Legislative ethics addresses the difficulties arising out of this public/ private dichotomy. Ordinary ethics, sufficient for guiding a private citizen through whatever dilemmas he may face, cannot solve the special problems of elected representatives. The public identity a citizen gains when elected to public office brings with it new ethical responsibilities. Moreover, the tension between the public and private identities of a legislator itself gives rise to new kinds of ethical pitfalls: private interests may come into conflict with public duties; public duties may demand action contrary to private values and beliefs. A useful framework of legislative ethics must take into consideration the interplay and interaction between legislators' public and private responsibilities.

Many have agreed that elected officials should be held to a higher standard of behaviour than ordinary citizens.[12] Yet the framework of legislative ethics cannot consist simply of a few additional restrictions tacked onto the ethics applied to ordinary individuals.[13] Legislative ethics prohibits some behaviour allowed by ordinary ethics – primarily since legislators have access to, and may potentially misuse, powers not available to ordinary citizens. But at the same time, a system of legislative ethics must be permissive enough to allow legislators to serve particular interests ahead of the general interest. Legislators are expected, and elected, to represent the interests of their constituents, party, or geographic region, even if such interests are contrary to the wider public interest. An MP who is perceived as insufficiently thorough in pursuing the particular interests of his constituency may lose his seat, or may even be deselected by the local party organization. What MPs are not permitted to do, however, is to advance their own personal interests to the detriment of those interests they represent.

Additionally, a consistent theory of legislative ethics must recognize that legislators are fundamentally different from other citizens. This requirement rests in part on the Burkean notion of an elite – individuals elevated by election to public office are in some sense "special." Moreover, according to Heinz Eulau, it is an error to assume that the "chosen," whether elected or selected, are or can ever be "like" their choosers. The very fact of their having been elevated through some mechanism of choice from one position into another makes the "chosen" fundamentally different from their choosers. Having been chosen, representatives have at least one attribute that distinguishes them from the rest, no matter how socially or psychologically similar they may be in all other respects. Status differentiation is a crucial tenet of any representational relationship.[14] Such a difference in status further necessitates a special system of legislative ethics.

How then should the scope of legislative ethics be defined? One starting point is the principle that legislators – those who make the laws – should not break the laws. But, as has already been emphasized, legislative ethics must consist of more than just statutory prohibitions. Provisions must be established to address the potential ethical dilemmas that arise in the routine daily conduct of legislators. A further fundamental principle prohibits the use of public office for personal gain. Public office has been traditionally viewed as a "public trust."[15] Central to this trust is the requirement that legislators serve the interest of the public: in their role as public trustees, legislators are asked to place the interest of the public before their own when operating in the political arena. When legislators base their conduct on the potential for personal financial reward, the public's trust in them has been clearly betrayed.

Legislative ethics, narrowly defined, consists of these two prohibitions: legislators must break no laws and must not allow personal interest to affect their public trust. The elected member's personal interest is usually defined in narrow pecuniary terms, as it is difficult to identify and regulate other psychological or emotional rewards that might influence an individual's actions. Once outside the boundaries of bribery or overt self-dealing, there may be very little agreement about what constitutes a legitimate or illegitimate business or political transaction.[16] In Britain, where there are few formal injunctions beyond "don't break the law" and "don't take bribes," and where there are many unregulated but ethically suspect opportunities available to MPs, an effective ethical regulatory framework is dependent on the existence of a consensus as to which of these questionable activities should be judged corrupt. As will be seen, it is doubtful that such a consensus can be found.

Indeed, it will be argued that in this realm the approach adopted by the British House of Commons conforms to what Bruce Jennings terms "minimalist ethics."[17] Such an ethical system is based almost exclusively on the identification of financial conflicts of interest. Further restrictions or inquiries are viewed as unnecessary; a declaration of interests is assumed to be sufficient. The House has never questioned the propriety of members possessing outside interests, only the means and timing in which they should be disclosed. Accordingly, although ministers have been subject to certain restrictions, no backbench or opposition frontbench MPs have been required to divest themselves of interests that might conceivably prejudice their public duties. Instead, the House has addressed itself to the question of whether, and if so how, those outside interests should be revealed. Being sensitive about individual members' privacy, the House has traditionally required the disclosure of interests only when an MP actually speaks or votes upon a matter in which his or her action might be influenced by personal interest.

This ethical minimalism does not, however, imply that the framework of British legislative ethics is inconsequential or trivial. The House has in place a complex but, as will be seen, chaotically and inconsistently developed system of formal and informal means to ensure ethical propriety in its members' conduct. It is this system that is to a large degree responsible for shaping legislative behaviour. The legislative environment and institutions determine the degree to which, and the ease with which, members can fulfil their ethical obligations.[18]

BRITISH LEGISLATIVE ETHICS: THE CURRENT SITUATION

The functional characteristics of ethical systems in legislatures consist of a combination of most or all of the following components:

- formal ethics regulations
- informal moral traditions
- discipline, punishment, sanctions
- electoral retribution
- political incentives and rewards

British legislative ethics includes elements of each category, although some are relied upon far more heavily, almost to the exclusion of the others. Each component will be examined to ascertain how it shapes MPs' ethical standards.

Formal Ethics Regulations

Richard Crossman observed that "politicians have never regarded Parliament as a profession with its own code of ethics."[19] Thus, unlike most professional societies – law, medicine, accountancy, engineering – parliamentarians do not adhere to and uphold a set of formal ethical rules. While ministers are governed by a firm set of directives, MPs have been reluctant to promulgate their own set of ethical guidelines. Ethical guidance for ministers is contained in the cabinet document "Questions of Procedure." Shortly after his election in 1992, John Major decided to make public for the first time the rules that govern the financial interests of ministers.[20] According to this manual, ministers are required to relinquish all directorships and controlling interests they may have in companies and corporations, and to cease playing a day-to-day role in the management of partnerships or professional firms. MPs, in contrast, have almost nothing but an unwritten code on which to rely. Their behaviour is guided and framed by a set of resolutions, Speakers' rulings, recommendations from committees of privilege, and what Alan Doig describes as "some ill-defined standards concerning individual integrity and the reputation of the House."[21] According to the Salmon Commission, MPs should avoid "activity inconsistent with the standards the House is entitled to expect from its members." The problem remains that these standards are not stated explicitly, nor are they detailed or presented in a consolidated, cohesive manner.

The one explicit rule with which members are confronted is the requirement to file an annual declaration of outside interests with the Register of Members' Interests. Both ministers and MPs file a written disclosure of their financial interests under a number of headings, including directorships, shareholdings, property, gifts, and foreign travel (see table 1). The operation of the register is entrusted to the registrar of members' interests, who is appointed from the Clerk's Office. The registrar, aided in his duties by a Select Committee on Members' Interests, considers irregularities and offers advice to MPs on the completion of their declarations. There are no permanent provisions for dealing with unethical behaviour. Many acknowledge that the register was weakened by the absence of sanctions for non-compliance, but members were reluctant from 1976 to 1987 to take action against the most persistent offender, Enoch Powell. Powell claimed that he had never consented to be governed by the rule requiring declaration and argued that members-elect must be informed of the rule by means of a statutory provision, before such a rule could be considered binding.[22] His refusal to comply with the requirements of the register seriously diminished its importance. Until his defeat in the 1987 general election, he was a constant reminder that an MP could refuse to file with impunity and that the register was effectively a voluntary feature of parliamentary life.[23]

In recent years the register has developed and experienced its share of growing pains, as attempts have been made to extend and refine it. The first discussion of significant changes to the register came in December 1986. Parliamentary debate centred on whether there was any need to extend the registration and declaration requirement to lobby journalists (in Canadian terms, members of the Parliamentary Press Gallery), research assistants, secretaries, and officers of all-party groups. Based on the assumption that a pass granting entry into the House and its halls can be, if used astutely, a tool for making money, the House decided in favour of the extension. Staff, it was decided,

Table 1
Categories of the Register of Members' Interests

Heading	Specific Classifications
1 Directorships	Remunerated directorships of companies, public or private
2 Employment or office	Remunerated employments or offices. Ministerial office and membership of the European Parliament, Council of Europe, Western European Union, and the North Atlantic Assembly do not need to be registered.
3 Trades or professions, etc.	Remunerated trades, professions, or vocations.
4 Clients	The names of clients when the interests referred to above include personal services by the member which arise out of or are related in any manner to his membership of the House. These services include, as well as any action connected with any proceedings in the House or its committees, the sponsoring of functions in the palace, making representations to ministers, civil servants, and other members, accompanying delegations to ministers and the like.
5 Financial sponsorships, gifts, etc.	Financial sponsorships (a) as a parliamentary candidate where to the knowledge of the member the sponsorship in any case exceeds 25 per cent of the candidate's election expenses, or (b) as a member of parliament, by any person or organization, stating whether any such sponsorship includes any payment to the member or any material benefit or advantage direct or indirect. This subsection includes gifts in relations to a member's parliamentary duties, other than those received from abroad to which category 7 applies. It is, however, not necessary for a member to register the fact that he is supported by his local constituency party.
6 Overseas visits	Overseas visits relating to or arising out of membership of the House where the cost of any such visit has not been wholly borne by the member or by public funds. Overseas visits undertaken on behalf of the Inter Parliamentary Union, the Commonwealth Parliamentary Association, the Council of Europe, the Western European Union, and the North Atlantic Assembly, or by any institution of the European Economic Communities need not be registered.
7 Payments, etc., from abroad	Any payments or any material benefits or advantages received from or on behalf of foreign governments, organizations, or persons.
8 Land and property	Land and property of substantial value or from which a substantial income is derived. The requirement is to register the general nature of the interest rather than a detailed list of the holdings. A member's home need not be declared, unless he also receives income from it.
9 Declarable shareholdings	The names of companies or other bodies in which the member has, to his knowledge, either himself or with or on behalf of his spouse or infant children, a beneficial interest in shareholdings of a nominal value greater than one-hundredth of the issued share capital.

Source: Register of Members' Interests on 12th January 1987 (London: HMSO 1987). The categories were somewhat modified and extended in June 1993. See chapter 7 for a discussion and the new registration form.

have access to information and documents, and the opportunity to listen to and spread gossip. This required the registration of their outside interests. In the December debate the House approved the extension, and in January 1987 it took effect.

In the Select Committee's *Third Report* (1 March 1988) it was noted that an overall review of the operation and efficacy of the register had not been conducted in the more than ten years since its inception. The committee suggested that it was time to examine how registration could be made more effective. Circumstances had changed – the public wanted more information about elected representatives; an increasing number of members regarded their job as a full-time occupation; and recent privatization legislation had meant that MPs were increasingly voting on legislation that could lead, and in some cases had led, to a direct personal gain – and the committee considered a review to be prudent.[24]

The Committee generated many reform possibilities – including disclosure of outside income; identification of Lloyd's syndicates, clients, and trust beneficiaries; and making the register legally binding on members. The committee voted, however, not to adopt these specific proposals as recommendations, but instead contented itself with reporting them to the House. It appeared somewhat reluctant to conduct a major inquiry into the current register. Instead, in what might be interpreted as an attempt to divert attention from MPs and their interests, the committee launched an investigation into a further extension of the registration requirement to lobbyists. It embarked on a study of whether a register of lobbyists would be desirable, and how such a register could be operational. The committee began conducting hearings and considering evidence in March 1988 and published a final report in September 1992. It essentially recommended that the House should decide in principle to establish its own register of professional lobbyists, and that the explicit form and content of the register and the details of the accompanying code of conduct should then be discussed with interested parties. To this end, the report included a draft register and a draft code of conduct. As of January 1994, however, the report had not yet been debated by the House.

In the meantime, the committee's attention was forcibly returned to the register by the case of John Browne, MP, who was accused in 1990 of failing to list all his registrable interests. Fallout from the case led not only to sanctions against Browne, but also to modifications in the operation and extent of the register (see chapter 7).

It is evident that the formal ethics regulations that pertain to MPs revolve around declaration and registration rather than restriction and avoidance. Virtually anything is permitted as long as it is made public.

Most recently, this motto has been applied to research assistance paid for by an outside source and to subsidies given to MPs for the operation of their constituency offices by companies and councils. The tradition of orally and informally declaring an interest in debate in the House or its committees has to some extent been formalized by the introduction of the register, which was not intended to supplant, but rather to complement the requirement of oral declaration.

Informal Moral Traditions

The second element in the system of legislative ethics in Britain is the body of unwritten, informal traditions and conventions – principles of etiquette for parliamentarians – which buttress the formal declaration requirements.[25] Parliament has exhibited an implicit faith in the ability of forces of social and cultural evolution to generate efficient informal rules. Moreover, it is assumed that this process functions optimally when it is unfettered by written rules and statutes, since these cannot possibly anticipate all the ethical problems a member could conceivably face. Instead, it is assumed that members will quickly become acquainted with the norms and expectations that bear on ethical behaviour simply through the socialization process undergone by all MPs when they enter Parliament: ethical standards are instilled as if by osmosis. To codify them would restrict their evolution and deny Parliament the opportunity to exercise flexibility in their interpretation.

The foundation of the etiquette that governs British parliamentary behaviour is honour. No effort is made to outline expected ethical behaviour in the situations MPs face on a daily basis. The individual's discretion is relied upon, and decisions are made accordingly. It is expected that members' honour, and their innate common sense, will lead them to make the proper decision. MPs are encouraged to believe that they belong to a privileged elite, one whose behaviour is governed by a standard not intended for others.[26] With this comes the presumption that MPs have moral insight into public affairs. While they are drawn from the electorate at large, it is assumed that election bestows a measure of ethical intuition. Members may choose to ignore moral urgings but, at a minimum, they have the ability to recognize the ethically correct course of action. The critical dictum is the requirement that MPs place the public interest before their own private advantage. The concept of honour permits MPs to use their discretion in the application of this principle to concrete situations – no explicit instructions are needed.

In her work on conflict of interest, Sandra Williams describes the tradition of British MPs being "honourable gentlemen" as a historical residue of a political culture born out of the aristocratic tradition in government.[27] Historically, the House of Commons has been viewed as a meeting place of gentlemen who saw membership of Parliament as a public service and not as a job. Politics was viewed as an amateur pursuit, which led to a reliance on integrity, character, discretion, and, above all, honour in the establishment of standards of behaviour.

This tradition of the "honourable gentleman" is reinforced by the collegiality that envelops the House of Commons. Elected persons, regardless of political persuasion, all feel an affinity towards one another: they are all MPs, and this alone provides them with common bonds. Many legislators share common background characteristics – they are as a whole less diverse than the constituencies they serve.[28] They are collectively participants in a socialization process that binds them to the institution to which they have all been elected.[29] This common legislative experience and circumstance encourages adherence to a shared perception of acceptable behaviour.[30] As a result, there is a great reluctance on the part of MPs to impugn and question the standards of their colleagues. Yet MPs remain the primary custodians of the system, since no one else enjoys the presumption of honourable behaviour.

The absence of statutory requirements, and the paucity of formal opportunities to become acquainted with and consent to the informal rules of ethical conduct, do not, of course, preclude the possibility that MPs are following an unwritten set of rules known only to them. Indeed, the idea that they are following such a code is central to the British system. Unfortunately, most research on the subject does not support this presumption. Canadian MPs disagree about what constitutes corrupt behaviour, and their disagreements can be traced to partisan affiliation, parliamentary experience, and spatial cleavages.[31] Similarly, British MPs and candidates for parliamentary office are divided over alternative interpretations of the constitution. Donald Searing warns against exaggerating these divisions, but he also suggests that "too much may be expected of cultural variables like consensus on the rules of the game" and that "constitutional constraints," among other things, might be required to compensate for the weakness of unwritten rules.[32]

Informal rules are a firmly entrenched component of the British system of legislative ethics. More than any other component, they are responsible for determining the ethical climate of the House of Commons. The system is thus dependent on the presumption that members can readily identify the ethical implications of their behaviour and properly resolve any dilemmas which arise therefrom.

Discipline, Privilege, Sanctions

In the British system there are few, if any, institutional means of investigating and disciplining unethical conduct. This third element of legislative ethics thus remains underdeveloped. No permanent bodies exist to serve as a focal point of an investigation, to determine reasonable punishment, or to act as the adjudicator in the case of an appeal. To cope with gross ethical misconduct by MPs, where the misdeeds are seen as serious or potentially a source of scandal, the House typically appoints a special committee or board of inquiry.[33] Normally, such bodies are staffed by legislators themselves. If an investigator is appointed from outside the legislature, a judge or a retired politician is the preferred choice. No set procedure is followed in these cases, and accused legislators are generally unaware of available means of recourse. These special committees possess the authority to make recommendations, but there are no assurances that what is recommended will be adopted. Moreover, no established penalties exist for contravention of the rules. Each case is decided as if it were an exceptional situation.

In Britain there is virtual unanimity in the belief that only the House of Commons, and not the criminal courts, is responsible for establishing and upholding its own ethical standards. It is accepted that it is the sole right of the House to adjudicate upon the conduct of its members in their parliamentary capacity. The claim to this right in part derives from the historical origins of Parliament as the High Court of Parliament, the highest court in the land. Thus it would be contrary to the supremacy of Parliament for its proceedings to be regulated or challenged in any other court. MPs then are the sole guarantors of acceptable conduct in the House. They are responsible for identifying and punishing corrupt behaviour and for monitoring one another's conduct.

Even in the one area where legislation exists – bribery – it would seem that MPs are able to circumvent it. In Britain, bribery is outlawed by antiquated legislation that specifically excludes from its scope Parliament and the office of MP.[34] It would seem that MPs in their parliamentary capacity are outside the ambit of the law for these purposes, since the legislation does not recognize Parliament as a public body nor an MP as a public person.[35] Moreover, Article 9 of the Bill of Rights further protects the position of MPs by providing them with parliamentary immunity. It asserts that "freedom of speech and debates or proceedings in Parliament ought not to be impeached in any court or place outside of Parliament." This provision removes any MP from the reach of the statutes and common law that restrict corruption.[36] Graham Zellick argues that this is a phrase of uncertain scope and that "there is a distinct possibility that the acceptance of payments by an MP in certain circumstances, hitherto thought to lie within the exclusive cognisance of Parliament, may constitute criminal offences, which the House could instruct the Attorney General to prosecute, Article 9 of the Bill of Rights notwithstanding."[37] But as evidenced by the Poulson case, the House has yet to interpret Article 9 in this way.

As a sanction against unacceptable behaviour, the House retains powers to exclude and expel members who are in contempt of Parliament, although only the power to exclude has been used in recent times.[38] Until 1666 the House relied on the imposition of fines, and select committees in 1969 and 1977 proposed that this lapsed power should be revived by legislation. Past practice, however, has shown the House to be reluctant to punish members involved in acts of corruption. MPS who have been charged with contempt of Parliament are still expected to "do the honourable thing" – resign. In some instances resignation has been avoided by a prompt apology for an error in judgment; chairs of committees or official party positions have also been relinquished in lieu of resignation from Parliament. The Commons seems to regard the personal misfortune suffered in resignation a sufficient penalty in itself and seldom acts to impose further punishment.

As this description indicates, the British Parliament is a solitary and reluctant disciplinarian. It employs a set of ill-defined rules that no one is effectively responsible for enforcing. The members of the House avoid initiating charges of misconduct. Initially, at least, they prefer to leave allegations of impropriety to outsiders: the media, electoral challengers, legislative officers, or the police.

Electoral Retribution

One of the strongest arguments against moving towards an institutionalized ethical framework is the assumption that the electorate will punish those individuals guilty of misconduct or impropriety. If asked, most citizens would probably say that corrupt politicians should not be re-elected. Traditionally the House has left it to the electorate to decide whether an MP's actions are so reprehensible that they no longer can continue to support him. Yet this belief that corrupt politicians will be subject to electoral retribution is undermined by research which shows that politicians have been re-elected by large majorities even after accusations and convictions for blatant violations of the public trust.[39]

American researchers Peters and Welch offer a number of explanations for this anomaly. The first is the possibility that voters may be uninformed or misinformed about candidates. A voter may simply not know of a candidate's misconduct, or if they are aware of the allegations a sample of the electorate is liable to misperceive, selectively perceive, or even refuse to believe the charges.[40] The second is that voters may knowingly vote for a corrupt politician by trading their vote for an economic advantage. This assumes that the voters themselves are capable of being corrupted.[41] A third explanation is the functional approach to corruption, which claims that corruption is a necessary evil.[42] Finally, charges of corruption are only one factor voters must weigh in making an electoral decision. Peters and Welch find most persuasive the argument that voters "trade" votes for a corrupt candidate for other desirable benefits, such as a preferred stance on a policy issue.[43] Regardless of the explanation, evidence exists which illustrates that the British electorate has been willing to trade off, or simply ignore, allegations of impropriety at election time.[44] And as the case of Cecil Parkinson illustrates, a member can be re-elected with an increased majority even after serious charges of impropriety have been made against him.[45]

Political Incentives and Rewards

Following this discussion of punitive measures it would seem appropriate to determine whether there is in effect a system of rewards or incentives to encourage high standards of ethical conduct. In general, the British parliamentary career structure, while not as clearly defined as the American equivalent, has fewer built-in incentives. Rewards can include the chairs of the prestigious Public Accounts, Treasury and Civil Service, and Foreign Affairs committees, membership on the Selection Committee, and, of course, ministerial office. There is also some discretion applied in the allocation of other rewards, notably assignments to parliamentary delegations and foreign travel. In the British House of Commons the use of political incentives as a deterrent to corrupt behaviour is not in any way structured or formalized. MPs are not generally rewarded primarily on the basis of ethical probity or exemplary conduct. The Whips are well informed as to what each member is up to, and if an individual is engaging in dubious activity he can find himself excluded from the remunerative perks associated with ministerial office, private parliamentary secretaryship, or the Whip's office. Of course the Whips must decide to regulate his behaviour.

The Whips office is responsible for recommending MPs for advancement and for overseeing their behaviour.[46] In *Rebels and Whips*, Robert

J. Jackson indicates that the Whips actually keep a record of misconduct. From his interviews with a large number of Whips and former Whips, Jackson discovered that the Tory Whips in particular were responsible to the Chief Whip for any private information they might learn in the House. Such information was actually filed in the form of written reports called "dirts," kept in the Chief Whip's office.[47] Labour Whips supposedly report verbally to the Chief Whip any rumblings they might pick up, and their comments are no less significant. In addition, both Whips' offices scan the national newspapers for reports of MPs' behaviour.[48]

This is not to suggest that members who are serving in ministerial office or as Whips are pure or above corruption. Indeed, such members are, owing to their position in the disciplinary structure, more insulated from potential retributions for unethical behaviour. The system of party discipline certainly has the capability of punishing ethical misconduct or rewarding exemplary actions. But since the incentives and disincentives it can apply are also used to reward or discourage an entire range of other political activities – compliance with party positions, securing of campaign contributions, recognition of accomplishments on behalf of the party – the effectiveness of party discipline in ensuring ethical standards is unclear. Ethical behaviour is only one factor in the preferment decisions made by the Whips. Just as the voters can weigh the importance of allegations of corruption against other political considerations, so do the Whips.

BRITISH LEGISLATIVE ETHICS: THE PROBLEM

The British House of Commons maintains a framework of legislative ethics that is complex but incoherent. This systemic ethical confusion only compounds the ethical dilemmas MPs face: given the absence of clear, concise, written guidelines, all MPs must construct their own interpretation of the ethical rules that apply to behaviour. No one is responsible for identifying and communicating the crucial unwritten rules. There is no institutionalized means of informing members of their ethical duties, and there are precious few opportunities for members to confront the rules directly or to test their understanding of them. Moreover, compliance with the rules is effectively voluntary, because members are free to designate themselves as interpreters of their responsibilities. Under these circumstances, ignorance of the rules becomes a plausible defence and members are relieved of the moral responsibility that comes with knowledge.

The Report of the Select Committee in the Poulson case and the ensuing debate revealed that members were unaware of ethical expectations or sanctions that could be applied in the event of a breach. In failing to act on the recommendations of the report, the House ignored an opportunity to repair deficiencies in its framework of legislative ethics, and, in doing so, demonstrated a lack of concern for the problems these deficiencies pose. This lack of concern is a fundamental problem of British legislative ethics: weaknesses in the ethical foundation of the institution may be noticed from time to time, usually when a particular scandal draws attention to them, but they are on the whole dismissed as unworthy of the effort required to shore them up.

Furthermore, in allowing so much ethical discretion to the individual MP, the British system is vulnerable to failure in one of its most basic goals: the safeguarding of the public interest from private concerns. Parliament assumes that all MPs will instinctively and automatically place the interest of the public before their own. But this process depends on the individual MP's unbiased judgment as to what exactly constitutes the public interest, and a clear perception of the point at which personal interests begin to impinge upon it. Should this perception be incorrect or unclear, or the judgment not completely autonomous, the MP has no systematic guidelines to refer to in resolving the conflicts.

The Problem of Autonomy

A fundamental need in a system of legislative ethics that grants so much latitude to the individual legislator is that the judgments of its members be free from illegitimate or inappropriate considerations, especially considerations of personal gain. The system must preserve the autonomy of legislators against influences that seek to bias or corrupt their decision-making, influences that can originate from without and within the legislative environment itself. Only when legislators are fully independent are they capable of representing constituent interests and assessing political claims on their merits.

Unfortunately, the process of representation does not accommodate the notion of legislative independence particularly well. MPs can never be entirely autonomous. They are expected to respond to the demands of citizens, constituents, and party colleagues – people with whom they share common objectives. Indeed, in a representative assembly, all members are both representatives and legislators, and the demands made on representatives impinge upon and circumscribe the autonomy they have as legislators. As legislator, an MP is a parliamentarian

– a member of the legislative assembly, a member of certain committees, a potential sponsor of bills, a voice in parliamentary debate, a
vote in the division lobby. As representative, an MP is the honourable
member from a certain constituency in a certain region, subject to the
Whip of a particular party, a voice for a sponsoring trade union or
professional organization, a spokesman for societal issues.

MPs execute their representative function primarily in the arena of
a deliberative assembly, where the actions of cohesive political parties
are expected to reflect the salient divisions within society. The British
party system, and associated party discipline, encourages MPs to pledge
their primary loyalty to the party leadership.[49] Thus many of an MP's
representative responsibilities are discharged by accepting the direction of party leaders and engaging in parliamentary debate on
national issues.[50] MPs operate without their own electoral mandate in
a system based on national party competition. The fusion of the choice
of executive and legislative candidates fosters a "team mentality,"
rather than the "every man for himself" mentality nurtured in systems
that have an institutionalized separation of executive and legislature.[51]
To a large degree MPs owe their election to the party, not to their
personal efforts, and bear collective responsibility for government
performance.

The autonomy of MPs is further circumscribed by the imposition of
institutional constraints on an MP's role in the legislative process.[52]
Individual MPs do not possess the authority to amend or delay legislation; they do not control the parliamentary timetable; the opportunity to introduce a private member's bill is severely restricted; and it
remains the prerogative of the government to obstruct any bill it finds
objectionable.[53] In addition, parliamentary committees are not
accorded wide investigative powers, and the staff and resources they
are allocated are not generous. Operating under constraints such as
these, the MP has only a limited ability to protect and advance the
interests of constituents, and can claim to affect legislation in only the
most diffuse way.

On the other hand, these structural limitations on an MP's legislative
autonomy shift much of the burden of responsibility and accountability
for legislative action onto the party or legislature as a whole and afford
the individual MP greater freedom to give expression to societal interests
that are not necessarily defined in territorial terms. The party political
battle is largely about interests that are unattached to constituency or
to persons as such. Examples drawn from the ongoing Conservative
agenda include law and order, family values, trade liberalization, and
the principle of privatization. The parliamentary system restricts the
formal legislative autonomy of MPs, but at the same time relaxes the

parameters of interest representation; indeed, by channelling individual MPs' autonomy away from the legislative agenda, it encourages the association of MPs with interests outside their constituency.

That MPs have little power to determine the course of legislative action should not, however, be interpreted to mean that MPs are powerless and that any impropriety they engage in is necessarily trivial. On the contrary, it is in this area of representing outside interests that MPs have their greatest discretionary latitude in the exercise of their autonomy. There is nothing to limit or even guide MPs' involvement in activities outside the House and no shortage of opportunities for involvement, many of which come to them solely because of their position.

Often these outside involvements include the representation of organized interests in Parliament. In exchange for a retainer, MPs can advise and assist clients: they obtain parliamentary papers, submit written and oral questions, secure unrestricted passage to the corridors of Westminster, and in general facilitate access. Some outside groups promote interests that are localized in specific geographic constituencies, in which case association with these groups can be defended as another means of furthering constituency interests. But when these outside interests are broadly based, and associations advance particular points of view on national issues, MPs who accept retainers are essentially allowing their responsibility for national concerns to be co-opted by an external influence. Yet this is not considered a problem.

In fact, the nature of the parliamentary career encourages emphasis on national issues as well as these other forms of employment. From 1677 to 1912 MPs received no payment for their service,[54] and an image of the politician as a public-spirited amateur persists. This image has its uses: MPs call upon this tradition of part-time public service and collective representation to help justify their acceptance of outside employment as a means of supplementing their meager parliamentary incomes and making up for the relatively poor facilities available to them.

The acceptance of retainers and outside salaries raises the possibility of an ethical dilemma. Once MPs receive money for the representation of an interest, it becomes difficult to ascertain whether they are advocating a position out of pure conviction or for direct pecuniary benefit. In addition, consideration must be given not only to the repercussions such payments have on legislative autonomy, but also on the time members spend in their outside business. Time spent promoting outside interests is time not spent on public business – time during which the public's interests go unrepresented. When MPs attend to their private affairs at the expense of the concerns of their constituents, there is a conflict between the interest of the public and that of their representatives.

When private citizens become MPs, they gain an additional, public persona. They are then not only people with their own private associations and interests, but also representatives of the public and all its interests. When the dealings and deliberations of an MP's private persona interfere with the functioning of his or her public persona, ethical dilemmas result. Problems of legislative ethics proceed, in a sense, from the confusion and competition between the various roles an MP must play as both a public and a private person. As we shall see, the situation is even more complex, in that these two basic roles are multifaceted and can be divided into more specific orientations.

The Problem of Multiple Roles

MPs must in fact make a choice of which role to emphasize in a given situation, a choice that will depend on what else is happening in the legislature, on the actual conduct of other MPs, and on the general features of the political system as a whole.[55] In their efforts to respond to or communicate with their constituents, MPs must choose among their roles and at times play a number of them simultaneously. MPs have legislative responsibilities that can be quite different from, and even conflict with, their representative duties. But MPs are also employers, and thus need to hire staff and administer the day-to-day operations of their Westminster and constituency offices. MPs are candidates: they have to help raise party funds and cope with the advantages of incumbency. MPs are also required to act as boosters for their local constituency and geographical region, as loyal members of their party caucus, as adherents to certain organized religions, and as members of their profession or social class. The problem is that MPs are expected to play these different roles concurrently, and at times they conflict. Unfortunately, analysis of these roles does not reveal which one will be pre-eminent in any given situation. Complicating the problem further is the interaction between MPs – a member's choice of role will be affected by the roles being played by others in the legislative environment.

In the interplay of these traditional roles alone there is potential for activity of an ethically questionable nature: MPs may, and many do, hire their spouses as secretaries, thereby channelling a portion of their staff allowance back into their household coffers. When MPs adopt additional roles such as corporate director or parliamentary consultant, the problem of sorting out the various roles and avoiding impropriety can become intractable. To avoid compromising their legislative autonomy, MPs must exercise their discretion. There are no rules to guide MPs in choosing whether to accept retainers, gifts, travel, entertainment, hospitality, computers, or other benefits from interest groups, corporations, foreign governments, or "grateful constituents." It remains up to the individual MP to determine when such involvement constitutes unethical behaviour.

What remains to be considered is which aspects of an MP's roles are vulnerable to corruption. As Dennis Thompson points out, the ethical scrutiny of legislative life can and should be based on a thoughtful, balanced appraisal of the opportunities as well as the limitations that political realities create.[56] Consideration must first be given to the degree of influence MPs are able to exert in the legislative process. MPs are limited in their ability to shape the legislative agenda. Therefore, it is often argued, they are less exposed to situations of conflict of interest with the risk of corruption,[57] since there exist constitutional limits to members' abilities to confer direct financial benefit on their constituents or other individuals or groups. Yet a serious threat to legislative independence is posed by those who understand these limits and who are not pursuing direct pecuniary payoffs, but are rather seeking access to the centres of public debate and to the information that MPs can provide. In exchange for such access or information, they are prepared to pay MPs who are willing to be a conduit for these indirect benefits.

To gain some insight into the issue of MPs' influence, real and perceived, Sandra Williams asked thirty MPs which aspects of being an MP provided, in their view, opportunities for conflict of interest and possible corrupt activity.[58] The general consensus confirmed the popular image of the powerless backbencher, all but excluded from the decision-making process. However, this did not prevent MPs from recognizing potential opportunities for advancing outside interests and acknowledging the importance of maintaining the appearance of impeccable standards of conduct. According to Williams's findings, two main aspects of an MP's role were cited by members as providing opportunities for advancing outside interests: an MP's behaviour on the floor of the House or in committee, and the unique opportunity of having access to ministers and civil servants.

Whether or not it is exploited, there is scope for a member to engage in ethically questionable behaviour. By virtue of election, MPs are granted immediate entrance to the Palace of Westminster and all its resources. These include parliamentary papers, reports and proceedings, access to the parliamentary timetable, and advance warning of emergency debates. MPs have the parliamentary library and its research staff at their disposal. They also have the opportunity to mingle with and approach, both on an informal and formal basis, ministers and civil servants. On an individual level, MPs can make arrangements with the in-house caterers to reserve meeting rooms and dining rooms for entertainment purposes. MPs also are accorded franking privileges, the opportunity of foreign travel, gifts, and, at their discretion, they allocate staff salaries and claim travel and living allowances. The office of MP comes with its own perquisites, and there are few rules to guide the members in the administration of these privileges. MPs may not only exploit the privileges of access and information for themselves, but they can also confer these benefits on outsiders. Public relations firms, consultants, and interest groups are undoubtedly able to operate far more effectively when they have the immediate availability of parliamentary papers and unrestricted access to Westminster that only an MP can provide.

And even if MPs themselves know the limits of their formal political influence, outsiders may not. Thus as Alan Doig has written, the use of the letters 'MP' after one's name becomes a legislator's most important commodity.[59] Various firms may employ MPs solely for the fact that they are MPs, and have prestige value as such, regardless of any influence they may or may not possess.

Even in their routine activities, MPs face the demands of a confusing multiplicity of roles. They are tugged in many directions at once by pressures and interests and responsibilities originating from both within and without Parliament. Yet they must choose between these roles largely on their own, as Parliament itself offers little formal help in sorting out the role conflicts that inevitably arise.

CONCLUSION

MPs would not be relieved of the responsibility for the propriety of their conduct if the House of Commons adopted written ethical guidelines. They would still be required to make discretionary judgments. If there are no rules that contain specific prohibitions or precise requirements, MPs cannot be reprimanded for making personal decisions that others find objectionable. But currently there is no basis for questioning these judgments.[60] Ignorance of the law is never an excuse for illegality, but ignorance of informal, unwritten norms can be advanced as a plausible defence for misconduct.

Unfortunately, the very system in which MPs operate leaves them vulnerable to ethical impropriety in the grey areas on the fringe of the formal political process, where there are few formal and explicit standards of ethical behaviour. In the House of Commons there is neither a coherent framework of legislative ethics nor the belief that the absence of such a framework is a problem. As we will see, the stigma of corruption is reserved for the most blatant cases of bribery and illegalities, while subtler forms of ethically dubious behaviour go undetected and unrestricted.

While major scandals attract most public attention, it is the day-to-day behaviour, and the relative propriety of that behaviour, that sets the ethical tone for the legislative environment. Indeed, if an MP can legitimately make a tidy sum by accepting a retainer, he will never need to resort to accepting an outright bribe. Because the acceptance of a retainer, and the terms on which it is accepted – what the member will do in exchange for his remuneration – are entirely up to the individual MP, proper discretion is paramount. The confusion and multiplicity of roles that an MP must play hampers the exercise of discretion by those who would do right and masks abuse of discretion by those who would do wrong. Because of the importance of individual discretion in the ethical process, the attitudes and perceptions of MPs become of crucial interest to those who seek to understand British legislative ethics.

CHAPTER TWO

A Typology of MPs

The crucial variable in Parliament's ethical equation remains unknown: How do MPs make their ethical choices, and do they all make them in the same way? To settle these questions the MPs themselves must be consulted. One way of determining the attitudes that inform these choices is to present MPs with a series of situations that require them to make an ethical decision. By thus quantifying the ethical standards operative in the House, it becomes possible to determine the degree of ethical consensus or dissensus among MPs. This chapter explains the process used to measure and categorize the attitudes and perceptions of members of parliament. Based on the wide variation observed, an organizational schema will be used to encapsulate and explain four divergent ethical outlooks prevailing in the House.

THE RESEARCH INSTRUMENT

The questionnaire used to compile data for this book was modelled largely on a study carried out in 1978 by the American political scientists John Peters and Susan Welch. Peters and Welch mailed questionnaires to 978 state senators in twenty-four states.[1] A similar study was conducted in the Canadian House of Commons in 1984, but personal interviews with eighty-four MPs in their Ottawa offices took the place of a mail-out survey.[2] This study also made use of the personal interview technique.

Interviews were conducted with one hundred British MPs[3] over the period from March 1986 to March 1988. While a few interviews were not completed until after the 1987 general election, all MPs in the sample were selected for interview before dissolution. Since the completion of the interviews, no substantive ethical reforms or major scandals have taken place, and the internal demographics of the

House have remained fairly constant. It is therefore highly unlikely that any significant shift in attitudes has occurred. While some MPs commented specifically on Margaret Thatcher's role and her responsibility for setting the ethical tone of the House, there are no indications that John Major's accession to the leadership has caused a rethinking of the Conservative ethos. A change in government might tip the overall ethical sentiment of the House towards a more restrictive attitude, but the internal dissensus of MPs would undoubtedly remain. The implications of recent cases involving the Register of Members' Interests will be discussed in the context of members' attitudes towards the register.

The MPs were contacted by mail asking for their assistance with a study on morality in government and, more specifically, a perceptual study of MPs' attitudes towards political corruption. While the number of interviews completed was high, the interviews proved quite difficult to schedule, given that some MPs still operate without a secretary or even an office, and many MPs, with their hectic agendas, were evasive about pinpointing a meeting time.

Initial letters were sent to 250 randomly selected backbench MPs, of whom 27 (11 per cent) failed to respond. Of the 223 MPs who did respond, 110 (44 per cent) agreed to be interviewed; 100 interviews were eventually completed. Of the 113 MPs (45 per cent) who declined interviews, many (55) claimed to be too busy to spare the interview time, only 13 offered no reason for the refusal and 12 thought they would have little to say about political corruption, other than that they were against it. Other refusals were ascribed to various factors, such as the member's inundation with requests for interviews of this kind, the researcher's not being from the member's constituency, or the topic not being related to the member's areas of specialization.

The initial contact sample of 250 MPs was randomly selected and numerically weighted by party to reflect the relative number of backbench seats then held by each of the parties. Of 650 seats in the House, as of March 1986, 76 were held by government frontbenchers, and 3 by the leaders of the Labour, Liberal, and Social Democratic parties; these seats were removed from consideration. Of the remaining 571 seats, the Conservative Party held 321 (56 per cent), Labour 208 (36 per cent), the SDP/Liberal Alliance 21 (4 per cent), and other parties 21 [4 per cent]). The completed sample of 100 MPs included 54 Conservatives, 40 Labour members, 5 MPs from the Alliance, and 1 from the other parties.

The only exception to this weighting by party was that all twenty-six female MPs were included in the contact group, in order to facilitate the testing of gender-based differences in ethical attitudes. Unfortunately, since only seven women MPs (27 per cent of the women) agreed to take part in the study, perhaps the only gender-specific trait that can be identified is the greater reluctance female MPs have to participating in surveys. This is probably due to their being scarce (26 of 650 MPs).[4] As representatives of an interest group that equals half the population, there are probably many demands made on their time.

The average interview lasted approximately fifty minutes, with the shortest being fifteen minutes and the longest more than two-and-a-half hours. The majority of the respondents were cooperative and hospitable, despite the potentially sensitive nature of the topic. Most of the interviews were conducted within the precincts of Westminster – some were held in MPs' business offices in London – at varied times throughout the day. Most MPs, despite their busy schedules, were able to appreciate the vagaries of the London-Oxford InterCity rail timetable. By the latter part of the interview schedule, I was a familiar face to the security staff at the St Stephens Street entrance to Westminster and the clerks manning the Central Lobby who kindly pointed out my targeted MPs as soon as they came into view (whether they wanted to be pointed out or not).

The interview schedule (fully reproduced in the appendix) was divided into four sections. The first contained a series of open-ended questions on a broad range of ethical issues. These questions were designed not only to ease the respondent into the topic, but also to obtain a general sense of the member's attitudes to serve as a context for the more specific questions of later sections. In addition, by beginning the interview with broad generalities – questions on which every MP has an opinion, but rarely an opportunity to express it – the respondents were encouraged to "open up" and relax. In this way, the respondents were reassured that the researcher did not pose a threat, that the interview was not to be conducted in an adversarial manner, and that it was their own views and opinions that were important to the study.

The next section consisted of ten statements about corruption in general (see table 2), to which the respondents were asked to indicate the extent of their agreement or disagreement on a seven-point Likert-type scale, where 1 indicated strong agreement and 7 strong disagreement.[5] These questions were designed to elicit MPs' perceptions of various topical ethical issues. They will be used to construct a quantifiable perceptual profile of the MPs.

The third section of the questionnaire was a series of fourteen hypothetical scenarios (see table 3) depicting activities that some might describe as corrupt, and others not. The respondents were asked to indicate the degree to which they deemed the activities corrupt, once again using a seven-point Likert scale, where 1 indicated

Table 2
General Perceptual Profile

Statement	Text
15	Political corruption is not a widespread problem.
16	In so far as citizens distrust elected officials, it is because they do not understand what politics is all about.
17	Dishonesty is more widespread in politics than in business.
18	Political corruption is more widespread at the local than at the national level of government.
19	No matter what we do, we can never eliminate political corruption.
20	The corruption that exists in the political world simply reflects the standards of the rest of society.
21	If it hadn't been for the Poulson scandal, we would hear a lot less about corruption in government.
22	MPs are sufficiently well informed to act as the sole guarantors of acceptable conduct in the House.
23	Once allegations of corruption are made, MPs in their parliamentary capacity should be brought within the ambit of criminal law.
24	Britain's libel laws inhibit the uncovering and reporting of political corruption.

that the respondent saw the activity as very corrupt and 7 as not corrupt at all. For each scenario, the respondents were also asked to indicate on the same scale to what extent they thought the public would find the activities corrupt, to what extent their colleagues would find them corrupt, and finally whether they themselves would engage in the activities described. This hypothetical scenario format has been proven successful by a number of academics writing in the field of political corruption.[6] No study of the attitudes of British MPs has used this method.

The questionnaire concluded with a number of questions designed to elicit background and personal information. Some of these items were not actually posed as questions to the respondents, as the information was publicly available from sources such as *The Times Guide to the House of Commons, Dod's Parliamentary Companion,* Robert Waller's *Almanac of British Politics,* and the 1987 General Election Data Set.

The fourteen scenarios formed the core of the questionnaire and it is on these items that the remainder of this chapter will focus. As one of the primary goals of this study was to ascertain what MPs believe to constitute corruption, the scenarios were presented unadorned by explanation. No further details were provided, and elaboration was confined to clarifying the intent of the questions to avoid egregious

Table 3
Hypothetical Scenarios

Name	Text
CAMPAIGN	A cabinet minister promises an appointed position in exchange for campaign contributions.
SCHOOL	An MP uses his position to get a friend or relative admitted to Oxford or Cambridge, or some other prestigious institution.
DRIVEWAY	The driveway of the chairman of the City Council's private home is paved by the council's District Works Department.
CONTRACT	A cabinet minister uses his influence to obtain a contract for a firm in his constituency.
RETAINER	An MP is retained by a major company to arrange meetings and dinners in the House at which its executives can meet parliamentarians.
PLANNING	A local councillor, while chairman of the planning committee, authorizes a planning permission for property owned by him.
LORRY	A Ministry of Transport heavy goods vehicle examiner obtains £10 from the owner of a lorry to pass the vehicle.
SECRETARY	An MP hires his wife or other family member to serve as his secretary.
GIFT	At Christmas, an MP accepts a crate of wine from an influential constituent.
KNIGHT	A major company makes a substantial donation to the government party. Later, the chairman of the company is knighted.
TRAVEL	An MP is issued a first-class airline ticket as part of a parliamentary delegation. He exchanges the ticket for an economy fare and pockets the difference.
ALL PARTY	An all-party group on the aged secures the services of a full-time research assistant at the expense of Age Concern.
ORDER PAPER	A member on retainer to a PR company representing a foreign government submits several written questions for the Order Paper on British industrial development in that country.
PASS	An MP requests and receives a House pass for a lobbyist, to act as a research assistant, although his services are paid for by an outside source.

errors of interpretation. The clarifications were consistent – everyone who asked was told the same story. While the items are somewhat stark and unvarnished, the range of responses available gave the respondents an opportunity to reveal subtle differences in the degree of corruption they detected in each act.

WHAT CONSTITUTES CORRUPTION: THE MPS' PERSPECTIVE

We will now consider the MPS' perceptions of the scenarios and some of the reasons they advanced to support their decisions to judge an act corrupt or not corrupt. The fourteen scenarios are listed in table 4

Table 4
Scenario Responses and Statistics

Name	Text	Corrupt (%)	Not Corrupt (%)	Mean	Std Dev.	Median
LORRY	A Ministry of Transport heavy goods vehicle examiner obtains £10 from the owner of a lorry to pass the vehicle.	100	0	1.0	.10	1
DRIVEWAY	The driveway of the chairman of the City Council's private home is paved by the council's District Works Department.	99	1	1.1	.69	1
CAMPAIGN	A cabinet minister promises an appointed position in exchange for campaign contributions.	98	1	1.2	.70	1
PLANNING	A local councillor, while chairman of the planning committee, authorizes a planning permission for property owned by him.	96	3	1.2	.96	1
TRAVEL	An MP is issued a first-class airline ticket as part of a parliamentary delegation. He exchanges the ticket for an economy fare and pockets the difference.	87	9	2.0	1.6	1
SCHOOL	An MP uses his position to get a friend or relative admitted to Oxford or Cambridge, or some other prestigious institution.	61	26	3.3	2.3	3
PASS	An MP requests and receives a House pass for a lobbyist, to act as a research assistant, although his services are paid for by an outside source.	58	29	3.4	2.2	3
KNIGHT	A major company makes a substantial donation to the government party. Later, the chairman of the company is knighted.	53	35	3.6	2.5	3
CONTRACT	A cabinet minister uses his influence to obtain a contract for a firm in his constituency.	40	40	4.1	2.3	4
ORDER PAPER	A member on retainer to a PR company representing a foreign government submits several written questions for the Order Paper on British industrial development in that country.	40	49	4.4	2.5	4
GIFT	At Christmas, an MP accepts a crate of wine from an influential constituent.	31	50	4.7	2.2	4.5
RETAINER	An MP is retained by a major company to arrange meetings and dinners in the House at which its executives can meet parliamentarians.	20	72	5.6	2.0	7
ALL PARTY	An all-party group on the aged secures the services of a full-time research assistant at the expense of Age Concern.	11	82	6.1	1.8	7
SECRETARY	An MP hires his wife or other family member to serve as his secretary.	2	91	6.6	.98	7

Key: "Corrupt" equals responses of 1, 2, or 3 (as a percentage of valid responses). "Not Corrupt" equals responses of 5, 6, or 7 (as a percentage of valid responses).

by the percentage of MPs who viewed them as corrupt.[7] Many of the items showed a good deal of variance in the scoring, but the low standard deviation of the first four items (LORRY, DRIVEWAY, CAMPAIGN, PLANNING) emphasized the virtual unanimity of the respondents in viewing these situations as corrupt. This unanimity indicated that MPs did not have much difficulty recognizing and condemning acts involving bribery and the misappropriation of public funds. In Britain the one activity that is explicitly forbidden is bribery; it was not surprising that MPs were aware that such an act was deemed reprehensible by their political culture.

In LORRY, the action was a flagrant case of bribery and 100 per cent of the MPs deemed it corrupt. MPs attached much more significance to the fact that it was a bribe than to the size of the favour. Despite the almost trivial sum (£10) involved, the MPs were overwhelmingly clear on the corruption inherent in the act. The harshness of this judgment stood in stark contrast to the responses to a number of other scenarios that involved more substantial favours, but elicited more tolerant reactions from many MPs.

Ninety-nine per cent of the MPs viewed the DRIVEWAY item as corrupt. In this case the benefit directly accrued to an elected member. While strong in their condemnation, they were quite certain that this sort of thing went on all the time. But there were a few MPs who were not so sure that the situation was as completely corrupt as LORRY. Some MPs thought the scenario did not rule out the possibility that the chairman paid a reasonable price for the paving, and another thought that the paving of his driveway might well have added to the beautification of the community. Thus some MPs offered a rationalization for this scenario.

The nearly unanimous condemnation of CAMPAIGN would seem to indicate the value and the sense of propriety MPs attached to the raising of campaign funds. MPs also expressed great faith in the strength of their campaign finance laws – a number asserted that this situation would just not be permitted under the legislation. Yet 5 per cent of the respondents did admit that they themselves would engage in the activity.

The last item in this group, PLANNING, was perceived to be corrupt by 96 per cent of the MPs. This scenario was thought to be highly improbable by a number of the MPs, as they would expect the local councillor to excuse himself from any decision that affected property he owned. Those who found no corruption in this scenario were not convinced that the councillor was exploiting his position, nor did they like the implication that his actions were underhanded. The benefit in this scenario, however, was just too personal and direct for many to support this alternative contention.

Clearly MPS were in substantial agreement about the corruption inherent in the activities depicted in these four scenarios. For the rest of the hypothetical items, however, this ethical consensus unravelled. These remaining situations fell primarily into two broad conceptual categories: acts involving constituency service and acts involving a conflict of interest. These were clear examples of the "hard choices" MPS have to make in the course of their political career. It was these ethical dilemmas over which British MPS were most divided.

Constituency Service

By definition, legislative representation encompasses acts of constituency service. MPS are elected to serve and represent the interests of their constituents. They are expected to protect and advance the rights and interests of their constituencies in Parliament, ensuring that the government and the rest of the country are aware of the desires and concerns of their regions, town, or city. MPS are thus supposed to bias their judgments in favour of the interests of their constituents. How biased their judgments should be with respect to the national interest is both a political and an ethical question. Are MPS permitted or expected to go to any lengths to advance the interest of their electorate? Or is there a point past which serving one's constituency at the expense of the nation as a whole becomes ethically dubious?

There has been a continued growth in the literature on the topic of constituency service, initially in the United States with Richard Fenno's landmark work *Home Style,* and more recently in Britain with Donald Searing's *Westminster's World* and Radice, Vallance, and Willis's *Member of Parliament: The Job of a Backbencher.* A comprehensive study comparing constituency service in the two nations is Cain, Ferejohn, and Fiorina's *The Personal Vote.*[8] While British MPS are not as closely tied to their constituency as US Congressmen – they need not even reside in the constituency that elects them – MPS do get involved in many aspects of constituency life: local amenities, local history and traditions, the environment, and development of the economic infrastructure.[9] Because of this involvement, they are presented with situations in which they must exercise their responsibility to their constituents without compromising their duties as members of the national legislative assembly.

There are two scenarios in the research instrument that can be considered acts of constituency service: SCHOOL and CONTRACT. A majority of the MPS interviewed (61 per cent) considered SCHOOL to be corrupt. Most of these MPS saw it as an example of the "old boy network" and objected to a system in which personal merit counts for less than who one knows. Others were apprehensive about the feasibility of such an act. They suggested that any intervention by an MP, either by letter or by phone, could conceivably do more harm than good to an applicant's chances.

On the other hand, there were a number of MPs who did not find SCHOOL corrupt at all. These individuals argued that this was the way things were done, that you were expected to take advantage of university connections and, if need be, your position as MP to influence the admission process. MPs who had attended Oxford or Cambridge said they would not hesitate to write to the principal of their former college urging consideration of a constituent. Many of the MPs who scored SCHOOL as not corrupt indicated that this type of activity was not understood at all by the public. They were also very concerned about the disadvantages their children and friends have to suffer because of their public position. They asserted that they should be permitted to write to a college, just as any parent is entitled to do. When asked whether this meant they would be writing in an unofficial capacity – not on House letterhead or with the abbreviation "MP" after their signature – they insisted on their right to identify themselves as MPs.

There was a great deal of dissensus among MPs over how to score the CONTRACT item. Exactly the same number of MPs (40 per cent) scored the act as corrupt as scored it not corrupt. The members who drew the line on the side of corruption thought that the question implied that the minister was using his privileged position to lobby civil servants and other ministers on his constituency's behalf. This was perceived to be an unfair advantage, and presumed success on the part of the minister exerting influence.

Those who scored the act as not corrupt believed that ministers are expected to use their influence to obtain contracts for firms in their constituency, as are all members of parliament. Every member wants to secure contracts in order to facilitate employment and revenue for his constituency, thereby increasing his own visibility and chances of re-election. In this instance, the minister was perceived to be acting within the bounds of his influence, presumably adhering to the entrenched tender system that governs the granting of government contracts.

The lack of consensus on this question would seem to indicate that members are not at all sure how far they can go in the name of constituency service. In responding to this item, several members expressed concern whether the minister was seeking to exert his influence within his own department. These MPs did not look favourably on a cabinet minister choosing other than the lowest bidder for a contract. Bids, they felt, should all be considered fairly, and not just awarded to the minister's constituency because of his ministerial position.

In both these scenarios, and in constituency service situations in general, the ethical dilemma arises out of a conflict between two roles played by MPS: legislator and representative. In this type of situation, the MPS' representative persona – their motivation to act so as to benefit their constituents, and thereby reaffirm their constituents' confidence in them – affects the judgment of their legislative persona – the discretionary powers they hold by virtue of office. Alternatively, they use the powers of their role as legislator to benefit the interests of their role as representative.

This role conflict is, of course, fundamental to the process of representation – legislators who ignore any consideration of constituents' interests are not being representatives. But, as the scenarios discussed illustrate, MPS who allow representative considerations too much sway over their legislative autonomy run the risk of being labelled corrupt. It is a question of degree: for any respondent, there is a point at which use of legislative power for the benefit of constituents is seen as corrupt. Thus CONTRACT was viewed by some as "going too far," while others felt that the behaviour described was within the bounds of acceptable conduct and justified by the obligations of representation.

Conflict of Interest

Conflict of interest may also be seen as a process of role conflict. In this case, however, an official's private persona – his or her role as private individual, concerned with the maximization of personal benefits – affects the performance of public legislative duties. Or to put it in more familiar terms, a conflict of interest situation is one in which a public official has the opportunity to use public office to benefit personal interests.

An important distinction must be made between "conflict of interest" and "conflict of interests." Unfortunately, this distinction is often not clear. Parliament is in one sense a forum in which the confusion of opposing viewpoints is resolved into a coherent policy. Conflict of interests is thus inherent to Parliament, for without disagreement on important issues, no deliberative assembly would be needed. Conflict of interest, in contrast, is a situation that arises when an individual MP's legislative autonomy is compromised by personal concerns. Conflict of interest interferes with Parliament's task of resolving conflicts of interests, by biasing the judgments of members and rendering their public deliberations dependent on private considerations. Identifying a conflict of interests is as easy as distinguishing between government and opposition; identifying a conflict of interest is a more formidable and subjective task, which necessarily involves analysis of MPS' motivations.

The condition of conflict of interest is not by definition an ethically untenable situation. It is possible to resolve a conflict of interest by eliminating it; this can usually be done by abstention or recusal, either of which nullifies the official power being influenced by private considerations, or by divestiture, which removes from consideration the interest that might influence judgment. But conflict of interest can just as easily be left unresolved, and as such can be ethically perilous. Just as in the case of constituency service, however, culture-bound norms of perception can permit a certain amount of private influence over public judgments. Different MPs will draw the line between acceptable and unacceptable conflicts of interest at different locations, as is evidenced by the contentiousness of the respondents with respect to the remaining scenarios.

The scenarios that depict conflict of interest situations are TRAVEL, PASS, ORDER PAPER, GIFT, RETAINER, ALL PARTY, and SECRETARY. These scenarios all involve, in one form or another, the interaction of private interests with official duties, privileges, or opportunities, often resulting in a monetary gain. Unlike the constituency service scenarios, the "payoff" goes only as far as the MP involved and does not extend to the constituency at large. While it is possible that the scenarios may be described as alternative types of corrupt behaviour – misappropriation of funds, nepotism, influence peddling – the broad term "conflict of interest" will be used to denote these types of activities. In each, the MPs disagreed on where the line should be drawn between acceptable and unacceptable behaviour.

For the MPs surveyed, the whole issue of foreign travel was contentious. There were means of participating in foreign travel that were perceived as more legitimate than others. Parliamentary delegations, either in connection with a committee, all-party group, or friendship group, were thought to be acceptable means of travel. It was when individual MPs were approached by foreign governments or interest groups that suspicion arose. As one MP pointed out: "There are proper and improper ways of engaging in foreign travel. When travelling with a select committee you receive an invitation, everything is registered and above board. But foreign governments also invite individual MPs to visit their country for a few days every two years. This has implications. It has to be considered whether the trip is being used as a bribe to get an MP to adopt a particular point of view." A colleague put forward this contrary point of view: "Foreign trips are a source of irritation to some. Most MPs do not want to go unless the trip is fully paid for. This does not mean that the sponsoring group or country has bought you. We are not such a gullible lot. A free trip does not ensure opinions."

Still, the great majority of MPS thought the TRAVEL scenario to be corrupt and the mean score of 2.0 indicated fairly serious condemnation of this activity. In explaining this assessment, they emphasized not the danger of being beholden to a foreign government, but the act of "pocketing" the difference between the prices of the two tickets. Members suggested that such activity did go on, and some attempted to provide as justification the hardships MPS endure because of their elected position. Some MPS condoned the practice of exchanging tickets by claiming it as one of the perks of the job: if they were willing to suffer the discomfort of economy-class travel, they felt entitled to the savings.

Members also suggested that it was common practice for an MP to exchange the ticket and use the difference to take his spouse or children along. As one admitted: "I have done this in the past, but did not pocket the difference. I used the extra money to take my wife along with me. This would probably be small 'c' corruption, as would be any actions which supplement my meagre allowances. I don't like the notion of pocketing the difference; you should spend the money on matters related to the trip itself." But as one of his colleagues pointed out, "I really don't see the difference between taking your wife along and pocketing the cash." Spousal accompaniment on trips is neither restricted nor regulated. According to the MPS, the extent to which it is accepted is due to its regularity.

The next item, PASS, was deemed corrupt by 58 per cent of the MPS. The activity described in the scenario is a recent phenomenon and is closely connected to the proliferation of lobbying done at Westminster and to the number of MPS themselves working for public relations firms in some capacity for remuneration. In considering the question, MPS distinguished between the type of organization the lobbyist was connected to, expressing more reluctance to apply for a pass for a commercial firm than for a charity or cause group.

In addition, many MPS wondered whether the lobbyist would be doing any actual research for the member who provided him with the pass. MPS who scored the act as corrupt felt it smacked of unfair advantage, and that the MP involved was in essence selling guaranteed access to Westminster and its hallways. With a pass a lobbyist has unrestricted clearance past the main entryway and its rigorous security check. Once inside, the pass guarantees him the ability to roam the halls, use the library, and obtain parliamentary papers. These are all privileges a member of the public or members of other lobby and interest groups are not accorded.

It was this favoured status which led one member to claim that this was "an undesirable and unwise practice which leans toward criminality," and another to suggest that "this type of situation can't be right.

A research assistant ought to be just that, nothing else." Members who evaluated the act as corrupt also objected to someone other than the member or constituency party paying the salary of a research assistant. They felt that only assistants paid by the member directly out of the staff allowance should be entitled to Westminster passes, not those who are funded by interested, outside organizations. The Select Committee on Members' Interests thought this practice to be worrisome enough to merit study. As one MP complained: "This is a shocking abuse which has become all too common."

Members who justified the granting of a research pass to assistants whose salaries did not come out of their own budget did so by claiming that salaries and allowances had to be supplemented in some fashion. Since passes were normally requested for lobbyists employed by firms with which MPs have a relationship, either as directors or consultants, many felt that the remuneration they received merited the awarding of a pass. Several admitted to requesting such passes and stated they would be much more obliging if such requests were for a group or a firm with which they had sympathies.

Those MPs who deemed ORDER PAPER corrupt considered the submission of questions on behalf of clients to be an abuse of position. In their view the MP was only seeking information because he was being paid to obtain it, not because of some belief or firm commitment to the issue at hand. The MPs, it seemed, were also especially wary of any activity that involved a foreign government. This could be attributed to memories of those MPs who, in the late 1960s and early 1970s, were implicated in scandals involving foreign governments.[10] In addition, members who scored the act corrupt worried that the MP's interest was not legitimately declared, and remarked that it was not always clear from examining the order paper whether a member possessed a direct financial interest. The Select Committee on Members' Interests has actually studied this problem and considered the possibility of placing an asterisk beside those questions on the order paper in which a member has a pecuniary interest. Several of the members who were dissatisfied with the current situation would be supportive of such a measure, as evidenced by their remarks:

MPs should mark written questions in which they have an interest. People should know whom they are seeking information for.

Material reward of some kind for putting questions to other representatives in Parliament, in or outside the House, or in the framework of the bureaucracy, should not be permitted.

Those members who thought the act was not corrupt based their assessment on the premise that the interest was declared and hence acceptable. These MPs thought it perfectly acceptable for members to seek written information for their clients in return for monetary compensation, as long as the relationship was declared. As with PASS, many MPs considered such information procuring to be a legitimate service provided by MPs to those who retain their services.

In the course of their job, all MPs are offered gifts of varying value from grateful constituents, interest groups, and foreign governments. No rules exist to help MPs determine which gifts can be accepted and which cannot. The only requirement is that any gift accepted should be registered. In contrast, the guidelines for ministers impose value limitations on gifts accepted. Gifts can assume many guises – meals, theatre tickets, hotel rooms, and so on. Only occasionally is money offered: "Once I was sent £500 but I sent it right back. When I became Minister I waited for a buxom Swedish blonde with a short skirt to appear, but to no avail." One MP indicated that the GIFT scenario was for him not at all hypothetical:

When I was Minister, I once worked very diligently on a particular piece of legislation which eventually was passed into law. An individual connected with the bill from one of the lobby groups sent me a crate of wine as an expression of gratitude. Not knowing what to do, I accepted the wine and gave each person who was involved in the report a bottle, from the secretary on up. Later, the lawyer involved thanked me profusely for the extravagant bottle of wine saying it was very good. "Extravagant?" I said. He then informed me that it sold for approximately £48 per bottle.

Members are very reluctant to offend anyone – especially a constituent – by refusing a gift. Some try to avoid embarrassing the bearers of gifts by accepting them and then turning them over to a local charity.

Of the MPs interviewed, 31 per cent considered the GIFT item to be corrupt. These MPs saw gift-giving as encroaching on the boundaries of bribery and did not think that MPs should allow themselves even to be perceived as beholden to a benefactor. They felt that by accepting a gift, an MP compromised his independence. Some refused gifts of any kind: "I do not accept gifts from anyone as I don't want anything to influence a decision … This whole area of gifts can be regarded as corrupt and is a cause for concern." Others were less stringent, but still insisted that MPs must employ their discretion to avoid gifts given in the expectation of some consideration in return: "I once had a sizeable sum of money sent to me. I sent it back. MPs should be able to distinguish between a courtesy and something intended to influence one's judgment."

Most MPs, however, viewed the GIFT scenario as not corrupt and appeared to view most gifts as simple tokens of appreciation, unlinked to any expectations. These members also doubted that MPs could fulfil any *quid pro quo* expected of them. As one MP said: "I should be so lucky that someone would send me a crate of wine. I just do not believe that MPs are in a position to influence anything. But I will concede that it is all a matter of perception – whether you can convince people that you are a person worth influencing." In addition, several members mentioned cultural considerations. In a variety of cultures the offering of gifts to public officials is thought to be highly acceptable and the proper way of conducting business. To refuse such a gift could conceivably cause more harm than good. Almost all the MPs, whatever their opinion of this particular scenario, appeared to weigh considerations of size or value, type of gift (money, meals, entertainment, or material goods), and origin (individual constituent, interest group, or other organization) in their decisions about how to deal with gifts.

Barely one-fifth of the MPs deemed RETAINER to be corrupt. Some of these MPs felt that the member involved had reduced himself to little more than a booking agent in a catering firm. They also complained about members who booked rooms for a fee, which in some instances could be a considerable sum of money. They especially objected to MPs sponsoring what were essentially lobbying efforts – effectively providing their "stamp of approval" in hopes of drawing a larger number of their colleagues into attending, perhaps unwittingly, an occasion designed to influence their opinions.

The MPs who did not object to RETAINER saw no difficulty with such activities. They pointed out that the relationship of the MP with the corporation would have been declared – and thus the intentions of the event would be clear. They felt that such meetings were an acceptable means of informing parliamentarians of the concerns of interested groups, and pointed out that such sponsored dinners occur all the time.

The item ALL PARTY was viewed as corrupt by only 11 per cent of the respondents. An all-party group on the aged and on Age Concern could be expected to garner the support of many MPs. Age Concern is a conscience group, and many people support their aims and objectives wholeheartedly. Assistance from Age Concern can be seen as a harmless and beneficial aid to an all-party group low on the resources needed to promulgate its humanitarian concerns. At the same time, the scenario depicts an interest group clearly purchasing privileged access to the legislative system via the all-party group.

A few MPs condemned the scenario on principle: "It is quite wrong for charities or groups of any kind to pay for any services of an all party group." But the majority of MPs either accepted this sort of behaviour in the abstract, or allowed their sympathies for the group depicted to determine their tolerance for the behaviour. One MP's comments illustrated the latter hypothesis: "People would tend to see it very differently if any other group had been used. Age Concern is too humanitarian. It evokes everyone's sympathy, unlike the Nutrition Group which has researchers hired by every food manufacturer in Britain. This group is a very slick operation. The acceptance by all party groups of assistance from outside interests is a very risky business and it needs to be curbed." This MP, like many of his colleagues, identified the "risky business" involved in this scenario, but allowed his final determination to depend on his personal support for the causes and interests involved. This scenario may have been a difficult one for the MPs to evaluate, for while few of them deemed it corrupt, only 57 per cent were prepared to say that they themselves would engage in the activity.

The scenario deemed corrupt by the lowest percentage of MPs (2 per cent) was SECRETARY. Eighty-four per cent of the respondents saw absolutely no hint of corruption in the scenario (score of 7), and the two MPs who did, felt it was only mildly corrupt (score of 3). This is surely a reflection of a legislative system in which there are no restrictions on nepotism, either by law or by convention. MPs defended the decision to hire their spouse or family member by citing the low salaries they received and the burden of having to spend so much time in London, away from the family home. They suggested that MPs who employed their spouses were able to spend more time with them. As one member said: "The practice is justified by the convenience. MPs are away from their family so much. This way there is the added advantage of the same timetable." Also, several members pointed out that spouses were prime candidates for secretarial jobs – they knew the constituency inside out, were aware of the personality and idiosyncracies of the member, and had first-hand knowledge of the member's schedule and preferences. This, the MPs argued, made them invaluable, notwithstanding the fact that not every MP's spouse has formal secretarial training. What the MPs said they would not condone would be putting a spouse on the payroll for work that was not performed. While a few suspected this was still common, most MPs thought this practice had been eradicated with the establishment of new, central payroll and allowance offices. It is still, however, left to the discretion of an MP how much of the staff allowance will be paid to the secretary, and it remains within the MP's prerogative to award the entire sum.

Many MPs were curious as to why such a situation was included among the scenarios, because in their minds it was clearly not corrupt. Most were unaware that in many other legislatures this activity is viewed as a clear conflict of interest and is restricted, if not completely prohibited. When informed of this, a number of MPs refused to acknowledge an inherent conflict of interest in the situation. They did not agree that hiring one's spouse was similar to lining one's own pocket, even though in most instances the spouses were hired automatically: the position was not advertised; interviews were not conducted; the spouse was merely put on the public payroll. Interestingly, however, while the MPs did not condemn this act, only 64 per cent said they themselves would hire their spouse. Perhaps these members had other reasons for this decision, such as the difficulties they might encounter in both living and working with their spouse.

The final scenario, KNIGHT, is neither a conflict of interest nor an act of constituency service. Strictly speaking, the act depicted is one of political patronage. Whether such acts can be considered corrupt was not conclusively settled amongst the MPs: responses covered the spectrum from one to seven and all points in between; this scenario also had the highest standard deviation of responses (2.5). Those who judged the act corrupt objected to the direct relationship between the campaign contribution and the knighthood. A number of the MPs expressed concern that the honour should be bestowed for reasons other than a sizeable contribution. In their opinion, political service and merit could be a criterion employed in the dispensation of patronage, but there should be no *quid pro quo*. Those MPs who judged KNIGHT not corrupt regarded patronage as an acceptable prerogative of the prime minister and government of the day. A number of the members excused the practice by claiming that this was the way the system operated. As one observed somewhat cynically: "The awarding of Knighthoods in this fashion happens three times a day after lunch." Another offered: "This is the time honoured way in which the game is played on both sides of the House." A number of the members explained that political parties had to raise money somehow and that honours could be used as an incentive to donors. This they could tolerate as long as there was no system of "honours for sale" in operation.

It was apparent that MPs were not in unanimous agreement as to those acts that could and could not be considered corrupt. Members seemed to draw the ethical line between acceptable and unacceptable behaviour in different places and they advanced a host of reasons to defend their judgments. In the following section a typology will be constructed to help organize the responses of the MPs so that further comparisons and distinctions can be presented.

WHAT CONSTITUTES
CORRUPTION: A TYPOLOGY

Having examined each of the scenarios in the questionnaire, it is now possible to proceed to the construction of the typology. The first step was to remove the four items – LORRY, CAMPAIGN, DRIVEWAY, and PLANNING – the MPs overwhelmingly found corrupt. In these scenarios there was a lack of variance to explain. Their distinctive quality was the degree of consensus the MPs expressed in deeming them corrupt.

The KNIGHT scenario was also removed, but for different reasons. In the first place, it does not fit either of the categories of constituency service or conflict of interest which organize the subsequent discussion. Second, responses to this item were very closely correlated with party affiliation: Conservative MPs felt it was quite acceptable; Labour MPs were strong in their disapproval. Unlike the remaining scenarios, the large variance in this case was primarily due to a single factor.[11] This result was not unexpected, given the well-known attitudes of the two major parties towards the honours system.

The next step was to determine if the previously discussed conceptualization of the remaining nine items could be supported by the data. A Pearson correlation matrix was produced to determine the strength of the relationship between the various scenarios within each of the two conceptual groups. The matrix indicated that the two scenarios in the constituency service item – SCHOOL and CONTRACT – were related statistically as well as conceptually. The significant correlation coefficient of .43 (p < .01) indicated that the acts were evaluated in a similar manner by the MPs.

The matrix also revealed a number of statistically significant relationships between the seven conflict-of-interest scenarios (see table 5 for the cross-correlations of TRAVEL, PASS, ORDER PAPER, GIFT, RETAINER, ALL PARTY, and SECRETARY). The item that correlated with the greatest number of others was RETAINER. It was significantly correlated (at p < .01) with GIFT (coefficient of .44), TRAVEL (.24), ORDER PAPER (.37), PASS (.31), and SECRETARY (.40). Each of the other items correlated significantly with at least one other item in the conflict-of-interest group.

Tolerance Scores

Previously, the scores for each scenario have been discussed in absolute terms: the percentage of respondents who scored an act corrupt. Since "corrupt" was never defined for the respondents, and since no examples of acts that would be given particular scores were provided,

Table 5
Pearson Correlation Matrix for CONFLICT scenarios

Scenario	Retainer	Secretary	Gift	Travel	All Party	Order Paper	Pass
RETAINER		*.40*	*.44*	*.24*	.12	*.37*	*.31*
SECRETARY			**.19**	*.16*	−.04	.11	−.01
GIFT				**.19**	.11	*.31*	*.38*
TRAVEL					**.16**	*.15*	.09
ALL PARTY						.12	*.15*
ORDER PAPER							*.24*
PASS							

Key: Coefficients in ***bold italics*** are significant at p < .01. Coefficients in **bold** are significant at p < .05.
Coefficients in *italics* are significant at p < .10.

decisions on where to draw the line between corrupt and not corrupt remained subjective and variable from respondent to respondent. Still, while some MPs may have been much more tolerant than others of certain behaviour, a picture of the general acceptability of each of the scenarios emerged. At the same time, the absence of a pre-defined scale allowed each respondent's set of answers to generate an implicit definition of corruption – a definition that varied from respondent to respondent. This inherent relativity in the scoring must be taken into account when classifying the respondents. If the mean scores of the whole sample are examined, it is possible to determine the relative tolerance each MP held for the activities described in the scenarios – in other words, compared with the average MP, whether a particular respondent was more or less tolerant of a particular act. For example, the mean score for the entire sample on the RETAINER item was 5.5. Respondents who gave RETAINER a lower score than the average can be said to have had a low tolerance for the activity depicted in the scenario, while those who gave a higher score had a high tolerance.[12]

Based on this idea of a tolerance score, two additive scales were constructed.[13] The first is a combination of SCHOOL and CONTRACT, both of which depict constituency service situations. This new variable SERVICE has a mean of 3.7 and a standard deviation of 2.0. The second scale combines TRAVEL, PASS, ORDER PAPER, GIFT, RETAINER, ALL PARTY, and SECRETARY, and is labelled CONFLICT, since each of these situations involves a conflict of interest. CONFLICT has a mean of 4.7 and a standard deviation of 1.1. As previously noted, correlations between items within each of the scales was relatively high.

The mean value of CONFLICT divides the sample into groups of high and low tolerance for conflict of interest, just as the mean values for the individual scenarios break the sample into tolerant and intolerant

Figure 1
Ethical Locations of the Sample

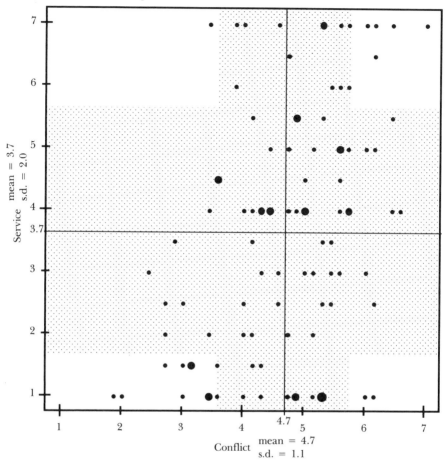

'1' = "Corrupt" = low tolerance
'7' = "Not Corrupt" = high tolerance
Area shaded is within one standard deviation of the mean scores.
A ● is plotted at the ethical location of each MP.
A ● signifies two MPs at the same location.
A ● signifies three colocated MPs.

groups. Similarly, SERVICE splits the sample into groups of high and low tolerance for generalized constituency service. By combining these two bifurcations, a four-fold typology of MPs, based on their tolerance of these types of activities, is produced. This is depicted graphically in figure 1. Each respondent is represented by a point on a scatter graph whose y-coordinate is his SERVICE score and x-coordinate is his

CONFLICT score.[14] A horizontal line at SERVICE = 3.7 (the mean value) is the border between high tolerance for constituency service above the line, and low tolerance below it. The vertical line at CONFLICT = 4.7 divides MPs with high tolerance for conflict of interest (on the right) from those with low tolerance (on the left). The intersection of these mean lines describes the "ethical location" of a hypothetical average MP. The spread of points across the graph illustrates the diversity of ethical tolerances and attitudes evident in the sample.

The Typology[15]

Each quadrant of figure 1 contains MPs with similar attitudes towards political corruption. MPs in the lower left quadrant have relatively low tolerance for both constituency service and conflict-of-interest scenarios. These twenty-eight MPs will be classified as *Puritans*, a name that signifies their apparently restrictive approach to ethical decision-making. These MPs found corrupt both types of activities described to them. They were members who operated from a very stringent set of values that precluded such activities. They were unwilling to tolerate any deviance from the straight and narrow, even in the name of constituency service. These MPs ran the risk of being too restrictive in their views: they saw the potential for corruption inherent in almost every "hard choice" they had to make. This propensity to see any shade of gray as darkest black could in the long run be to the detriment of their constituents. But there are powerful indicators that explain why the Puritans are so rigorous in their evaluations.

Sixteen MPs with a low tolerance for conflict of interest, but a high tolerance for constituency service, are found in the upper left quadrant and will be termed *Servants*, to emphasize their willingness to give primary consideration to the interests of their constituents in their ethical determinations. The Servants were more willing than their Puritan colleagues to see constituency service activities as acceptable and even necessary aspects of an MP's job. While they were willing to bend with respect to constituency-related activities, they were not particularly pliable on matters of conflict of interest. These acts they considered to fall outside the accepted duties of the British MP.

Twenty-one MPs populate the lower right quadrant of the ethical graph, indicating a conceptually intriguing combination of relatively high tolerance for conflict-of-interest situations with a more "puritanical" attitude towards constituency service. This group of MPs will be given the name *Muddlers*, as their responses and remarks in the interviews indicated that they were in many ways confused about the ethical issues they confronted as MPs. The Muddlers felt that trying to get contracts for their constituency or using their position and influence to gain admission to a university would be violations of acceptable means of carrying out their representative responsibilities. These were items in which the MP himself would not derive a direct, personal benefit. But many Muddlers found situations that involved monetary payments to MPs in exchange for services to be perfectly acceptable. Whereas Servants were willing to bend the rules for the benefit of their constituents, Muddlers were willing to tolerate dubious behaviour when it suited their own interests, but felt no obligation to do so for the sake of their constituents. While the Muddlers offered a host of explanations to account for this viewpoint, these rationalizations were not accepted by all MPs.

The remaining thirty-five MPs, who occupy the upper right quadrant, will be classified as *Entrepreneurs*. The largest of the four groups in the sample, they found both constituency service and conflict of interest relatively more acceptable than did their colleagues. These MPs viewed their office almost as a business, rather than a calling, and felt that the activities described were relatively legitimate and within the boundaries circumscribed by the standards of the House. In the grey areas of conflict of interest, and in determining the scope of activities that can be conducted in the name of constituency service, these particular MPs were guided by the principle of "anything goes." These MPs best exemplified the minimalist approach to ethics with which Britain has been previously identified: they were willing to accept almost any activity as long as it did not contravene some written statute. Given the paucity of statutory restrictions that apply to MPs, this allowed them a great deal of latitude.

Figure 2 is a graphical summary of this typology, showing the tolerances of the four types. In addition, four points have been plotted to depict the positions of hypothetical average members of each type (as defined by the mean Service and Conflict scores for each type taken as a whole). In the following chapters, these abstract points will be embodied into composite profiles in order to illustrate the various types of MP, by aggregating common characteristics, traits, and perceptions shared by the MPs who make up each type.

CONCLUSION

The range and variation of responses to the hypothetical scenarios demonstrate that the MPs interviewed were by no means in ethical lockstep with one another. The expectation that all members would evaluate the scenarios in a similar manner, with similar responses, was not borne out. Analysis of the data did not reveal a monolithic consensus

Figure 2
The Typology

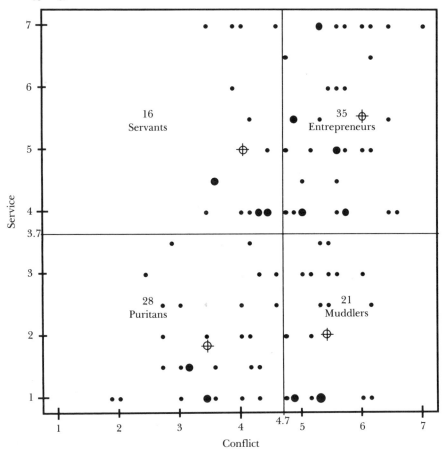

'1' = "Corrupt" = low tolerance
'7' = "Not Corrupt" = high tolerance
A ⊕ signifies a hypothetical "typical" MP.

on ethical issues, but rather distinct and divergent subpopulations. These subpopulations are encompassed in the typology.

Each type of MP will be analysed in detail in chapters 3–6. This examination will begin with a discussion of the MPs' explicit definitions of corruption and their responses to the general perceptual questions in the research instrument. These sources will indicate the basic ethical attitudes of the type. Next, background data, spatial information, and political characteristics will be used to provide a clearer picture of the different types of MPs – where they come from, on which side of the House they sit, their educational and occupational background. The reflections of the MPs on various specific ethical issues will then be used to illuminate and flesh out the general perceptual profile. Finally, a discussion of the basic ethical outlook and strategies of the type will provide understanding of the totality of the type's ethical motivations and concerns.

Similarities and differences among the four types will be examined, as well as variation within each type. Outliers in the categories will be examined and reasons advanced to explain their deviation from the categorical norm. What the profiles will reveal is that different types of MPs draw the line between acceptable and unacceptable ethical conduct in different places. Each uses discretion to shape and uphold a set of ethical standards that is personally comfortable. Through their choices and comments, the MPs indicate the kinds of activities their standards permit them to tolerate, those they are unable to tolerate, and the ethical boundaries within which they function.

CHAPTER THREE

The Puritans

The Puritan category consists of the twenty-eight respondents who displayed low tolerance for both constituency service and conflict of interest. These MPs drew the boundaries of ethically acceptable behaviour more narrowly than other members. They zealously and rigidly safeguarded their legislative autonomy, and were determined to allow neither their private interests nor their roles as representatives to exert undue influence on their functioning as legislators. Unlike many of their colleagues, the Puritans were well aware of their distinctiveness in this regard. Most Puritans expressed confidence in their standards and a firm belief that these standards were above reproach. Several described their approach to legislative ethics as "prudish," or actually "puritanical."[1]

These self-described Puritans were guided by a clearly defined sense of right and wrong, and their ethical judgment flowed from a well-developed and oft-consulted set of values. Ethical introspection was an important part of their daily routine and ethical probity formed the foundation of their public trust. One Puritan suggested that in any situation which might lead to compromise or the perception that one has compromised one's trust, "it is best to be like Caesar's wife." The Puritans had difficulty with the idea that there can be a grey area between acceptable and unacceptable behaviour, and tended towards a manichean view of ethical matters: an activity either conformed to the standards that must be adhered to, and was thus acceptable, or did not, and thus could not be condoned. The Puritans were the most consistent of the four groups in their ethical outlook, but their unwillingness to compromise deprived them of flexibility in their judgments. Like their namesakes, they were at times dogmatic in their treatment of ethical questions and ignored subtleties.

The clearest example of this ideological approach was the Puritan's strong support for a total ban on the practice of MPs pursuing other employment in addition to their legislative duties. While many MPs were concerned about the increasingly close relationship between legislators and outside employers, such involvements have always been a feature of the British system, and many MPs today maintain additional employment. The Puritans considered the arguments put forward by their colleagues – that poor parliamentary salaries and facilities make outside employment a necessity – to be specious and misleading. As one Puritan explained, "MPs should not have outside interests other than the people who elected them."

In many ways, the Puritans' stringent attitudes have made them outsiders in their own House. They believed that the collegiality of the legislature inhibited not only the detection but also the punishment of ethical transgressions, and provided strong disincentives to MPs who try to monitor the conduct of others. The Puritans, guided by strong ethical convictions, were frustrated by a system they saw as ad hoc and unwilling to discipline any but the most extreme offenders, and even then, reluctantly. Some Puritans went as far as to suggest that the system had failed, and that the office of member of parliament was open to serious abuse. At the same time, they felt powerless to curb practices they found unacceptable yet prevalent. All they felt they could do was to continue to ensure that their own behaviour conformed to their own high standards.

PURITAN PERCEPTIONS

The basic ethical perceptions of the MPs will serve as a starting point for the elucidation of the Puritan perspective. The most fundamental was their stated definition of the term "political corruption." This qualitative examination will be buttressed by a quantitative analysis of a battery of perceptual questions. This general perceptual profile exemplifies the consistent differences of opinion that were associated with the ethical tolerances on which the typology is based. Puritans stood out not just for their tolerance levels, but also as a group with coherent opinions and beliefs about a wide range of ethical issues.

Puritan Definitions of Political Corruption

The responses of the MPs to the individual scenarios formed an implicit definition of political corruption, but the members were also asked explicitly for a personal definition of the term. The definitions offered by the MPs can be classified broadly into three kinds: those that centred around the notions of betrayal, abuse of office, and inducement. Betrayal definitions were those indicating that an act becomes corrupt when it involves the abnegation of an MP's personal principles or responsibility to the public – the most common idea was that corruption involves a betrayal of the public trust. Abuse of office definitions emphasized the exploitation of privilege: when an MP misuses the powers or opportunities afforded him by his position, he has engaged in a corrupt act. Inducement definitions indicated that corruption occurs when an illegitimate influence causes an MP to compromise his legislative autonomy. The four types of MPs differed in their perceptions of the distinguishing characteristics of a corrupt act.

One-third (32 per cent) of the Puritans, more than any of the other types, offered betrayal-based definitions. Under such a definition, motivation is paramount: an action can be considered corrupt even if it breaks no laws and does not involve any illicit financial transaction; and even an otherwise acceptable act, performed for improper reasons, can become corrupt. This definitional theme is in keeping with the Puritans' commitment to principles and ideological tenets. In their opinion, compromise of self or constituents was indicative of corruption. As one put it: "Corruption is a betrayal of one's pledges and promises and understood political viewpoint for the sake of personal advancement." Another Puritan's definition might even include the process of legislative compromise and political expediency: "Corruption is changing one's perception of what the right course of action is." To most other MPs, such definitions seemed unnecessarily restrictive: only 7 per cent of the non-Puritans defined corruption in terms of betrayal.

Thirty-six per cent of the Puritans (as opposed to 26 per cent of the others) defined corruption as the result of inducement. This type of definition, in which the MP is seen as a victim (albeit a somewhat willing and too weakly principled victim) of corrupting influences shifts some emphasis away from the idea of the public trust and towards the idea of a *quid pro quo*. One MP defined corruption as the "acceptance of money or preferment of some kind which would influence someone to alter their opinions – trim their views." In this type of view, corruption occurs when an MP performs an act, which he would otherwise never contemplate, directly as a result of the promise of reward or benefit. Corruption is thus specifically linked to an inducement – it has a "cause" – and springs from a reciprocal relationship between the MP and an outsider.

Finally, whereas most MPs (53 per cent) equated corruption with abuse of office, only 29 per cent of the Puritans did so. This type of definition is conceptually the narrowest, as it ignores motivation and concentrates on the act itself, and whether it crosses a threshold between legitimate exercise of authority and illegitimate misuse of opportunity and influence. This definition can be seen as a modification of the betrayal theme, in that "abuse" assumes a betrayal or subversion of accepted "use" of office, such as "taking advantage of your position for your own personal or party gain." Unlike the inducement definition, the abuse definition portrays the MP as initiator of the corrupt act – he chooses to overstep the bounds of acceptability for his own self-centred reasons – and does not clearly imply an external partner. But while betrayal definitions involve an injured party – the public or the MP's honour – abuse definitions are "victimless." The identification of corruption is dependent upon how much discretion MPs are afforded in using their powers – only when certain undefined limits are exceeded is an act deemed corrupt.

The view of corruption as an abuse of office ultimately reduces the issue to a question of scope: certain acceptable acts, taken to extremes, become corrupt; unacceptable conduct, if reduced in scale, can be tolerated. Whether an MP abides by or exceeds a discretionary limit on official power determines the judgment. A betrayal definition accepts no such reductionism. Each act, no matter how consequential, must be examined for adherence to ethical standards and responsibilities in order to be deemed acceptable. The relative popularity of betrayal, as opposed to abuse, definitions among the Puritans reflected their restrictive ethical viewpoint. That more Puritans offered definitions based on inducement than any other notion suggested that many saw Parliament as endangered by external influences it may no longer be able to resist. The Puritans were the one type especially worried about the ethical climate of the House of Commons.

General Perceptual Profile

In order to obtain a general estimation of their attitudes towards political corruption, the MPs were asked to indicate their agreement or disagreement with a series of statements about the issue. Mean responses were computed for the Puritans and for the sample as a whole (see table 6). These figures provided an indication of what the Puritans thought about corruption, its prevalence in Britain, and what, if anything, could be done about it.

Two-thirds of the Puritans agreed that political corruption was not a widespread problem. The Puritans did not think corruption ubiquitous, but compared with the rest of the sample, they were significantly less sure ($p < .01$). In fact, the mean Puritan response to statement 15 was a weak, almost neutral agreement, while the sample as whole indicated stronger agreement. Those Puritans who did think political corruption to be widespread painted a somewhat bleak picture:

Table 6
Puritan General Perceptual Profile

Statement	Text	Agree (%)	Disagree (%)	Mean	Std. Dev.	Median	Significance
15	Political corruption is not a widespread problem.	67	26	3.2	1.7	3	**t:** p < .01
		82	*15*	*2.5*	*1.6*	*2*	**F:** *p < .05*
16	In so far as citizens distrust elected officials it is because they do not understand what politics is all about.	56	37	3.7	1.9	3	
		66	*28*	*3.2*	*1.9*	*3*	
17	Dishonesty is more widespread in politics than in business.	4	85	5.7	1.1	6	**t:** p < .10
		4	*89*	*6.0*	*1.2*	*6*	
18	Political corruption is more widespread at the local than at the national level of government.	70	19	3.0	1.8	2	
		73	*12*	*2.7*	*1.6*	*2*	
19	No matter what we do, we can never eliminate political corruption.	74	22	2.9	1.8	2	
		80	*13*	*2.5*	*1.7*	*2*	
20	The corruption that exists in the political world simply reflects the standards of the rest of society.	52	33	3.6	1.8	3	
		55	*31*	*3.4*	*1.9*	*3*	
21	If it hadn't been for the Poulson scandal, we would hear a lot less about corruption in government.	38	50	4.2	2.1	4.5	**t:** p < .10
		29	*64*	*4.8*	*2.0*	*5*	**F:** *p < .01*
22	MPs are sufficiently well informed to act as the sole guarantors of acceptable conduct in the house.	33	59	4.5	2.1	5	**t:** p < .05
		52	*40*	*3.7*	*2.2*	*3*	**F:** *p < .05*
23	Once allegations of corruption are made, MPs in their parliamentary capacity should be brought within the ambit of criminal law	89	4	1.7	1.1	1	**t:** p < .001
		70	*23*	*2.7*	*2.1*	*2*	**F:** *p < .01*
24	Britain's libel laws inhibit the uncovering and reporting of political corruption.	67	26	3.3	2.1	3	**t:** p < .001
		37	*53*	*4.5*	*2.2*	*5*	**F:** *p < .001*

Key: Values in *italics* pertain to the entire sample of 100 MPs. "Agree" equals responses of 1, 2, or 3 (as a percentage of valid responses). "Disagree" equals responses of 5, 6, or 7 (as a percentage of valid responses). "Significance" equals significance levels for t-statistic (difference between Puritan and non-Puritan means) and F-ratio (analysis of variance across the four types of MPs).

Political corruption is taking place all over Britain – local governments, Parliament, the bureaucracy, the work place.

I do think significant corruption exists in Britain and that many of the situations described are real life scenarios. While I have my suspicions, I just do not have enough information to go on.

One offered a possible explanation for why his view was in the minority: "Corruption goes on all right. But because it happens in secret it is very difficult to discover." Some of the difference of opinion within the Puritan group seemed to be based on the visibility of corruption: some, seeing only a few well-publicized incidents, assumed that there was nothing to worry about; others saw the problem as the tip of an iceberg and inferred a large number of incidents that would never become public knowledge.

The Puritans were also less willing to agree that dishonesty was more widespread in politics than in business. While most MPs strongly defended the integrity of politicians, the Puritans were the least firm in their defence ($p < .10$). Combined with the results of statement 15, this suggests that, notwithstanding their conceptual objections, Puritans, compared with other MPs, were more willing to concede that political corruption could be a problem for Parliament.

Some have suggested that the problem of corruption, if it exists, lies implicitly with the citizens rather than the politicians – that is, the public's perception of MPs as untrustworthy may be due to their lack of knowledge of political realities. The Puritans were less likely than other MPs to blame the public for its general distrust of politicians (statement 16), but not to a significant degree. Nor were the Puritans' responses to statement 20 significantly different from the sample as a whole. These two statements probed the MPs' opinions on whether societal values and constraints were important in encouraging or inhibiting political corruption. Apparently there was no link between this issue and relative tolerance for potentially corrupt activities.

The Puritans were slightly more optimistic than their colleagues that political corruption could be eradicated. Fewer Puritans than non-Puritans agreed with statement 19 that corruption could never be completely eliminated. Some Puritans, while conceding that some corruption was inevitable, expressed the opinion that it could be more strictly limited and controlled: "While we might not be able to eliminate corruption, we certainly could do better in tightening things up." Another added: "Much more could be done, such as the introduction of guidelines, or even legislation. A government that was critical of abuses would be necessary as well." Interestingly, the Puritans were at once the most cynical of the four types of MPs about the extent of corruption in the House, and the most idealistic about whether it could be curbed.

The Poulson Affair was the one notable scandal in Britain which implicated a number of parliamentarians. The scandal has been credited with awakening Britons to the fact that political corruption occurred not only in the United States but also at home, and involved their own politicians. Most MPs in this study tended to downplay the role of the Poulson scandal (statement 21). The Puritans, however, displayed significantly greater agreement with the statement (p < .10). This insistence on the importance of Poulson reflected the importance the Puritans attached to ethical matters in general. The Poulson revelations may even be credited, in part, with the development of the stringent ethical standards adhered to by the Puritans.

The Poulson scandal not only awakened people to the reality of corruption in Britain, but it also forced Parliament to examine its standards of conduct in public life and the mechanisms that exist to investigate and sanction errant members. Statement 22 was an attempt to find out whether MPs believed there was a need for an external regulatory agency or whether the disciplinary function should remain within the parametres of Parliament. The Puritans were significantly less willing than their colleagues to accept MPs as the sole guarantors of acceptable parliamentary conduct (p < .05). Unlike their colleagues, the Puritans thought that the job of ensuring ethical conduct among MPs should not belong to MPs themselves. While the Puritans expressed pride in their ability to keep their own personal behaviour above reproach, many indicated that they felt their colleagues to be either unwilling or unable to avoid compromise. Currently MPs are the only individuals responsible for monitoring standards; the Puritans here tacitly acknowledged that this arrangement is no longer sufficient.

Given this finding, it was not surprising that the Puritans overwhelmingly agreed that MPs should be brought within the ambit of criminal law. Significantly more than the sample as a whole, the Puritans objected to the notion that MPs can be, or appear to be, above the law (p < .001). Under the existing corruption legislation, Parliament is not considered a public body, nor is the position of MP thought to constitute public office, and thus the House and its members are effectively excluded from the purview of the law (see chapter 1). Once again this was a situation the Puritans found especially untenable.

The Puritans were also quite distinctive in their opinion that Britain's libel laws did indeed inhibit the uncovering and reporting of political corruption. The difference between the Puritan position on this issue and that of the other types of MPs was dramatic and statistically significant (p < .001). Clearly the Puritans saw this legislation as yet another factor hampering the effective investigation of ethical misconduct. Some Puritans drew explicit comparisons with the United States and suggested that investigative journalism was not accorded the same degree of freedom in Britain. The Puritans felt that libel laws deterred journalists from pursuing allegations of corruption. The one exception mentioned was *Private Eye* – the publication that first brought the Poulson scandal to light. Apparently the Puritans would endorse a more intrusive press as a means of ensuring better compliance with parliamentary standards of ethical behaviour.

The Puritans' general perceptions of corruption illustrated once again their unique ethical point of view. The Puritans were aware of abuses occurring in Britain and were concerned about ethical matters. The issues on which they most clearly stood out from other MPs were those pertaining to the management of ethical misconduct. On this score the Puritan position suggested that the current system was inadequate to this task. The Puritans saw MPs as having too much responsibility for their own discipline and too much insulation from outside scrutiny. While this does not mean that they would welcome the intrusion of an external agent or body into the ethical concerns of MPs, they did concede that self-policing was not the best possible solution and that recourse to the criminal laws might be of assistance.

WHO ARE THE PURITANS?

To appreciate the Puritan mindset fully, it is useful to examine common traits and characteristics as well as shared perceptions. An MP arrives in the House as the product of a particular background. Experience as a member of parliament builds upon this background, and both shape the manner in which an individual responds to questions of ethics. Previous attitudinal research has suggested that certain personal characteristics and prior experiences are important in determining the ethical predispositions of legislators.[2] Background characteristics in this book will be divided into three categories: political, spatial or territorial, and socioeconomic. Political factors include party affiliation, self-perceived scales measuring the respondent's degree of liberalism and left-right position in the political spectrum, legislative tenure, previous governmental experience, and retention of additional employment outside the House. Spatial factors include regional location and degree of urbanization of the constituency. Socioeconomic factors include age, education, religious affiliation, and religious attendance. These characteristics will be examined systematically for any commonalities that might be associated with the Puritan viewpoint.

Figure 3
Party Affiliation

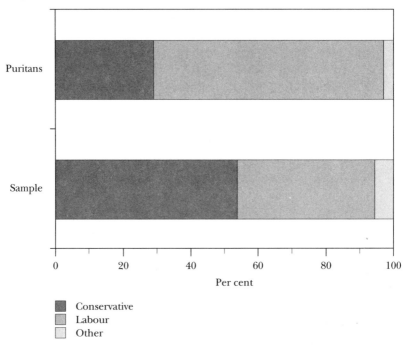

Political Characteristics

The importance of party affiliation to the Puritan category is demonstrated graphically in figure 3. Of all the MPs surveyed, 54 per cent were members of the Conservative Party and 40 per cent were Labour members. Of the Puritans, however, more than two-thirds (68 per cent) belonged to the Labour Party and only 29 per cent were Conservatives. This high proportion of Labour members in the Puritan category was significant ($p < .05$). Clearly membership in the Labour Party was closely associated with identification as a Puritan. Labour members were more likely than other MPs to display the low tolerances for conflict of interest and constituency service that defined the Puritan category.

However, the Puritan type and the Labour Party are not synonymous. Almost a third (32 per cent) of the Puritans were members of other parties, and over half (52 per cent) of the Labour members in the study were not Puritans. On the other hand, the concentration of Labour MPs in the Puritan group might indeed be expected for several reasons. One is the ideological underpinnings of the Labour

Party: socialist principles and philosophical understandings may shape and determine how MPs view ethical issues. Low tolerances for conflict of interest and constituency service activities can be seen as an extension of Labour's preference for economic and social interventionism and egalitarianism. It is also not surprising that members of a Conservative government that has championed the entrepreneurial values of self-interest and initiative tend to be found in groups that are more forgiving of situations in which an MP's personal interests, or those of the constituents, are advanced at the expense of others. This ideological argument finds support in the findings of a study of Canadian MPs, in which the New Democratic Party (NDP) members were found to be the least tolerant of a similar series of corruption items.[3]

Moreover, Puritan MPs of both major parties perceived themselves as being on the left wing of their respective parties. Asked to estimate their own left-right ideological position within their party, Labour Puritans placed themselves further to the left than Labour members in general. At the same time, the Conservative Puritans considered themselves to be "wetter" than the party mainstream.[4]

An alternative explanation for the predominance of Labour members in the Puritan category has to do with proximity to power. The closer an elected representative is to the apex of power, the more tolerant one might expect the MP to be of abuses. Government positions bring with them power; power creates opportunities; and routine exercise of power might dull one's sensibilities about what constitutes inappropriate use of power. The opportunities to engage in potentially questionable activity are greater for a government backbencher than a member of the opposition. A Conservative Whip advised: "You should take into consideration when examining the responses of my Labour colleagues the fact that Labour has not been in government for ten years. They just are not in a position to influence government policy at all. Companies who want to offer an MP a retainer do so to government backbenchers, not those in opposition. It is a frequent practice for companies to ring the Whip's Office and ask for the name of an MP willing to act as an adviser." Members of the governing party are by no means necessarily more corrupt, but they are presented with more opportunities to engage in activities that could be considered unethical. Even if it is assumed that members of all parties begin with equivalent standards, the standards of government members might be expected to erode under the influence of these opportunities. Alternatively, opposition members, bereft of opportunities to indulge, might raise their standards – adopting a position of "if I can't do it, then no one should be able to."

A major decision for British MPs is whether they will pursue additional employment outside the House. This issue is at the centre of much of what ethical controversy exists in Westminster. The Puritans again stood in sharp contrast to the remainder of the sample: only 43 per cent of the Puritans reported an outside occupation, as opposed to 71 per cent of the sample as a whole. In fact, in all three other types more than three-fourths of the MPs were so employed. Of the twelve Puritans with outside occupations, half were employed as parliamentary consultants or corporate directors, while the remainder were either journalists, authors, or farmers. As we shall see, the proportion of consultancies and directorships was significantly higher in the other categories (see figure 4). This distinction in type of employment is important in that parliamentary consultancy and corporate directorship can have much greater potential for creating conflict of interest situations than other types of employment. While an MP who is a journalist might be able to use his position as MP to enhance his byline, it would be difficult for him to profit greatly from such exploitation. On the other hand, the director of a company can reap significant benefit if a particular legislative decision allows that company to increase its revenues.

Historically, outside employment for MPs was accepted, if not actually expected, as part of the representative process. Members were expected to represent not only their geographical constituents, but also their trade or profession, and it was felt that these attachments helped to sharpen parliamentary debate and make it more relevant to the real needs of the nation. For much of Parliament's history, members received little or no payment for their parliamentary services and thus were dependent on sources of income outside the House for their livelihood. This traditional view, however, does not allow for the increasing commoditization of parliamentary position in recent times. Whereas members once contributed practical expertise, garnered from involvement in outside pursuits, to the governing process, now many outside involvements sap Parliament of attention and resources while returning no benefit to the institution.

That less than half the Puritans engaged in outside employment – and that even fewer were employed in positions that might lead to serious conflict of interest – could help account for the intolerant attitudes the Puritans expressed towards the conflict-of-interest situations presented. Whether the Puritans' intolerance was expressing itself as a refusal to risk their legislative autonomy by being beholden to an outside interest, or whether their lack of outside employment was inducing more restrictive attitudes towards conflict of interest, is a motivational distinction. The fact remains that of those few MPs

Figure 4
Outside Employment Types

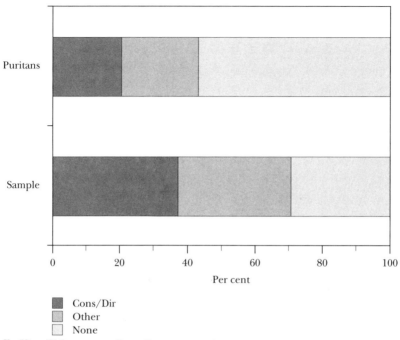

Key: "Cons/Dir" MPs engaged in parliamentary consultancies or corporate directorships.
      "Other" MPs engaged in other forms of outside employment.
      "None" MPs with no outside employment.

(twenty-nine) who avoided outside employment, 55 per cent were
Puritans. The association between Puritans and lack of outside employment was statistically significant (p < .01), and thus outside employment appeared to be an important indicator of "Puritan-ness," even
when party affiliation was controlled for. Thus, within the Labour and
Conservative parties themselves, lack of outside employment was still
significantly associated with membership in the Puritan category.

Puritan opinions on the issue of outside employment were strongly
worded. One saw the holding of outside interests as inevitably resulting
in neglect of public duties and misrepresentation of the public interest:
"You can't represent the constituents' interests and be the director of
a company. You should put forward a line in Parliament because you
believe it not because you are paid to do it. You can't be paid by two
masters. MPs should have one job. Moonlighting as an MP is not
acceptable. This is the root cause of all corruption in Parliament."
Another Puritan agreed with this line of reasoning: "There are so many

members on retainers to P.R. companies who are receiving payment for advancing specific causes, it would be interesting to see whether they would be supporting the same cause or side of an issue if they were not receiving payment." In general, the Puritans felt that permitting MPs to serve as parliamentary consultants opened the door to abuse of position. One suggested that this practice had recently escalated and that vast sums of money were now involved: "Some members are paid £20,000 to be consultants. You have to ask what the company is getting out of it – parliamentary papers, access, written questions, sponsored lunches and receptions?" Other objections were similar: "I am totally against MPs using their name as an entré. We should not have individuals selling their membership in the House to outside interests." Outside employment remains one of the most contentious ethical issues facing the Commons and its members, and examination of the comments of the other types of MPs will illustrate the controversy.

Puritans rejected the idea that trade union sponsorship was equivalent to consultancies. Payments from trade unions go directly to the constituency party of the sponsored MP, normally to help defray campaign costs and the operating expenses of the constituency office. The member himself is not personally remunerated. A parliamentary consultant, in contrast, is paid directly, and the funds he receives may be used entirely at his personal discretion. Although a union-sponsored MP might receive a sum to help defray personal expenses, it is usually nominal, and many give this to the constituency as well, as one Labour Puritan explained: "Usually trade unions provide a sum which goes to the constituency party, in my instance £600 and then £100 for the personal use of the MP. This tradition is traced back historically to the time when members were not provided with a salary, thus something was contributed to their personal expenses. I think this is a custom that should be ended. I personally give that money to the constituency party as well."

Parliamentary experience – the number of terms or years a member has been in Parliament – might also affect ethical standards. A large number of Puritans (39 per cent, versus 31 per cent in the sample as a whole) were first-term MPs, with four or fewer years legislative experience. The hypothesis that freshman legislators are more stringent in their views than colleagues who have been longer in the legislature has been supported by other studies of legislators and their attitudes towards political corruption.[5] While this hypothesis finds some support in the data for this study, the association is not strong enough to be statistically significant. This result provides a preliminary indication that Puritans are unlikely to lose their ethically restrictive orientation as time goes on.

While many Puritans were relatively new to the House, most were no strangers to politics. Half the Puritans had experience as local councillors prior to their election to the House, and 29 per cent had served as ministers or party Whips. Ministers, Whips, and local councillors, unlike backbench MPs, are subject to and must uphold formal codes of conduct. It might be expected that exposure to such codes would tend to cause individuals to develop more restrictive ethical views, especially since there exists a large amount of confusion in the House about just what is and what is not acceptable behaviour. These Puritans with prior code-of-conduct experience had, at least at one time, been told more precisely what their ethical boundaries were. If the three Puritans who sat on the Committees of Procedure, Privilege, and Members' Interests – all of which deal with matters of conduct and ethics – are added to the above numbers, fully 82 per cent of the Puritans can be said to have had exposure to and experience with formalized ethical regulation via codes of conduct. Such exposure, consistent across both sides of the House, was quite rare among the other types of MPs, and although the effect of previous experiences is difficult to measure, it may be that this was a crucial factor holding the Puritans together as an attitudinally cohesive group.

On these political characteristics alone, the Puritans formed a distinct subpopulation in the House. While, as might be expected on ideological grounds, many of the Puritans were Labour MPs, the Labour Puritans were distinguishable from their fellow partisans in a number of ways, as were the Conservative Puritans. More than half the Puritans held no occupation besides MP; one-third were members in their first term of office. In addition, with one exception, every Puritan who did report an outside occupation had at some point had to adhere to and uphold a written code of conduct. Thus virtually all the Puritans either had prior experience and standards to follow in making decisions in ethically grey areas, or chose to avoid having to make such decisions, by refusing to accept outside employment.

Spatial Characteristics

Research in the United States and Canada has suggested an association between legislators' ethical attitudes and the spatial character of their districts or constituencies. Just as the Puritans shared certain political characteristics, it might be reasonable to expect that particular regions or types of constituencies would tend to elect more puritanical MPs. From where do the Puritans come?

One discernible regional accumulation of Puritans was found in Scotland, which supplied 14 per cent of these MPs. This was the highest concentration of Scottish MPs (40 per cent) in any one type. These Scottish Puritans all conveyed the belief that their constituents were more intolerant of impropriety than the constituents of members from elsewhere in the United Kingdom. This is a common stereotype: the Scot as an aggressively thrifty and morally rigid Presbyterian. Michael Johnston, in research on the attitudes of the British public towards right and wrong, found Scottish respondents to be the least tolerant of a number of ethical situations presented to them.[6] The Scottish Puritans thought this would be especially true with respect to sex scandals. As one explained: "The repercussions of a sex scandal would depend on one's party and where in the United Kingdom the MP's constituency is. A sex scandal for me being from Scotland would be disastrous. I would have to resign forthwith." They were also quite candid in their comments on the ethical atmosphere of Parliament:

Its like being in public school again with people breaking the rules. The types of activities described to me in this questionnaire happen all the time. I find most of them abhorrent.

There are things going on around here – the awarding of contracts, fiddling, dinners, passes – which are abuses. Others regard them as acceptable, but I do not.

A similar regionally based ethical intolerance was reported in the aforementioned study of Canadian MPs: those from western Canada – a region, like Scotland, on the periphery of national politics which has traditionally seen itself as separate in culture and attitude from the national "core" – were found to be significantly less tolerant of corrupt acts.

The data were also examined for broader regional biases in the distribution of Puritans. One particularly interesting possibility was that the geographical and socioeconomic divide between North and South would be seen to have an effect on the ethical attitudes of MPs.[7] This suggestion, however, was not supported by analysis of the data. Puritans were not significantly more common in either northern or southern Britain. Alternative partitions of the United Kingdom into three or more large regions also failed to find significant distinctions.

Despite this lack of apparent regional grouping, the Puritans were not distributed uniformly throughout the country. Examination of the nature and settlement of constituencies – how urbanized or rural they were – showed the Puritans to be concentrated in particular types of constituencies.[8] The relationship between an MP's type and the rural-urban classification of the constituency was significant ($p < .02$). But this association was not a simple linear one. Puritans tended to be found in mixed, very urban, and inner-city constituencies, while there were relatively few rural Puritans. This trend towards urbanism was somewhat surprising, given that previous attitudinal studies had found intolerant legislators to come predominantly from rural ridings or districts. Urban areas, often having been subjected to long periods of machine politics, were assumed to have been "conditioned" to accept ethical behaviour that would not be tolerated in the countryside.

This is a hypothesis for which examination of subsequent types will provide support despite the somewhat contradictory association of Puritans with urban areas. Since most of the well-known corruption cases in Britain have occurred at the local level, and 61 per cent of the Puritans have previous local council experience, their lower tolerance level might be partially attributed to direct experience in dealing with, or cleaning up, cases of corruption. As local councillors, these MPs would also have had to abide by a written code of conduct. The standards they followed during their local council tenure may have been carried over into Westminster to aid ethical decision-making. These standards would naturally tend to place them at the "puritanical" end of the ethical tolerance scale.

Background Characteristics

Personal traits and values, as well as political and spatial factors, can be expected to bear upon an individual's attitudes towards corruption. These personal factors, while somewhat more nebulous than party affiliation or constituency region, assess the most basic ethical decision-making of an individual. Education, religion and religious observance, and age will be examined for what affect they may have on classification of MPs.[9]

The Puritans were a relatively well-educated group (89 per cent had attended a college or university), but no more so than most MPs (88 per cent of the sample were university attendees). This was not surprising given that in the House as a whole, a university education is the norm rather than the exception. While the situation is changing, especially in recent elections, it is still the more educated who are elected to Parliament: "I think that the background of MPs does influence what they are able to do, how they perceive things, and their reactions here. In Britain, we have a history of working men becoming MPs only in this century. It is still not the norm for miners, plumbers, fitters, to become MPs. The class bias predominant in Parliament is the upper middle, wealthy classes, the educated. It is still not easy for the 'man in the street' to gain access to the House of Commons." It is not only their having been elected that differentiates MPs from their constituents, but also a higher general level of education.

Age was not significantly associated with membership in the Puritan category. The mean age of the Puritans was the same as that of the sample (fifty-one years, with a standard deviation of twelve years in both cases).[10] Further analysis was suggested by the number of Puritans in their first term of parliamentary service. Perhaps the Puritans, though indistinguishable from their colleagues by age alone, might stand out in the House by the age at which they first were elected. However, the mean age at which Puritans entered the House (age forty) was not noticeably different from that of the sample (age thirty-nine). This result does not negate the importance of the Puritans' relative inexperience, but a blanket statement about any particular stage in life being more "puritanical" than others does not appear to be possible. In fact, any hypothesis suggesting that the propensity to acquire Puritan attitudes grows or diminishes with age finds no support in these data.

Only 32 per cent of the Puritans claimed membership in the Church of England, compared with 47 per cent of the sample. At the same time, 32 per cent of the Puritans were agnostic, in a sample which as a whole was only 17 per cent agnostic. In addition, 9 per cent of the Puritans were atheist, versus 6 per cent of the sample. These were the highest percentages of atheists and agnostics, and the lowest percentage of Anglicans, of any of the four groups – more than half of the professed atheists and agnostics in the sample were Puritans. This detracts from the hypothesis that individuals belonging to an organized religion might be less tolerant of corruption than those who evince no religious affiliation.

Of course, membership in a particular church does not guarantee ethical probity – those who rarely attend services will likely be less influenced by the ethical teachings of their faith. An attempt was therefore made to measure the frequency of religious attendance.[11] One might expect avid church-goers to be less tolerant of corrupt acts than non church-goers, but in the case of the Puritans this was not substantiated. Half attended services only infrequently, and only 14 per cent frequently, as many as never attended at all. Apparently the MPs with the strictest ethical standards were not, as a whole, regular church-goers, casting some doubt on claims that moral and ethical legislative standards are founded on organized religion.

While there is no uniform standard Puritan, the commonalities so far discovered suggest that a reasonably accurate composite may be constructed. Such a "typical Puritan" might be a first-term Labour MP, from an inner-city Scottish constituency. A former local councillor and journalist, this individual now devotes his full attention to the proceedings of the House and scrupulously avoids the offers of the numerous organizations wishing to employ parliamentarians. While not especially religious or irreligious, he has strong opinions about what constitutes acceptable behaviour and is proud of a commitment to probity that occasionally makes it difficult for him to compromise even on political issues. This composite may help to vivify the abstract notion of the Puritan type, but what remains to be analysed, in order to appreciate the Puritan mindset, are the detailed views and specific comments of Puritan MPs on a range of prominent issues associated with legislative ethics.

REFLECTIONS

The Puritans' distinctiveness as a group was evident not only in their general perceptual profile, but also in their opinions about various ethical issues and concerns. The strongest impression given by the Puritans was that they were well aware that they adhered to especially restrictive ethical standards. Most of the Puritans readily acknowledged that, compared with most of their colleagues, they were intolerant of questionable behaviour. This relatively clear position had two consequences. First, the Puritans were imbued with a sense of ethical superiority – they tended to perceive themselves as lone voices of propriety crying out in an ethically desolate wilderness. The Puritans could be quite contemptuous of the motives behind their colleagues' activities, and even doubted whether most other MPs were fully capable of discerning the appropriate course of action in an ethical dilemma. Second, the Puritans were prone to a kind of ethical isolationism. Though seriously concerned about activities they considered violations of the public trust and existing parliamentary standards, and ardent in their calls for more comprehensive ethical regulation, many had come to believe that significant reform could not be realistically expected from the House of Commons. In response, since they despaired of uplifting the standards of the House, they had retreated behind their own "purity" and contented themselves merely with ensuring that their own behaviour remained above reproach.

The Public's Image of MPs

The majority of MPs interviewed (61 per cent) thought that the public find them to be untrustworthy. The Puritans were slightly but not significantly more critical than MPs as a whole, since 64 per cent thought the public consider MPs to be untrustworthy. The consensus seemed to be that a certain amount of public disfavour was the inevitable lot of politicians: "As a group the public sees us as untrustworthy – they always have and they always will. They generally view us as self-serving individuals." While the Puritans were not able to indicate precisely why the public had these perceptions, they did use a number of adjectives to describe themselves that were entirely unflattering: "In general the public finds us a shifty, slimy lot. We are not held in high esteem in the public eye."

While they thought the odd cynic might claim that every member was in politics merely for what he could get out of it, one-third of the Puritans were confident they were viewed as at most inefficient, rather than untrustworthy: "I don't think the public see us as being bent or having our nose in the trough." Another member thought that the public appreciated that MPs do a good job and that they must endure long and socially taxing hours. A few felt the media played an important role in the way the public perceived parliamentarians: reports and stories that depict MPs as shifty, selfish womanizers do nothing to enhance their reputations. But, they added, these are the types of stories that sell newspapers.

No matter how they felt the public viewed them, however, the Puritans generally did not see MPs as any less trustworthy than ordinary citizens: "Parliament is no different from other groups of people – there will be hard workers and lazy workers. There will be honest individuals and corrupt individuals. There is nothing unusual in that." While a few thought that there were individuals in Parliament who were there only to "make money while they could," most revealed their idealistic nature by insisting that MPs were somewhat more principled: "What motivates MPs to come here in the first place is the extension of life and some commitment to a particular philosophical stroke or perspective. We came here to do a job, to represent the people and to pursue the prospect of real social change." A number of the Puritans thus saw the overall public perception of untrustworthiness as an undeserved slight on their integrity, but recognized the difficulty of convincing the public of their worthiness: "While we have our own ideas of integrity, it is the same type of thing as an audit: we want someone else to know." The problem was that "MPs, unlike shopkeepers, deal in words not goods. But integrity is not measured by words, but by your ability to do your job with other people." While complaints about this misperception were common, no plans for correcting it were offered.

The Register of Members' Interests

The Register of Members' Interests is the sole formal regulatory mechanism adopted by the British House of Commons. MPs are required to file an annual disclosure of their holdings and interests under certain specified headings. Two-thirds (67 per cent) of the Puritans expressed dissatisfaction with the current register (compared with 52 per cent of the sample). The Puritans' relative disapproval of the register was significant (p < .05). This result confirms the overall Puritan impression that the current system for resolving ethical dilemmas was not satisfactory.

Some Puritans did claim to be happy with the register, but they seemed to do so almost by default. One admitted to never having looked at the register, another indicated that there was no reason to query it, while a third viewed it as a reasonable compromise. Behind their professed satisfaction lay a principled objection to the basic premise of the register: these Puritans rigidly upheld a view of ethics as an important issue that each individual member should spend time thinking about personally. Unlike their fellow Puritans who were disappointed by the register, they felt the protection of this principle was more important than the need to buttress the registration process. They perceived the register to be an invasion of privacy and in direct contradiction of the presumption of honour that comes with election to Parliament. One stated bluntly: "Yes, I'm satisfied with the operation of the Register. It is a waste of time anyway. I do not approve of inquiries about MP's interests." Another offered that "to improve the Register would be intrusive of the member's privacy." In their minds, MPs were supposed to be "honourable" members. To have a register was to insinuate otherwise.

Given the Puritans' views on outside employment and attachments, however, it was not surprising that a majority of them expressed dissatisfaction with the register. The first criticism levelled by a number of Puritans was that declaration was simply not enough. To say that one has a particular interest is not in itself completely informative. Value amounts are not disclosed in the register, nor in the case of corporate directorships and consultancies are clients listed. This makes it very difficult to evaluate the size and scope of the interest, or to determine its precise nature and extent: "The register does not disclose enough information … What is declared does not reveal the full extent of a relationship." And some Puritans claimed that unidentified clients were receiving preferential treatment from their retained members: "Declaration is meaningless. There are MPs here who use their membership in the House to invite clients in to get introductions to senior civil servants. This is ridiculous. You can't get constituents in this way. These people are using their dual roles as company director and MP to abuse Parliament and line their own pocket." Another asserted that the register omitted the most important information: "The register does not necessarily ask the right questions. It asks for a list of directorships ... but does not ask how much they receive, whether they are formal directorships or consultancies. More questions need to be asked." The Puritans were frustrated by a register they felt lacked the "teeth" necessary to function effectively and efficiently. They advocated a number of changes to the operation of the register and clearly believed it was not functioning optimally.

A few of the Puritans suggested cynically that the register was created merely to lull the public into thinking that the House was doing something to address questions of ethics: "The Register is a joke, a cover. It tells you nothing. People are receiving an annual salary of between £20,000 and £100,000 as well as being an MP." Another suggested that "I don't even think the register mitigates against corruption." These Puritans viewed the register as no more than a public relations ploy designed to reassure, or perhaps even mislead, the public.

The other major objection raised by the Puritans was that the register remained voluntary. In fact, this common perception is incorrect. As a resolution of the House, the register is a compulsory regulation, and in theory to defy such a resolution constitutes contempt of the House. But this has not proven to be the case, as most members readily volunteered, given Enoch Powell's unpenalized refusal to file a declaration ever since the register's inception. It was Parliament's failure to discipline Powell, many Puritans claimed, which created the impression that the register is voluntary. One Puritan echoed Powell's argument that the register "should be compulsory and made a condition of office. People should know about it before they run for office and then they can't complain afterwards." Such a suggestion is currently under study by the Select Committee on Members' Interests. But perhaps the common perception of the register as a voluntary nicety is already being dispelled by the recent decision of the House to sanction John Browne, MP, for failing to disclose his outside interests fully and adequately. The suspension of Mr Browne in 1990 from the House for twenty sitting days may be a signal that the House will no longer tolerate violations of the register.

Their comments on the Register of Members' Interests reflected the prevailing Puritan view that MPs should not be permitted to engage in outside employment, or at least that the practice of MPs serving as parliamentary consultants and advisers should be terminated. As a group the Puritans had the lowest number of members with outside occupations (43 per cent). Forty-three per cent of the Puritans further stated that MPs should be forbidden altogether from holding consultancies. The Puritan declaration forms revealed trade union sponsorship, trips abroad, occasional writing and speaking fees, a few directorships, ties to family businesses, but they did not generally contain long lists of outside interests.

Of the groups of MPs it was the Puritans who were the most strongly convinced that declaration was not enough. They did not believe that public knowledge of a member's interests resolved the ethical quandaries created by MPs with outside employment and holdings that were not placed in trust. Simply declaring that an interest exists may satisfy existing requirements, but in fact does nothing to avoid potentially corrupting entanglements and attachments. Abiding by the declaration rules allows a member to avoid accusations of abuse of office. Yet for the majority of Puritans, who defined corruption in terms of inducement or betrayal, declaration did not mitigate against impropriety – it was the interest itself, not whether it was publicized – which was at the heart of the matter.

Discipline and Sanctions

For many Puritans, these definitions, and their concomitant dissatisfaction with simple declaration, led to a belief that the House must take a more active role in ensuring compliance with standards of ethical probity: "There should be some means of investigation connected to the Register. MPs should investigate each other. They should try to find out what people have done to deserve the directorships and consultancies they hold." The Puritans as a group were none too sure that MPs should be the sole guarantors of acceptable conduct in the House. Currently, however, this is the case – MPs themselves monitor one another's behaviour, as the House of Commons retains the prerogative of disciplining and sanctioning its membership. This duty is left largely to the Whips in each party, and the Committee on Privileges hears allegations against members. The Select Committee on Members' Interests assesses compliance with the register, checking to see that the declarations are returned and completed properly. The committee does not investigate the returns, but does sit to consider larger issues as they relate to the register.

The Puritans' attitudes towards discipline and sanctions reflected their low tolerance for transgressions and transgressors, and their distinctive distaste for the dampening effect collegial ties have on the processes of investigation and reprimand. The Puritans were frustrated by the absence of established procedures in these areas. What they saw as a black-and-white issue often became obscured behind numerous layers of rationalization and excuse-making, and was subject to so many roadblocks that it emerged as a uniform grey.

The majority of Puritans (63 per cent) agreed that MPs who fail to comply with the Register of Members' Interests should be subject to sanction. Once again, the Puritans were the most ardent supporters of sanctioning non-compliance (only 45 per cent of the sample agreed, a difference significant at p < .10). According to one: "Members who fail to comply should be subject to sanction. They should lose their seat ... In cases where there is doubt, a committee of member's peers should examine the case."

The majority position in support of sanctions was fairly straightforward – those who do not obey ought to be disciplined. The opposite view, however, seemed to be based primarily on mitigating factors, rather than direct objection to the punishment of transgressors. Most of those who objected to sanctions reiterated Powell's position that the register must be made a condition of standing for election. A few others rejected legislative punishment in favour of electoral retribution: if people know their MP has refused to sign the register, but they continue to re-elect him, then they are expressing their confidence in him, and no further penalty should be issued. A Puritan who had intense feelings on the issue expressed it this way: "I would think that voting for sanctions, especially expulsion, would be to deprive a constituency of their representative. I wonder whether only the electorate should have the position and the ability to make such a judgment. If they want to elect someone who does not declare their interests, that is their business. It is not to be determined by MPs."

Most Puritans felt that these concerns were outweighed by the need to enforce ethical standards in the House. As to how exactly those who failed to comply with the register should be disciplined, there was very little agreement. Suggestions included exclusion, suspension, denial of House privileges, formal apology, expulsion, or appearance before the select committee. The latter two sanctions received the most support. The Puritans were pointedly opposed to the imposition of fines or more minor sanctions such as censure, reprimand, salary suspension, or publicity.

What their suggestions revealed was that despite their strong reservations about the ability of MPs to police their own behaviour effectively and impartially, the Puritans were reluctant to countenance the involvement of an external agent in the disciplinary process: "The power of sanction should not be removed from the House. I favour the use of internal discipline – the suspension of privileges, to forbid people from speaking and participating in debates ... that kind of thing." No one suggested the involvement of the courts or an outside ethics commission. In other legislatures, notably the US Congress, external actors such as the Office of Governmental Ethics Laws, the Justice Department, and Common Cause all play a role in the monitoring and investigation of the behaviour of legislators.[12]

The current arrangement allows the Whip's offices to wield the bulk of disciplinary power in the House for ethical as well as party political matters. The following comments from two Puritan Whips convey the disciplinary procedures and processes in operation in the House. The first Puritan Whip served in the Whip's office for a greater length of time than the second. This might account for the more candid nature of his remarks:

It would not be up to me to discipline an errant member. It would be a matter for the Committee of Privileges. What I would do, would be to try and spot trouble early. If it looked like someone was in trouble, I'd drag him in and give him a talking to. If it was a serious scandal, I would advise the MP to issue a personal statement in the Chamber and apply for the Chiltern Hundreds.[13]

Some people are not aware that they are acting improperly. I also give advice about the Register of Members' Interests. My role as Whip is that of social worker. I have to impose discipline, which is difficult at times with this massive majority and try to persuade people to act honourably. There are rules about some things, such as the granting of research passes, the violation of which is punishable. But no one bothers. I can't ask people to behave in a manner that I am not prepared to behave myself.

The other Whip was more guarded in his response:

I am not able to tell you what role the Whip's office plays once allegations of corruption are made. I am not able to mention the chain of command that is followed. MPs look to the Whip as an example of the behaviour expected of them only in a negative sense. If a Whip misbehaves there will be double the repercussions of a regular MP. Yes, MPs come to me for advice on ethical questions. I think the older Whips receive a different response. MPs see me as a young Whip. It is difficult to say whether they would come to me more often if I was older.

These comments reveal that a nebulous chain of command, which begins with the Whip, is followed in the instance of a scandal. After this it is none too clear who is involved, although the first Whip did make mention of the Committee of Privileges, which presumably hears the allegations that are made against the MP.

Some Puritans objected to this unclear, internalized process. One spoke at length about the problems posed by collegiality and insularity:

You just can't crack the club-like atmosphere of the House of Commons. They make the rules and can throw you out. The existing system for making accusations is very unfair. In the Committee of Privileges you are not even allowed to hear the evidence against you. There are simply no incentives to pursue those guilty of improper behaviour. Once you do uncover something, your party, your colleagues, the Whips, all tell you to hush it up, that it will be handled internally, that we should avoid bringing the party and Parliament into disrepute. Thus there is nowhere to take your accusations, and in some instances, proof. It is just not worth it.

Another Puritan described the strength of collegial ties in the House, even across partisan lines:

There is a definite club-like atmosphere which surrounds the House of Commons. We make our own rules to suit us, or if we don't make them we are very arbitrary in their application, for instance Reggie Maudling in the Poulson case. I really believe he only got off because he was a former Minister and a member of the government. It is really frowned upon to challenge the collegiality of the House. When I voted on the Poulson case, I voted for the implicated members to be expelled. There were only 20 of us who voted this way. The looks I got as I walked through the lobby ... They wanted to spit on you.

There is apparently little encouragement or incentive for MPs to investigate or pursue suspicions, even when they have proof of their fellow MPs being involved in illicit activities. Perhaps if there was an institutionalized way for them to air their opinions, then self-monitoring would not be the futile and frustrating process it appears to be.

The Puritans' concern for the adequacy of disciplinary procedures may well be related to their suspicions that MPs were currently getting away with acts of impropriety. The great majority of Puritans (85 per cent) said they knew of or suspected corruption in Parliament. One major area of suspicion was parliamentary consultancies and retainers. Several of the Puritans thought these fraught with potential conflict:

There are worrying trends. Not important in a constituency sense. The shady areas are business appointments and parliamentary consultancies. There should be a blanket ban. People interpret their role in different ways. I personally distrust all parliamentary consultants.

MPs are basically honest. The biggest danger to the number of honest MPs who find their parliamentary salary insufficient, is that they then conclude that they do not have real jobs and thus take on some outside consultancies.

Others were concerned that outside interests were not being fully disclosed. Finally, one Puritan characterized the typical British MP as rather hypocritical: "I would suspect that the MPs interviewed came down very harshly on small things like the £10 bribe, but yet the lucrative dealing that goes on in the area of parliamentary consultancy is allowed."

Other Puritans discussed the nature of questionable activities going on in Parliament. Some spoke of them in a generic manner, while others related specific incidents with which they were concerned, such as the British Telecom incident: "Political corruption exists in Britain, but I am not sure it is significant. There are varying degrees of intensity. Three Tory MPs voted on a bill before they declared their financial interest. This is faintly dishonourable. As is an MP using his position to provide goods or services, in return for political favours." Others expressed concern over the awarding of contracts, and one was concerned about various instances: "Yes, I've certainly suspected corruption. A case in point is a private-hybrid bill which bounced through the House with ease. I have grounds to believe that there was some assistance. And without a doubt there is the Westland case. I do think there is corruption taking place in Parliament, nothing on a large scale, but it is happening none the less." The problem according to another Puritan was that "many of these activities are accepted by MPs. They are thus considered permissible action and no one is making efforts to restrict them." It was this behaviour which led one Puritan to predict that "there will be one or two scandals yet to come, that will be far worse than the Poulson Affair."

Interestingly, two Puritans admitted to engaging in "corrupt" activities themselves, although the activities were not of great consequence:

I would say that on average I have abused my position as MP 12 times or so in the past 4 years. I would hazard to guess that others are guilty on more occasions. Members are guilty of misusing their position as MP, of trading on their title to seek preferential treatment. It would be interesting to ask if MPs have phoned up a public utility like British Telecom and said "I am an MP, my phone is broken, can you come fix it." Is it corrupt for an MP to phone a hospital where his daughter is sick and ask for different visiting hours as he can't come between 5–8, as he has a 3 line Whip vote? Same goes for speeding tickets – do you say you are an MP rushing to vote?

Myself and probably several other members have cheated on their allowance sheets, on our living allowance. The limit is £7,000 and everyone tries to use up the limit, so I might estimate over the top. This is easiest to do with the food expenditures. If I overestimate, I won't be out in the end.

The first Puritan was upset by the practice of using one's elected position to exact additional consideration, even when that consideration was simply increased responsiveness from a telephone repairman. That this member considered such a minor misdeed to be an abuse of public office, and therefore corrupt, illustrates the importance Puritans attached to maintaining ethical probity, as well as their ideological approach to ethics.

It would seem that many Puritans either suspected or knew of corrupt activity taking place in Parliament. Their general sentiment was that these acts were acceptable to most of the rest of the House, and thus there was not much they could do as an individual MP other than refuse to participate: "The issue of corruption disturbs me. I do think there is abuse going on, but I don't have the time to snoop around myself." There just do not seem to be sufficient incentives available to those wishing to curb activities they find objectionable. One Puritan commented: "The grey area of financial inducement is not caught by our system. There is not even an attempt to try and control it. There is a hypocritical attitude prevalent – we can't eliminate it but we can control it. Yet there is not even an attempt to tackle it." The attitude prevalent among the Puritans seemed to be that they would keep their own noses clean, but they were not willing, or did not feel able, to initiate steps to prevent others from engaging in activities they themselves considered questionable.

Lobbyists and Lobbying: A Worrying Trend?

While pressure or interest groups have always been a part of British politics, it is only recently that there has been an influx of professional lobbyists into the corridors of the House of Commons. In other legislatures, such as the United States Congress, and more recently the Canadian House of Commons, registers of lobbyists have been introduced in an attempt to regulate the lobbying process. In Britain, the Select Committee on Members' Interests has investigated the issue of lobbying and the possibility of such a register. Their report has yet to be acted on by the House, but a number of the discussions from the committee's early reports parallel some of the suggestions and comments of the Puritans.

The Puritans were overwhelmingly in favour of the introduction of a register of lobbyists, with 81 per cent agreeing that one should be adopted. Support for this register was stronger among the Puritans than the other groups, although in all groups a solid majority of MPs were in favour of it (70 per cent of the sample approved). While the Puritans viewed the lobbying process in a positive light, they still thought that some measure of control was needed. The Puritans suggested that a register would help MPs to identify individual lobbyists, as well as which particular interests a lobbyist represents. Concern was evident that lobbyists were able to secure extensive access to Westminster and that steps needed to be taken to identify them. For some Puritans the development of the "art" of lobbying was happening just too rapidly.

Nearly all Puritans (86 per cent) said that they had received several personal approaches from professional lobbyists, as did most of their colleagues (83 per cent of the sample). Only two Puritans stated that they had not been approached or contacted by lobbyists. The most common method of contact reported was an invitation to dinner or lunch to discuss the lobbyist's views on a particular issue. A few Puritans indicated that they found the briefs circulated by the lobby groups useful and informative, but for the most part Puritans were not impressed with lobbyists and their profession: "There are people here who are buying the ears, minds and possibly the votes of MPs. There are lobbyists who claim to influence government opinion. If the success rate is only half of what the claims say it to be, it is ridiculous."

A few of the Puritans expressed views that some other MPs might find alarmist or exaggerated, but they illustrated the depth of concern of these Puritans: "Lobbyists are very powerful by and large. They are out to ruin the country. These powerful lobbies from the City are not wanted in the Central Lobby." One Puritan expressed it in simple terms: "The people ought to know who is paying to wine and dine their elected representatives." This particular statement implied recognition of the fact that the public would likely not appreciate specialized interest groups and corporations sponsoring elaborate dinners for their MPs. The Puritans also asserted that lobbying was only in a nascent state, and that additional concerns were bound to arise: "We are only now starting to move in the direction of more formal lobbying. Certainly not on the same scale as the U.S., but there are a growing number of outfits specializing in government lobbying. This has brought with it a growing expertise in the nature of lobbying." This concern for the professionalization of lobbying was expressed succinctly by one Puritan: "Lobbyists are not too worrisome at the moment. But they could be." Many Puritans feared that as lobbyists become more and more adept at finding ways to influence MPs, the House would become less and less able to protect its members' independence and autonomous judgment.

But what the Puritans were most concerned about was the possibility of a connection between the recent growth of lobbying and the increasing number of MPs on retainer to parliamentary consultancy firms.[14] They were the only group in the typology to suggest this link. Many worried that such consultants function as a lobby from within: "Most lobbyists operate through contacts in the House – through MPs they have on the payroll." In return for a retainer, some MPs are willing to organize dinners and meetings at which their clients can meet parliamentarians. A Puritan described his experience: "I have been invited to receptions by companies which have been sponsored by fellow MPs. I did not know what they wanted and was a bit hesitant about accepting the invitation, but after all it was hosted by one of my colleagues. Lobbying takes place not only at Westminster, but also at the party conferences. This is a new phenomenon." It was this aspect of lobbying – the conscription of MPs into consultancy firms – which was the most disturbing to the Puritans. This concern for a process that transforms representatives into paid advocates is perhaps warranted. The resources and opportunities which are only available to MPs, and which make them attractive employees to PR firms, also permit them to give advantages to their clients which are denied to the wider public. Firms, groups, or organizations that do not have an MP on their payroll might very well find the lobbying process more cumbersome, restricted, and time-consuming.

ETHICAL STRATEGIES

In the British system of ethical management, MPs are required to supply their own interpretation of prevalent informal norms and conventions. This means that members are adopting their own strategies and techniques for handling the ethical questions of legislative life.

The only written admonition guiding members in determining what is and is not acceptable behaviour is the oft-quoted dictum that members should avoid "activity inconsistent with the standards the House is entitled to expect from its members."[15] To Puritans this phrase meant a number of different things. To some it was an intentionally vague catch-all, designed to cover every conceivable indiscretion: "This is a club phrase which means anything for anybody. It is a posh member catch-phrase; a cosy club rule. If you can't keep the club secrets you get thrown out." The vast array of responses offered by the Puritans indicated that there was very little consensus among them as to what the phrase was intended to mean. The most common explanations provided were: undermining the reputation of Parliament, activity for personal rather than public ends, and concealment of an interest or advancing an interest for pay. Other responses included dishonesty, acceptance of an inducement, and even "profanity." The range of interpretations is demonstrated by the following quotations:

Well, I could give the political answer of the voicing of views so outrageous to go beyond the pale of normal democratic discussion; someone like Peter Bruinvels for instance. Or the expression of particular views or participating in particular activity in the House, not because of what you believe or your party, but because of financial advantage.

That would mean any conduct within the House which offends the rules of debate. Unparliamentary language, using offensive language during the course of debate. Acting in a way which offends parliamentary procedure.

Well, not departing from your integrity in the way you carry out your functions as MP. What is done in private, like a hotel bedroom, has nothing to do with me. There must be a distinction between public and private life.

At the moment this just means lying to the House. It is too loose of a phrase. Keith Best lied six times and still did not resign. It was appalling. Profumo resigned not because he had been sleeping with a prostitute, but because he had lied to the House.

Obviously it covers a number of moral questions. The abuse of each other physically and verbally. Clearly it would be very wrong to be found in the ladies toilet with the kitchen staff, even if both parties agreed.

This phrase apparently provides little consistent direction in the establishment of ethical standards for MPs. Each individual interprets the phrase differently, placing the emphasis where they determine it is meant to be. To one, the House's expectations may be primarily that all members maintain their autonomous judgment against all compromising influences, to another they may be simply that members avoid compromising situations in their private life.

If Puritans were not relying on this phrase in the formulation of their responses to ethical questions, where did they take their standards from? More than any of the other groups of MPs, the Puritans claimed to rely on personal standards they developed before entering the House. While they were certain that their own standards were impeccable, they were none too sure of their colleagues. Yet they remained reluctant to impose their own standards of conduct on their fellow MPs: "I don't like to make judgments about other people's behaviour. Ethics is about decisions and judgment. Common sense should prevail. It is not my place to inflict my values on others." Another affirmed this ethical solipsism: "No one has the energy to become involved or to question other people's activity." This insistence that no MP should impose his own standards on others was widely shared in the House. In the case of the Puritans, since most were comfortable, even proud, of their own probity, this isolationism was not a problem. But as will be seen in the discussion of other types, notably the Muddlers, there were quite a few MPs who were by no means sure of whether the standards they followed were the "right" ones, and who implicitly admitted that they would appreciate someone willing to give them ethical direction and advice.

The Puritans spoke of what they themselves did to avoid questionable situations. Surely some of their colleagues would have found their behaviour excessive, but it was how these individuals operated in the legislative environment: "I do not aspire to a job in government. I am not wining and dining like the others. I have not taken freebie trips all over the world. I avoid club areas, like all-party groups. These are examples of sloppy consensus." A more conventional strategy is offered by a fellow Puritan: "As my own personal standard I do not accept any gifts. The items I receive I take and donate to the Mayor's charity for that year. I never accept anything as a personal gift. Nor am I on retainer to serve as a consultant." The Puritans were the only group in the typology to offer details of the personal practices which they followed to avoid ethical dilemmas. They were the only MPs who consistently mentioned that they either refused gifts of any kind, donated them to charities, or abided by a self-imposed value ceiling on any gift. Many refused to accept retainers, and some Puritans indicated they were wary of foreign travel opportunities other than as part of a parliamentary delegation. These tactics revealed a consistent and well-developed ethical strategy on the part of the Puritans. When deciding a matter that had ethical implications, they were guided by *a priori* rules that helped determine what they should do, rather than *ad hoc* considerations and circumstances.

These personal standards were relied upon to cope with the ethical dilemmas MPs face. Half the Puritans indicated that they were faced with ethical dilemmas occasionally or even frequently. As one Puritan said: "There are situations which you have to watch. From little beginnings, big things come." Others recounted their experiences:

Occasionally one faces ethical dilemmas. Once I received a thank you letter with £50. Under those circumstances I sent the money right back. Or you could give the money to the charity of the donor's choice. Under other circumstances you might have to accept the gift. For example, a family once came to my surgery office. Their niece, a Polish girl, had leukemia. I helped the family to bring her over, so she could receive the tests and medical attention she needed. They were extremely grateful and in time there arrived from Warsaw an oil painting specially done for me. It was a thank-you present.

But what do I do – say "I'm terribly sorry but I can't accept gifts"? In the end I decided the family would be hurt if I refused it. So I accepted it and it sits on my surgery wall.

I have not been offered a bribe of sexual favours. Occasionally though, a developer wants an MP's help in a constituency to push a planning application through. I would agree that it is for the good of the constituency. But what happens if I accept lunch? Do I buy my own lunch or declare it to the local authorities? I have not yet stooped to selling my soul for sole. If I was offered £10 million, now that would be tempting, but not for a small sum of money.

Many of these dilemmas centred on the acceptance of gifts presented to MPs, foreign travel, and hospitality offered MPs such as meals, theatre tickets, and hotel rooms. While ministers have recourse to rules that outline what is acceptable and what is not, MPs are left to devise their own guidelines. One Puritan offered his view on the issue: "There are some things which you accept – pens, ties, bouquets of flowers – nothing over £50. There should be a minimum rule imposed for MPs like there is for Ministers. The current situation is ethically unsound. The member always has the option of accepting and declaring the gift and then donating it to the local hospital or charity." While another voiced his concerns as follows: "I am worried about foreign travel and hospitality. It is okay if you are going in a parliamentary delegation or all party group. It is when individual MPs are invited places that trouble arises. I worry about people compromising their principles. Everything should be registered and above board. I don't know that it always is."

The Puritans felt that the current situation for the prescription of ethical standards was disturbing. The existing rules were ignored and not adequately enforced. Thus behaviour they would deem questionable was permitted, since there were no rules that expressly prohibited it. But it was not just that the rules were outdated. Puritans detected real inertia in the House on matters related to ethical standards: "There are activities which should be restricted but are not. There never will be rules passed to outlaw it. The House never comes around to review things, such as standards in public life." Some Puritans were hopeful that since most legislatures in the Western world were addressing ethical questions, and several had introduced legislation, pressure would mount on Westminster to follow suit: "The rules which do exist are very nebulous indeed and there is beginning to be more of a grumble about things than there has been in the past." Perhaps in response to this grumble, the Select Committee on Members' Interests, in connection with its inquiry into lobbying at Westminster, has also studied a number of ethical issues including codes of conduct, improvements to the register, and the granting of research passes. But there has not been a full-scale review of ethical standards since the Salmon Commission in 1976. Apparently, the Puritans felt such a review long overdue.

Yet, despite this concern, the majority of the MPs interviewed were opposed to the introduction of a code of conduct. Only 26 per cent of the Puritans (24 per cent of the sample) were in favour of codification. But the Puritans also had the largest percentage of MPs (26 per cent) who were still open to the possibility of a written code. Puritans in favour of a code stressed that "declaration is not enough. It is only a start. Much more can be done. Guidelines would be helpful. I would go as far as to advocate legislation." Another added: "I think some sort of code would be helpful, but not like the local government code which is quite wordy." Even the support for a code was vague and unspecific – as has been seen on other issues, the Puritans were sure that something was wrong, but were not sure how to fix it.

The reasons that formed the basis of their opposition were varied, but seemed to centre on the rules actually being written down. Several Puritans feared that codification would inevitably encourage exploitation of loopholes: "The more you write down, the more gaps you create. The more details you provide, the more important the things left out become"; and "Once on paper, people begin to look for the small print." Other Puritans were not so sure that a code would be able to provide guidance for every situation an MP faces: "I would not be in favour of a written code. It would not cover every eventuality. You can't simply compartmentalize behaviour. Members should know the difference between right and wrong."

Other Puritans suggested that there was really no need for a code, that there were alternative sources of guidance for the MPs to look to:

I don't think a code is necessary. There are three sources of assistance – their colleagues, their party and themselves – available to each MP in acquiring a basic understanding about ethics in public life. If they are in doubt they can seek advice from the Whip's Office or from the Offices of the House. I would worry that everything not indicated in a code could be engaged in – there could be a reverse effect.

I don't think a written code of conduct would be helpful. New MPs hopefully have pretty strong standards before coming here. It is not something they acquire after. If this is the case, they will soon find themselves on a slippery slope.

It is apparent that in the minds of the Puritans, a formal, written code of conduct was not the answer.

While opposed to a code of conduct, a number of the Puritans were favourably disposed towards some form of guidelines, if not for themselves then at least for the instruction of their colleagues. One possibility is a system used in the American Congress. There, questions submitted to congressional ethics committees are answered by staff. The responses to queries of a generic nature are published in a handy book of rulings. These interpretive rulings provide a body of authoritative guidance on common situations faced by legislators to which Congressmen can refer when in doubt about how to resolve a situation. Perhaps a similar type of book or document would be appreciated by British MPs.

CONCLUSION

The Puritans took an aggressive approach to ethical matters. They made no secret of their dissatisfaction with the conduct of many of their colleagues, as well as with the means Parliament has adopted to regulate MPs' behaviour. Most refused to pursue outside employment and many called for an outright ban on the practice, or at least a prohibition against MPs accepting parliamentary consultancies. They scrupulously avoided accepting even small gifts in the course of their duties. To many other MPs they might appear extremist in their pursuit of ethical perfection, but the Puritans seemed to take a kind of pride in their own righteousness and probity.

The Puritans were particularly concerned about the operation of the Register of Members' Interests. They advocated that the register be made compulsory and they felt strongly that MPs who violate the registration requirement should be subject to sanction. The Puritans were also concerned about the lobbying process at Westminster and the influx of lobbyists into Parliament and its halls. They would support the introduction of a register of lobbyists and expressed that the House must ensure that it have some measure of control over the situation. Their responses illustrated that they had given prior thought to questions of ethics and that they had a ready course of action to follow in their day-to-day activities. The Puritans expressed frustration with the weaknesses in the system of investigation and sanctions and were notably distressed by Parliament's reluctance to punish transgressors or provide incentives for the pursuit of allegations of misconduct. Some indicated that they had in fact tried to follow up on their suspicions, only to be ignored or stonewalled.

It would seem that the Puritans are would-be reformers in a situation that makes reform especially difficult. The Puritans are convinced that they know what is wrong with the system, but are not sure exactly how to fix it. And even if they could agree on particular measures, they have serious doubts about their success, given that they see the remainder of Parliament as stubbornly opposing change. Many Puritans appeared to have given up the search for concrete solutions, and instead have concentrated on keeping their own ethical standards honed and their behaviour unassailable. Until motivated more strongly, the Puritans are left in their own ethical isolationism to grumble to themselves about the continuing decay of ethical standards in the House of Commons.

CHAPTER FOUR

The Servants

The Servants were those sixteen MPs who displayed high tolerance for acts of constituency service but low tolerance for conflict of interest. The Servants shared many Puritan concerns about the influence of external forces on the representative process, but unlike the Puritans they were willing to accept that MPs might exploit their position and the opportunities available to them as long as it was in the interests of their constituents. The Servants indicated that they felt a particularly strong bond to the people who elected them, and emphasized the process of representation and the dilemmas caused by conflicting obligations: "It is difficult for me to decide what to do when members of my constituency hold views with which I disagree. Yet, as a representative I am supposed to represent the interests and views of all my constituents. I find this difficult." Servants allowed their representative role much greater latitude in affecting their legislative function than did Puritans, but were still concerned about protection from the influence of extra-Parliamentary interests. While the Puritans strove to be pure legislators, uncompromised by personal or representative concerns, the Servants allowed complete legislative autonomy to take a back seat to the needs of those they represent. They were willing to engage in activity the Puritans would term corrupt as long it was their constituency, and not themselves or an outside group, that benefited.

Many offered explanations for their tolerance of the constituency service items. Most insisted that the CONTRACT item did not involve corruption, but was quite acceptable if not desirable behaviour:

Not only is this permissible, it is my duty to do so. There is nothing improper in this.

My constituents expect me to do this and would be fussed if I didn't.

The constituency should not be penalized because their MP is a Cabinet Minister. As an MP you are expected to do this.

This is difficult to do under the existing system as the civil service has the administration locked up. But it is the oldest thing in the game. I wouldn't hesitate to do it if there was a sporting chance.

The Servants also saw nothing untoward about the SCHOOL scenario. While they were somewhat doubtful they would be able to get a friend or relative admitted to either Cambridge or Oxford, most thought they would try. This was especially true of Servants who had attended one of these universities themselves: "Yes, I would do this. I would write to my old College. This is the way things are done." Another said: "While it is a bit naive to think that I could get someone in, I would try. This is the Old Boy Network and I would be unable to guarantee that anyone would get in." Most were willing to write a letter or to ring the warden or the principal and speak on someone's behalf.

In the eyes of the Servants, these constituency service acts were not only not corrupt, but actually part of their duties and responsibilities as MPs. The explanations they gave for their tolerance of these items were positive – they provided a reason why they should engage in the activity. In contrast, the Muddlers and Entrepreneurs were negative – they claimed there is no reason not to engage in the activity, and nothing explicitly prohibiting it. The Servants were willing to go the extra distance, and perhaps bend a strict rule here and there, for the benefit of their constituents.

The Servants were easily the most traditional of the four types of MPs. Throughout their responses and comments, they displayed a strong faith in the institution of Parliament, in the honour of its members, in the idea of the politician as public-spirited amateur, and in the competency and sufficiency of the existing ethical regulatory framework. Unlike the Puritans, many Servants held outside occupations, but few indulged in problematic consultancies or directorships. They agreed with the Puritans that some activities occurring in the House were cause for concern, but did not fault the House and its regulatory mechanisms. Rather, the Servants blamed primarily those involved for activities they found unacceptable. They admitted that there will always be some "rotten apples" in Parliament who will refuse to abide by standards of honour.

In addition, the Servants felt that most questionable activity could be attributed to MPs who, through either ignorance or neglect, had never been fully inculcated with the standards the House is entitled to expect from its members. They saw a lax and incomplete promulgation of these standards as the root cause of the ethical confusion and misbehaviour that afflicts the House. In the Servants' view, the standards themselves were sufficient and the expectation that MPs would use them in making their own determinations was reasonable. The individuals responsible for ethical leadership were lazy, however, and certain MPs were not willing to acquaint themselves fully with the standards expected of them.

Like the Puritans, the Servants viewed ethics as a personal matter and assumed that MPs should be guided by a strong personal code. The Servants, however, did not see themselves as essentially different from their fellow legislators. While the Puritans exuded a clear sense of ethical superiority and were at times disparaging about the ethics of their colleagues, the Servants seemed to regard themselves as typical MPs and expected that, barring the occasional and inevitable rotten apple, their own basic commitment to ethical probity would be shared by all members.

Ultimately, the Servants displayed a strong commitment to protecting and advancing the public interest, but in a more traditional patrician manner, as opposed to the Puritans' more radical ideological approach. Low tolerance for conflict of interest among the Servants came as much from the perception that such activity interfered with the proper representation of constituent interests as from a general ethical disdain. To the Servants, the represented alone have the right to request preferential treatment from their representatives. If representatives are doling out favours to anyone who provides pecuniary incentives, they are no longer upholding their representative responsibilities. Public service is not to be sacrificed for personal gain.

SERVANT PERCEPTIONS

Servant Definitions of Political Corruption

Most Servants (44 per cent) offered inducement-based definitions of political corruption. These definitions emphasized the deviation from the routine exercise of duties. It was this altering of an MP's actions for reward that Servants found objectionable:

Political corruption is the acceptance of money or preferment of some kind which would influence an MP to alter his or her opinions, trim his views because of material reward. To shape your opinion because of inducement.

Using the overall influence a politician has, whether voting on contracts or in the corridors of power, for a purpose he would not use it for if not induced.

This type of definition suggests that for an MP to engage in corrupt activities, he must be corrupted. In other words, he must be tempted to deviate from his normal acceptable behaviour and be unable to resist the temptation, which was usually characterized in monetary terms. The implication is that MPs are essentially ethical and well-intentioned, and that they succumb to corruption only when they lack the requisite moral fibre or, especially, guidance.

Only a few Servants (13 per cent) suggested, as did many Puritans, that corruption was essentially a matter of betrayal of principles and public trust. Definitions based on abuse of office were offered by 25 per cent of the Servants. The Servants' abuse-based definitions tended to emphasize that corruption also involved a degree of dishonesty: "Corruption is the deliberate manipulation of the truth or carelessness over facts, to achieve your predetermined goal." Or as one simply stated: "Corruption involves the abuse of the truth." This respect for honesty and openness was a continuing theme in the comments of the Servants.

Finally, one Servant offered a strict legalistic definition of corruption: "Any form of corruption – be it political, administrative, executive, trade union – is only defined strictly according to the law." Thus in this Servant's mind, corruption was isomorphic to illegality, and the determination of an act's propriety was accomplished by comparison with existing statutes. Two Servants did not provide a definition. They claimed they did not understand what the term "political corruption" meant and thus they were not prepared to comment.

The two types of definition that depicted the legislator as the initiator of the corrupt act were less favoured by the Servants than the one that involved an external entity. This did not mean that most Servants believed the public interest not harmed, or the office of MP abused, by corruption, just that the root cause of an instance of corruption was the diversion of an MP from the proper exercise of duties. This reflected their generally charitable view of the standards and behaviour of their colleagues. They viewed an external pressure as necessary before an MP would indulge in misconduct.

General Perceptual Profile

The Servants were nearly unanimous in their agreement that political corruption was not a widespread problem (see table 7). One Servant explained: "In the traditional sense, corruption does not apply to

Table 7
Servant General Perceptual Profile

Statement	Text	Agree (%)	Disagree (%)	Mean	Std. Dev.	Median	Significance
15	Political corruption is not a widespread problem.	93	7	1.9	1.4	1	**t:** p < .10
		82	*15*	*2.5*	*1.6*	*2*	**F:** *p < .05*
16	In so far as citizens distrust elected officials it is because they do not understand what politics is all about.	64	29	3.4	2.1	2.5	
		66	*28*	*3.2*	*1.9*	*3*	
17	Dishonesty is more widespread in politics than in business.	0	93	6.4	.91	7	**t:** p < .10
		4	*89*	*6.0*	*1.2*	*6*	
18	Political corruption is more widespread at the local than at the national level of government.	67	7	2.7	1.7	2	
		73	*12*	*2.7*	*1.6*	*2*	
19	No matter what we do, we can never eliminate political corruption.	73	20	2.5	2.2	1	
		80	*13*	*2.5*	*1.7*	*2*	
20	The corruption that exists in the political world simply reflects the standards of the rest of society.	57	29	3.2	2.0	2	
		55	*31*	*3.4*	*1.9*	*3*	
21	If it hadn't been for the Poulson scandal, we would hear a lot less about corruption in government.	53	40	3.9	2.3	3	**t:** p < .10
		29	*64*	*4.8*	*2.0*	*5*	**F:** *p < .01*
22	MPs are sufficiently well informed to act as the sole guarantors of acceptable conduct in the house.	73	13	2.5	2.0	2	**t:** p < .05
		52	*40*	*3.7*	*2.2*	*3*	**F:** *p < .05*
23	Once allegations of corruption are made, MPs in their parliamentary capacity should be brought within the ambit of criminal law	79	14	2.3	2.0	1	
		70	*23*	*2.7*	*2.1*	*2*	**F:** *p < .01*
24	Britain's libel laws inhibit the uncovering and reporting of political corruption.	53	33	3.7	2.3	3	
		37	*53*	*4.5*	*2.2*	*5*	**F:** *p < .001*

Key: Values in *italics* pertain to the entire sample of 100 MPs. "Agree" equals responses of 1, 2, or 3 (as a percentage of valid responses). "Disagree" equals responses of 5, 6, or 7 (as a percentage of valid responses). "Significance" equals significance levels for t-statistic (difference between Servant and non-Servant means) and F-ratio (analysis of variance across the four types of MPs).

Parliament. If it did, the place would have been depredated by the people who were engaging in the corrupt acts. Britain is not a corrupt society. It used to be." A number of Servants suggested that the parliamentary system itself effectively inhibited corrupt acts: "There is not much corruption in Britain because of the parliamentary system of government. There is just not the opportunity for corruption to take place." Of the four types of MP, the Servants were the ones most strongly in agreement with this statement, while the Puritans were the strongest dissenters. This perception bears out the Servants' faith in the robustness of Parliament's ethical framework. As will be shown, they were aware that ethical misconduct occurs, but considered it more an annoyance or embarrassment than a full-fledged problem.

Statement 18 met with the agreement of two-thirds of the Servants, slightly less than among the Puritans or the sample as a whole. Interestingly, a relatively large proportion (27 per cent, versus 14 per cent of the sample) chose the neutral response. Whether this indicated that they thought existing corruption to be divided equally among the two levels, or that they did not think corruption existed at either level, was unclear. But those who thought that there was more corruption at the local level attributed it to the relative power of an individual local councillor. Compared with an MP, a councillor has greater ability to make decisions that directly affect the public. In Parliament, effective power is concentrated in the hands of ministers; many Servants saw backbench MPs as excluded from the decision-making process and thus devoid of opportunities to engage in corruption. One cautioned: "Never forget how impotent an MP is." Another explained: "While MPs have the opportunity to engage in influence peddling, they remain powerless. They have influence but no power. In local government the chairman of the committee has power, the power to direct events. This is the same as a Minister. Many MPs sell their ability to influence events in government." This perception of backbenchers as powerless pawns in the parliamentary game helps to explain why so few Servants saw corruption as a serious problem – MPs who sell their influence were seen as selling something of marginal worth.

Not surprisingly, the Servants disagreed overwhelmingly and more strongly than the other types of MPs that political corruption was more widespread in politics than in business (statement 17). Not one Servant agreed with the statement. Most offered no explanation for their opinion, but simply disagreed quickly, almost instinctively; 60 per cent chose the "strongly disagree" response. Once again, as with statement 15, the Servants stood at the opposite extreme from the Puritans on this issue: whereas the Puritans were the group least convinced that British politics was free of corruption, the Servants were the group most confident of the ethical cleanliness of the House.

The Servants were also the type least pessimistic about the possibility of eliminating corruption entirely. While their responses were not far enough from the sample mean to achieve statistical significance, their answers revealed a strong undercurrent of idealism: "We will never be able to eliminate all of it. The same is true of all crime. But we can affect it. Limits can be imposed, codes introduced." Another added: "There will be some sin, but we can get rid of a lot of it." The Servants exhibited trust in Parliament's ability to cleanse itself and were not subject to the ethical despair that at times afflicted some Puritans.

The Servants placed even more importance on the Poulson scandal than did the Puritans, to a degree that was equally significant statistically. Indeed, a majority of the Servants actually agreed with statement 21. The Servants were generally willing to credit the case with focusing attention on standards of official conduct. As with the Puritans, it was not surprising that the Servants, with their low tolerance for conflict of interest, viewed the Poulson case as a particularly significant watershed.

The Servants' overall confidence in the virtue of MPs was sustained by their response to statement 22. Almost three-quarters of the Servants felt that MPs were sufficiently well-informed to act as the sole guarantors of acceptable conduct in the House. The Servants and Puritans were at opposite, statistically significant poles on this issue especially. The Servants felt strongly that it was the responsibility of the House and its individual members to maintain ethical behaviour: "It is a member's obligation to ensure acceptable conduct, both inside and outside the House." A colleague added that "there is no other viable alternative." These Servants asserted not only that MPs were well-placed to police their own conduct, but also that there was really no one else better placed to do so.

Most Puritans, in disagreeing with this statement, strongly questioned and even ridiculed the practice of MPs being subject only to their own oversight. Those few Servants who disagreed, however, seemed to base this opinion on quibbles with the language of the question: "I'm not so sure of this. There have to be others involved. For example, the Speaker, the Sergeant-at-Arms and other officers of the House." One Servant was comfortable with the concept of MPs watching over each other, but was not too sure about the "well-informed" aspect of the statement: "Overall, people are fairly honest here. But it is difficult. Not everyone knows the standards."

The Servants were clearly in favour of bringing MPS within the ambit of criminal law once allegations of corruption had been made, though not quite so clearly as the Puritans. Thus while insistent that the process of investigating and judging cases of alleged misconduct remain within the House, the Servants were still quite willing to make transgressors vulnerable to criminal charges: "MPS cannot be seen to be above the law. They should not be able to plead parliamentary privilege to cover up abuse." Others noted, however, that while they agreed in principle, they estimated that it would be very difficult to extend the ambit of the criminal law to include MPS. They felt that such a move would undoubtedly clash with Parliament's historic position as the highest court in the land.

The same pattern of responses – the Servants aligned with the Puritans, though not as extreme – was observed with respect to statement 24. A majority of the Servants thought that British libel laws inhibited the discovery of political corruption. The Puritans, of whom two-thirds agreed, were the only other group to display even the slightest agreement with the statement; only 36 per cent of the sample as a whole agreed. This suggests that libel statutes were seen more as an obstacle to the investigation of conflict-of-interest activities – as opposed to constituency service activities – since it was the MPS with low tolerance for conflict of interest who tended to agree with this statement.

The Servants expressed a number of views that were similar to those advanced by the Puritans. Where they differed markedly was on issues pertaining to the ethical insight of their colleagues in the House, and especially the desirability of having MPS as the sole guarantors of acceptable conduct. Unlike the Puritans, the Servants trusted their fellow MPS, or at least gave them the benefit of the doubt. But like the Puritans, the Servants were not willing to "look the other way" and were firm in the conviction that genuine offences should be punished, and that Parliament should not be seen as coddling its membership. The Servants indicated that they wanted to retain for members the traditional prerogative of establishing and maintaining ethical standards. The Puritans effectively broke with this tradition, however, and emphasized the need for additional controls.

WHO ARE THE SERVANTS?

Political Characteristics

Unlike the Puritans, the Servants were distributed fairly evenly on both sides of the House (see figure 5). Sixty-three per cent of the Servants

Figure 5
Party Affiliation

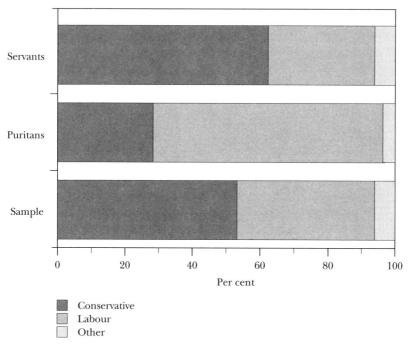

Conservative
Labour
Other

were members of the Conservative Party, 31 per cent were Labour MPs, and 6 per cent were from other parties. This distribution was not significantly divergent from that of the sample as a whole (54 per cent Conservative, 40 per cent Labour, 6 per cent others). Each of the major political parties had its share of constituency-oriented MPs. No party seemed to have a particular affinity for "Servant-ness."

The Servants saw themselves as more towards the left or "wet" end of the ideological spectrum within their party than did their colleagues in general. By far the most common response, however, was "middle-of-the-road," which was selected by 75 per cent of the Servants. This result, significant at the .05 level, indicated that Servants saw themselves as moderates within their own parties. The Servants had no particular ideological axe to grind. In a legislative environment where both the left and the right ends of the spectrum were inhabited by passionate ideologues, the Servants were the small "c" conservatives: cautious, trusting of conventional solutions and practices, and wary of speedy change in the routines of legislative life.

Not surprisingly, the Servants also saw themselves as the most puritanical of the four types. Asked to place themselves on a seven-point ethical scale from puritanical (1) to liberal (7), the Servants, with a mean score of 3.3, were the only group to record a mean below 4 (the sample average was 4.1), indicating that they see themselves as more puritanical than their fellow MPS with respect to ethical issues. In this sense, the Servants were even more puritanical than the Puritans, who actually placed themselves slightly towards the liberal end of the scale.

A large number of Servants were newcomers to Parliament. Thirty-eight per cent of them were first-term MPS and another 19 per cent were in their second term. Thus a majority of the Servants had yet to complete two terms in office. As was previously discussed with regard to the Puritans, this would tend to support the hypothesis that tolerance for corrupt activity tends to increase with years in service, at least with respect to conflict of interest.

As was the case with the Puritans, the exceptions to this trend were senior parliamentarians who either had ministerial experience or had served as frontbench opposition critics. Most Servants (63 per cent) had at one time held one or more of the following positions: minister, Whip, or private parliamentary secretary. In all these positions the members would have had to abide by a formal code of conduct. This experience might have predisposed them towards more restrictive standards of conduct regarding conflict of interest.

The Servants less closely resembled the Puritans with respect to outside employment (see figure 6). Fully three-quarters of the Servants had another occupation besides MP. As was the case with party affiliation, the Servants were not unlike the Entrepreneurs and Muddlers in the fraction who pursued outside employment – it was the Puritans who were the clear standouts. Of the twelve Servants with additional employment, five were barristers or solicitors, one was a Lloyd's underwriter, two were journalists, two consultants, and two corporate directors. That so many of the Servants were practising lawyers was striking – indeed, more than half of the nine practising lawyers in the entire sample were Servants. The law is a profession that carries with it a code of professional ethics, and, one might expect, a heightened sensitivity to issues of bias and prejudiced judgments, either of which might predispose lawyers towards low tolerance for certain types of corrupt activity, especially conflict of interest. At the same time, lawyers become involved in disputes specifically to advance the interests of those they represent. It should be noted for comparison with the remaining two types of MPS that while most Servants were employed outside the House, only 25 per cent of them engaged in consultancies or directorships.

Compared with their Puritan colleagues, the Servants were not as adamantly opposed to members engaging in outside employment or

Figure 6
Outside Employment Types

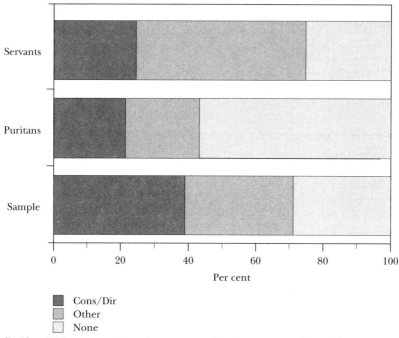

Key: "Cons/Dir" MPs engaged in parliamentary consultancies or corporate directorships.
"Other" MPs engaged in other forms of outside employment.
"None" MPs with no outside employment.

interests. Some were worried about the proliferation of retainers and outside employment: "I am concerned about members' outside interests and how they pursue them in the House – the representation of these interests." Another Servant was "very worried about the growth and extension of parliamentary consultancies. They are cause for trouble and that is what I would try to curb. MPs are trading on their name with influence they haven't got." And one Servant did echo a popular Puritan sentiment: "MPs should not be on retainer or hold outside financial interests. They should not even have an outside job. They should just be full-time members."

But most Servants, while worried and not all in agreement that such interests were desirable, were apparently confident that, if pursued in the open, outside interests presented no major problem: "Interests are okay as long as everyone knows about the interest. And they do here. People know who represents the Police or Automobile Association. It makes it redundant to have to declare it. This sort of representation is fine as long as it is not abused – done in secrecy. MPS can't be bought for the price of a lunch." It would seem that the Servants were more willing to accept the representation of outside interests, claiming that this had been a legitimate practice since the inception of Parliament. This view could help to account for the number of Servants who do have outside interests.

Yet despite the prevalence of outside interests among the Servants, only one attempted to justify the increased acceptance of retainers and outside employment by the poor salary and allowances provided to MPS: "I would emphasize that the situation is what it is today because of the abysmal pay, services and facilities provided to the British MP. This is true, especially in a comparative context having just returned from a visit to the U.S. Congress." For some reason, the great majority of Servants did not feel a need to rationalize the representation of outside interests by MPS. They merely seemed to accept this practice as part of the legislative and representative process. While most did not personally accept such retainers, only a few made disparaging comments about their colleagues who did: "I have very little respect for MPS who accept large retainers to act as consultants. It diminishes their independence." The Puritans were quite a bit more pejorative in their attitude towards colleagues on retainer. While all these attitudes might suggest that the Servants were more tolerant of outside employment than the Puritans, their responses to the scenarios show that they remained just as intolerant of the conflict-of-interest situations that such employment might create.

Finally, two Labour Servants raised some of the dilemmas related to trade union sponsorship (all of the Labour Servants were sponsored by at least one trade union). These Servants were apparently concerned with the ethical questions that arise when one accepts money from a trade union: "Trade Unions are placed in an unreasonably advantageous position in influencing the direction of policy affecting them." While they admitted the money from the unions did not go to them directly, they showed concern about their legislative autonomy: "Trade union sponsorship can be worrisome. There is concern about pressure once sponsorship is secured." Thus the Labour Servant members, like their Puritan counterparts, were well aware of the real and perceived implications of trade union sponsorship.

The political trait that most distinguished the Servants was their self-described moderation. This reflected their traditional outlook and ethical strategy. They shared with the Puritans a harsh disdain for MPS who involved themselves too closely with private interests, but accepted that the functional representation of external interests has always been, and remains, a integral part of the British parliamentary system.

Many Servants conformed to the time-honoured portrait of the MP as a professional – typically a lawyer – who dabbles in the affairs of the nation. Few have taken advantage of the rise of opportunities that trade directly on their parliamentary position. Thus the majority of those Servants who had another occupation avoided employment that might compromise their legislative autonomy.

Spatial Characteristics

As with the Puritans, attempts to uncover a statistically significant regional biasing of Servants were not successful. Servants were slightly more common in the northern half of Britain than were other types, and relatively few were found in the Southeast region. This tended to support the hypothesis that less tolerant legislators are more likely to come from peripheral regions than from the national core.

Once again it was the nature of the constituency that proved to be dramatically associated with MPs' tolerance scores. Analysis of the Servants' constituencies supported (at $p < .02$) the traditional notion that rural seats tend to produce representatives with more restrictive ethical standards. Sixty-three per cent of the Servants represented non-urban constituencies (Rural, Very Rural, or Mixed). In no other group did a majority of MPs represent non-urban constituencies. And of the six urban Servants, four were either former ministers or local councillors, as were many of the predominantly urban Puritans. It appears that this reversed tendency for some urban legislators to display low tolerances can at least be partially attributed to their prior experience with formal codes of conduct. Few Muddlers and Entrepreneurs had such experience.

Background Characteristics

More Servants (94 per cent) than MPs of any other category attended postsecondary educational establishments. This was not surprising given that most MPs have attended university, and especially considering the prevalence of lawyers among the Servants. More than half the Servants (63 per cent) were Oxbridge educated. This was the highest concentration of Oxbridge graduates in any of the groups and may help to account for their traditional outlook.

The age distribution of the Servants was similar to that of the sample as a whole. Compared with the sample, more Servants were in their forties or sixties, and fewer in their fifties, but the difference was not particularly striking. On the average, Servant MPs were slightly older when elected to Parliament (age forty-one) than their colleagues in general (mean age thirty-nine) or in any of the other groups. This might be expected given the number of practising lawyers in this type – they will have invested more time in establishing their career before entering politics than many individuals in other occupations.

Unlike the Puritans, a large number of Servants claimed membership in an organized religion. A majority (55 per cent) were members of the Church of England. All the Servants who gave a response to this question indicated that they belonged to some form of organized religion – none professed atheism or agnosticism – and all attended services at least occasionally. Seventy-two per cent reported going to church at least once a month; none of the Servants indicated that they never go. While the Puritan category seemed to contradict the hypothesis that firm religious beliefs would be associated with higher ethical standards, the Servants seemed to support it, as they were clearly the most religious group.

A portrait of the typical Servant begins to emerge. A middle-aged, Cambridge-educated barrister who still maintains an abbreviated practice, he is a moderate within his party caucus (whether he is a "high Tory" or a Labourite from the old school prior to the polarization of the early 1980s is equally likely). He represents several farming communities in the north of England and shares the views of his constituents on many of the issues of the day. He is strongly involved in community activities, especially those organized by his church. All these traits conspire to paint him as an old-fashioned member of parliament – he finds public service and the furthering of his constituents' needs to be reward in itself, enjoys his honourable association with an honourable institution, and, while intolerant of clear misconduct, implicitly trusts his fellow members.

REFLECTIONS

The Public's Image of MPs

The majority of the Servants (57 per cent) thought that the public find MPs to be untrustworthy. This was the lowest perceived untrustworthiness of any of the four groups. The Servants offered a number of reasons to explain why the public viewed them in this light. Several cited the low esteem in which politicians are held as the central factor:

This is the nature of politics. The public would view us as untrustworthy even if we were completely trustworthy. The public doesn't know. Politicians just have a bad name. Every general election there is the same old rubbish. My constituents trust me, but that is because I have been there a long time making promises.

Another Servant itemized the characteristics many politicians share, which accounted for the public's lack of trust:

1. Appear glib; tricksters.
2. Have the appearance of smooth, suave, confidence men.
3. When being questioned they are mentally agile and able to avoid the main thrust of the questions.

Other Servants blamed the media for this negative attitude:

We are viewed as untrustworthy chiefly due to the efforts of the media. Our public esteem has declined over the years. We are viewed differently by people who have actually dealt with us, through a committee or interest group. And our constituents who know us hopefully say "he is not as bad as the others."

Indeed, the Servants, even more than the Puritans, claimed that there was a difference between how the public perceives MPs collectively, and how constituents perceive their own MP.

The relatively large number of Servants who claimed that the public found MPs in general trustworthy still expressed some doubts about their public image: "While the public will trust an MP to help them, they equally believe that MPs will help themselves. What they distrust is not the individual but the individual's motivation." Another Servant felt that it was not that the public viewed them as untrustworthy, but rather that they disliked politicians altogether.

What did stand out among the Servants' responses was that, regardless of the public's opinion, they perceived themselves to be a trustworthy lot: "While the standard of honesty is fairly high here, the public views us differently." Many Servants referred to the "rotten apple" theory: "In any organization there will be one or two bad nuts." This was to be expected, they said, given that there were so many people operating in one environment: "Most MPs I would trust to go into the jungle with. The rest I wouldn't. If you have over 600 MPs of course you are going to have a cross-section of the public. It makes sense that some would be shady; others not." In the opinion of these Servants, Parliament was the same as any corporation, institution, or organization – there will be some individuals who engage in questionable activities.

The Register of Members' Interests

The Servants disagreed among themselves as to their degree of satisfaction with the Register of Members' Interests. While 31 per cent of
the Servants claimed to be dissatisfied with the register, 44 per cent
were entirely happy and another 19 per cent were somewhat satisfied.
One Servant admitted to never having looked at the register and thus
could not answer one way or another. While the Servants as a whole
were significantly more satisfied with the register than other MPs (p <
.10), this particular distinction may largely be due to partisan considerations: 89 per cent of Conservative Servants approved of the register,
while 60 per cent of Labour Servants disapproved.

Given the Servants' preoccupation with tradition and the firm
belief that the ethical system was operating effectively, it was not
surprising that a large number of them were satisfied with the register.
While the Puritans questioned the standards of some of their colleagues, the Servants placed their faith in the system of honour, which
permits them to have confidence in the ethical judgments of other
MPs. As one Servant pointed out: "Here the importance is placed on
tradition and convention, and the independence of MPs." Thus a
number of Servants deemed the register redundant: "I don't think
the Register is necessary. It was set up for the wrong reasons. I feel it
is wrong to impose on MPs demands to reveal personal financial
interests." Another added: "I think the Register is pointless. It is better
to allow MPs to rely on individual integrity." Because of their faith in
the existing system, some Servants objected to the presumption
behind the register that MPs cannot be trusted to reveal their interests:
"It is dotty to continue the convention of describing MPs as honourable gentlemen, when they are not even trusted to declare their
interests." Thus many Servants were satisfied with the operation of
the register because they had no expectations of it – they considered
it essentially unnecessary and therefore had no reason to identify
insufficiencies.

Other Servants agreed in principle with the register and were simply
content with its current status. Additional restrictions or demands
were considered by these Servants an invasion of privacy and they
seriously doubted that much could be gained by asking for more
information: "In general I am satisfied with the Register. It would not
be right for values to be disclosed or the names of clients. I'm not
sure it matters to know." Another Servant saw "no overwhelming
reason to make the Register compulsory." Whereas some of the Puritans were suspicious of the presumption that MPs were "honourable
gentlemen," and therefore favoured extension of the register, this

Servant defended the presumption as a basic principle of Parliament and rejected a compulsory register owing to its negative implications for the tradition of honour.

But not all the Servants supported this point of view. Some offered criticisms of the register which were largely of a housekeeping nature. They were most concerned with tightening up the register and improving its overall function. Many thought that if strengthened, it could identify those members operating on the fringe or engaging in questionable activities. These Servants were somewhat concerned about loopholes in the existing regulations:

There is no compulsory declaration. Not enough information is provided. The register does not cover all the aspects which are necessary if it is going to eliminate abuse. Value amounts and the names of clients should be included. It should be a specific declaration.

The register needs to show the nature of the interest – values and names of contributors. It should show the percentage of shares held and for how long they have been in the member's possession. Spouses' values and holdings should also be included.

Others mentioned that the register should be published more often and that a real effort should be made to keep it up-to-date. They pointed out that members could effectively conceal an interest by delaying an update in the register. One summarized the problem as follows: "There are people abusing the system and we need to ferret them out. If we give the Register the necessary punch, it should be able to do that." None of the Servants who were dissatisfied with the register suggested radical changes, but rather adjustments that would make it more suited to accomplishing its purpose.

Of all the groups of MPs, the Servants seemed to be the ones least interested in the register. The majority of Servants did not think the operation of the register was a major concern. Either they were satisfied that the current register was sufficient or they expressed disdain for the introduction of the register in the first place. Many Servants had faith in the ethical system as it operated before the introduction of the register, and thus in their opinion there was no need to tamper with something that was not broken.

This lack of interest in the register was countered somewhat by the overwhelming and intense support the Servants accorded to the recent extension of the declaration principle to include House researchers, secretaries, and lobby journalists. Sixty-nine per cent of the Servants favoured this extension, and many detailed their support:

I was in favour of the extension as these people have access to information – confidential information – before it is released to the public.

Entry into the House and its Halls is an opportunity to make money if used astutely – an opportunity to obtain information and documents and to listen to and spread gossip.

I favoured the extension, although the lobby journalists did not like it. I find it helpful, as it is worthwhile to know who you are talking to. I'm not too worried about secretaries, but with research assistants it can vary as to how influential they are.

The Servants were particularly interested in this reform, as they were the only type of MPs to elaborate significantly on their responses.

The Servants' views on the register reflected their essential contentment with existing arrangements. Whereas the Puritans thought declaration alone to be an insufficient basis for the management of ethical problems, the Servants defended it as a well-established and therefore effective method. Even those who suggested ways in which the register could be improved offered only additional forms of declaration and did not indicate that sterner measures were necessary.

Discipline and Sanctions

Compared with other MPs, and especially the Puritans, the Servants were significantly less supportive of sanctions for non-compliance with the register. Only 27 per cent of the Servants were in favour of sanctions, compared with 63 per cent of the Puritans and 47 per cent of the sample as a whole. These differences were significant at the .10 level. Those who disagreed with the imposition of sanctions did so for a number of reasons. A few thought such sanction would be unlawful, especially expulsion or suspension, as these measures would deny constituents of a representative. Another added that electoral retribution was sufficient to punish non-compliance: "The question of sanction should be left to the members in the first instance. Sanctions should not be written into the formal Register. It should be left to the constituents." Two Servants insisted, à la Enoch Powell, that the register must first be enshrined in legislation before sanctions could be levied for non-compliance. This legalistic interpretation of sanctioning was perhaps reflective of the number of lawyers in the Servant category.

Those Servants who favoured sanction were not afraid to recommend severe discipline. Their suggestions ranged from denial of House privileges to suspension and even expulsion from the House.

They justified these penalties as appropriate by arguing that the failure to disclose personal interests was an assault upon the public interest. But many of these Servants also reasserted that the register first needs to be compulsory: "The proper type of register should be established and then it would be obligatory. The question becomes how to establish this without resorting to Draconian measures. The answer lies with informal pressures. Enoch Powell holds out. He shouldn't be allowed to take his seat or vote. Pressure should be applied from behind the scenes." Another Servant saw the register as a contradiction in itself: "Either we should have a register or we should operate without one. Those failing to comply should be suspended until they do." While most Servants did not favour sanctions being attached to the register, those who did apparently believed that sanctions must be forceful to be effective. The Servants' concern for protecting the interests of their constituents was exemplified by the reasons they advanced for not applying sanctions – deprivation of representation – as well as their reasons for recommending sanctions: MPs were elected to represent the public interest.

The role the Servants gave to established disciplinary procedures in regulating ethical conduct was easily ascertained, given the large number of Servants with experience as Whips. It was apparent that individual Whips had their own perceptions of the significance of their role in the disciplinary process, and that this differed not only between Puritans and Servants, but also within the types themselves. Servant Whip 1 had these comments to offer on the role of the Whip's office:

The Whip's office is like the prefect's office. We do have a coercive role and that is to get the votes out. We are also in a position to advise on other areas. We really don't have a role in discipline – the MPs are ultimately answerable to their constituents. I feel sure I would speak to a member who was in trouble. If someone was involved in a dubious activity they would not see advancement. We advise the PM on appointments and we would not put forward the name of a drug pusher, homosexual, or womanizer. Members look to us not as an example but for advice.

This Whip believed that he played a minor role in the disciplinary process, limited to not advancing those who stray, rather than actually punishing them. He also agreed with many colleagues that punishment should come in the form of electoral retribution. Whip 2, in contrast, saw his disciplinary role as more substantial:

The Whips do a great deal with respect to discipline. If a member has a problem they go see the Whip. The Whips pick up the scent of someone in trouble. We are everywhere. If the matter affected a specific department the information would be passed on. Consultations with individual MPs is a continuing matter. The Whips are regarded as a source of advice and information.

These comments implied that the Whips were actively on the lookout for members who might be involved in worrisome activities. Both Whips agreed that with respect to ethical standards they were at least a source of information and counsel.

Whip 3 spoke frankly about ethics and his part in parliamentary discipline:

I have never regarded myself as the world's living symbol of ethical standards. I do not seek to impose my standards on other people. I hope I have ethical standards, but they are not something I want to talk about or export. A decision to discipline would be taken by the Chief Whip, not me personally. I would be consulted and would ask to have my views heard. I can't claim ethics and the enforcement of standards forms the centrepiece of my work.

This Whip, while he did not consider it to be his main task, would involve himself in the disciplinary process. While he preferred not to be regarded as a role model, he insisted on expressing his views when cases arose. He portrayed his involvement as active, but not central. Lastly, Whip 4 perceived his role to be both active and central. He credited the Whips with an instrumental role:

As a Whip it would be to me in the first instance that allegations would be told and it would be me who would approach the implicated MP. I would not just render advice, but could also take action. I could even call in the police if needed and if the scandal warranted it. I would know if anyone was up to something.

This "activist" Whip, unlike his colleagues, mentioned the involvement of outside regulatory agencies, such as the police force, in the disciplining of members of parliament. Given all these descriptions, it was certain that the Whips office was involved in the maintenance of ethical standards in the House. The extent of this involvement, however, depended on the viewpoint of the individual Whip.

Unlike the Puritans, the Servant MPs did not really raise any serious objections to the established disciplinary process. They were not perturbed by what the Puritans saw as a lack of incentives for investigating allegations against their colleagues. As one Servant said: "I am not interested in being Sherlock Holmes for everyone." Nor were they concerned by the effects of collegiality on discipline and standards.

Indeed, the Servants likely viewed the strong interpersonal ties formed between members as a useful tool in the establishment and maintenance of ethical standards, rather than as an obstacle to complete investigation.

While they might have felt distanced from the disciplinary process, the Servants did agree that there were or had been activities occurring in the House they would deem corrupt. More than half (56 per cent) of the Servants claimed to have knowledge or suspicions of corruption in Parliament, although 31 per cent qualified their admission by noting that the acts involved were minor. Some Servants balked at the term "corruption": "I have not seen corruption in Parliament. I have seen undue influence, for example, on the construction of the Channel Tunnel. There are things which happen which border on corruption." Another noted: "I am concerned about some of the things that go on in Parliament, but I would hesitate to use the word 'corrupt.' It is a very strong word. I would prefer to think of them as 'smelly' or 'stinky' or 'unacceptable.'" In addition, one Servant who said there was corruption in Parliament had other linguistic objections: "'Suspect' is a strong word. I have been 'curious' about people's outside interests. I don't think they are fully declared." Another insisted that corruption should only be discussed in terms of proof, not suspicion: "If MPs think there is corruption going on – that there are members who are corrupt – then they should be willing to name names, take action. They shouldn't make claims otherwise. Corruption only exists if you have evidence which says it does." Semantics aside, however, nearly all Servants expressed some concern over specific incidents or types of activities they found ethically questionable.

One Servant thought corruption particular to the current government. In his words: "There has been a general deterioration in standards in this administration. There have been Ministers with conflicts of interests, and Mrs. Thatcher herself has been caught in the foray with the Oman revelation and her son. There is a need for clearer rules and a Prime Minister who enforces them." Along these general lines, another Servant asserted: "People are openly and without reservation abusing the system. Trying to influence the course or direction of policy for a financial gain. MPs are concealing more than they are revealing." A few of the Servants mentioned in their replies specific cases and individuals they considered corrupt: "I have known of corruption in Departments and offices. The case of Keith Best was borderline, and Norman Tebbit has not always acted above board." Another indicated he was not satisfied with the Westland Affair: "I believe people are lying but I would need to see the documents to prove anything."

Others reported various activities of which they have been suspicious. One Servant thought that perhaps "we should look behind the operation of the various Friendship Groups. A few have third-party sponsorship which might be dubious." Another was concerned with the area of foreign travel: "There are proper and improper ways of engaging in foreign travel. When travelling with a select committee you receive an invitation, everything is registered and above board. But foreign governments also invite individual MPs to visit their country for a few days every two years. This has implications. It has to be considered whether the trip is being used as a bribe to get an MP to adopt a particular point of view." Additionally, some Servants had reservations about the acceptance of gifts, and a number proposed that there should be some value-limits established. Without a formal threshold of unacceptability, it was difficult for them to decide where to draw the line: "How do you quantify a gift? How do you place a value on it? Why is it corrupt to accept a crate of wine, but not a bottle?" One admitted that he only accepted diaries because after twelve months they were no longer any good.

But the greatest number of Servants voiced their suspicions about MPs acting as parliamentary consultants and their declarations of outside interests. One Servant suggested that a closer look should be taken at the areas and issues for which members have accepted consultancies. He thought that people were receiving "material reward of some kind for putting questions to other representatives in Parliament or outside the House in the framework of the bureaucracy." While he was suspicious of some of his colleagues, he added for his own benefit: "I have not been corrupted by money." Another Servant said that he was sure that "there are MPs here who give preeminence to their own commercial interests. I find this distasteful; whether it is corrupt is another question."

The Servants found it particularly difficult to apply the word "corrupt" to activities they did not fully approve. Many could identify behaviour they found questionable, but they also were reluctant to besmirch the honour of the House and its members by terming it corrupt. The Servants were loath to recommend sanctions for noncompliance with the register, but felt that discipline should be severe and unambiguous in instances where it was warranted.

Lobbyists and Lobbying

Most Servants (63 per cent) favoured the introduction of a register of lobbyists. The reasons offered were varied but centred on furnishing members with additional information that might aid them in the performance of their job. The register would enable members to know which interests a lobbyist was representing. While the Servants thought that the task of recognizing lobbyists got easier the longer an MP was at Westminster, such a register would be beneficial to new members and those on the backbenches: "Yes, I think we should know who the lobbyists are. A large number of backbench members don't know, particularly Labour MPs." Another viewed such a register as a further extension of the declaration principle: "There has to be full involvement. Anyone who has access to information should register."

A few of the Servants thought that the House would inevitably have to introduce such a register: "I suppose we will come around to this. Lobbying is a growing field which has become more professionally oriented in the last four years." Another saw potential for future abuses: "There are quite a number of lobbyists operating here. While I am not too worried at the moment, there are undesirable aspects developing." A few Servants insisted that lobbying was still a crude art in Britain, especially compared to its development in America: "I don't want to inhibit lobbying, as it informs the legislator of the concerns of groups and industries. But it should be done more publicly as opposed to secretly." Some Servants said that they valued the information provided by interest groups: "Lobbyists offer documentation, lunches, hospitality and meetings. You can accept them and not be corruptly influenced. They are a bore, not an inducement. It is a useful way to inform yourself." But at times the Servants objected to some of the tactics which were employed: "Such a register would certainly cut down on the number of cowboys around here."

Some of those who disapproved of a new register objected to the idea of a separate document. They did not want to provide lobbyists with a parliamentary stamp of approval they could use to their advantage to obtain clients. Once registered, firms could claim they were on the parliamentary register and thus a legitimate company with which to do business. But, these Servants maintained, if the register were included with the Register of Members' Interests, and the declarations filed by lobby journalists and members' staff, then the list of lobbyists would merely be seen as part of the larger effort to bring government into the open.

One Servant objected to a register on principle. While he stated that he frequently disapproved of lobbyists' activities and had as little to do with them as he could, he allowed that "my philosophical nature never likes to see other people spending their lives compiling registers. There is just no need for it." Another merely indicated that he had a mind of his own and was not easily persuaded by the efforts of lobbyists. In his words: "A lot of MPs like the freebies offered by lobbyists, but they are not bought by them. The lobbyists are just wasting the money of their clients." These Servants obviously felt that a lobbyists' register would provide marginal benefit, if any.

Almost all Servants (91 per cent) recounted approaches from lobbyists. According to the Servants the most common method of approach was by letter, usually containing an outline of the lobbyist's position and an invitation to a social event of some kind. Other methods included the receipt of documentation from an interest group, a telephone call, and the ever-popular invitation to lunch.

While concerned about the development of lobbying within Westminster, the Servants, unlike the Puritans, were not disparaging in their remarks. While they would have preferred that lobbying be done more openly, they were not in principle opposed to the work of these firms. In fact, they estimated that they benefited from lobbyist activity. As well, the Servants did not connect lobbying with individual MPs. Not one mentioned, in the context of the discussion on lobbyists, a concern over MPs acting as parliamentary consultants. It would seem that they did not consider such MPs to be a lobby from within. The Servants viewed lobbying as part and parcel of representation.

ETHICAL STRATEGIES

The Servants offered various interpretations of the phrase "activity inconsistent with the standards the House is entitled to expect from its members." Even among this, the smallest category of MPs, there was little consensus on what this guiding phrase is intended to cover. At one end of the scale was this comment: "The House is entitled to the truth at all times. It is a difficult point to separate the truth from political partiality in some cases, but there should be a common core of truth in every MP – the honesty of representation." At the other end was this response: "Gracious me ... the House expects members to be ladies and gentlemen and to observe the standards of courtesy, tolerance, good manners, punctuality, a proper standard of dress, a certain avoidance of foul language, moderation in drink and purity in family life." Through most of the definitions, however, there seemed to be a consistent thread: activity that violated the interests of their constituents.

While the Servants were confident they would recognize behaviour that was inconsistent with the standards of the House, they had trouble expressing or describing examples of such behaviour. This could have been, as one Servant suggested, because the phrase is not used by MPs, or as he put it: "It is not on their lips." One Servant even stated that whoever wrote the phrase "had lousy prose." A number mentioned honour and the admonition that MPs should behave as honourable gentlemen. They are to avoid activity that brings the institution of Parliament into disrepute. One explained: "We should not expect MPs to be angels, but they should be professional in all they do." As in the case of the Puritans, this phrase did not seem to offer much in the way of consistent ethical guidance for the Servants. Once again, individual members were supplying their own interpretation of what type of behaviour was inconsistent with the standards of the House. The Servants were aware of their responsibility in this regard. For the most part they felt that MPs should be able to make ethical decisions on their own. A number of the Servants indicated that MPs should have their own personal standards of ethics. "If they don't," a Servant warned, "they shouldn't be in Parliament." Another stated indignantly: "We don't need rules; we have values."

Unlike the Puritans, the Servants were not willing to discuss what they themselves did to avoid questionable situations. They were more prone to speak about the dilemmas they faced as representatives and the difficulties such dilemmas created for them. Thirty-three per cent of the Servants said they occasionally had to deal with such dilemmas. They spoke openly about the struggles they underwent with their conscience to arrive at the resolution of ethical questions: "The ethical dilemmas we encounter daily take you into the heartland. This is where you find yourself wanting to say something, or asked to say something related to commercial interests. This is a serious question." Or as one Servant related: "There are occasions when I should speak up but I don't. There are times when I have a strong opinion, but I tone down what I say to a public audience because of party discipline." A number of them indicated that several of the questions asked of them in the questionnaire resembled real-life decisions they have had to make.

The Servants raised several concerns that were constituency- related. These ranged from simple issues ("In my constituency, if I wanted to, I would not have to pay for anything: buses, in restaurants; everyone wants to pay for you. Is this corruption?") to more complex issues of competing loyalties:

The types of dilemmas I face revolve around conflicting pressures. Taking up individual constituents cases whether or not I am totally satisfied that it is a reasonable case. I must assume responsibility whatever the case.

It is difficult to decide what to do when members of your constituency hold views with which you disagree. Yet, as a representative I am suppose to represent the interests and views of all my constituents. I find this difficult.

Of the four groups of MPS, the Servants were the most bothered by this particular type of dilemma. Unlike a large number of the other members, the Servants did not interpret ethical dilemmas to be questions of conscience, such as the abortion issue or animal experimentation. More often than not, they ended up discussing dilemmas that arose because of their position as representative. A final illustration is this comment: "People in public life are very vulnerable. If I didn't pay my bus fare, it would be a headline in every newspaper. For the normal individual, this would not be of interest. I realize that this is a term of the political contract."

While the Servants expressed concern about the conduct of some MPS, they were not convinced that additional rules were the solution. Sixty-three per cent of the Servants opposed the introduction into the House of a written code of conduct. Their objections stemmed from several sources. Many thought that a written code was not a substitute for a highly developed personal sense of ethics: "There is no need for a written code. MPS are supposedly operating from personal values. We don't need written rules to tell us how to act in these circumstances." One asserted that MPS should already have developed standards before they enter the House: "Most professions have their own codes so you would get some sense of standards from your previous occupation." Others felt that formal rules would be redundant and ineffective: "Rules already exist in various forms. People place too much stock in a written code of conduct." Common sense was what these Servants said MPS should rely upon. There was already enough guidance available to MPS; it would be superfluous to codify it. Another simply stated: "Rules do not stop people from breaking them."

But the main objection to a code was the fear that it would inevitably prove restrictive and incomplete. The Servants suggested that such a code could not possibly cover all the areas of potential ethical conflict to which a legislator is exposed: "A written code would be restrictive. It couldn't match the whole range of activities MPS are involved in. We must apply principles to everything we do. It is impossible to reduce it to a code. The important traditions and conventions here are related to the independence of the MP – the MP's independence in situations." One Servant feared that a "code would create a regulatory framework, and that flexibility would give way to inflexibility." Another was anxious not to "create a regulatory edifice like that which exists in the United States." Finally, one Servant even doubted the possibility of writing a code: "A written code would not be possible. You couldn't write something loosely enough. It would be turning MPS back into schoolboys. We are wearing long trousers now, and have to accept responsibility and know how one should behave." Most Servants readily accepted that individual MPs should bear responsibility for resolving ethical dilemmas, and that the institution of Parliament should not try to predict solutions for every possibility.

Some Servants, while still opposed to a written code of conduct, mentioned that they would support the establishment of stronger guidelines – something less rigid than a code but more formal than the current situation. These Servants said that they would favour the outline of some general principles that could be applied – perhaps a set of ethical aspirations. They preferred to think in terms of an ethical statement rather than standards, as they indicated that standards are too detailed.

Those Servants who did favour a written code thought that its benefits would outweigh its drawbacks. Some suggested that since written rules were provided to ministers, they should also be provided to MPs. A few felt that standards of conduct were simply not being promulgated effectively. Thus some Servants were not so sure that all MPs could handle the discretion the system placed at their disposal. A few supported a code as a means of keeping the rotten apples from spoiling the rest of the barrel:

In the end it has to be written down because all MPs are well versed in splitting political and ethical hairs. Anything less than a hard fast rule will be avoided by those determined to do so.

A code of conduct would help in part, if we could agree what should go in it. We need to determine what the standards are going to be. The devious will stay devious unless there are established sanctions.

Even for these more cynical Servants, the ethical problems in the House were personal rather than systemic. They did not feel there was anything lacking in the ethical assumptions of the House; these assumptions needed only to be made more cohesive and communicated more clearly to all members.

CONCLUSION

The Servants fit well into the traditional model of Parliament and its members, and were on the whole quite comfortable with that model and its assumptions and corollaries. Servant MPs countered the pessimism of the Puritans with an optimism about the ethical strength and resiliency of the House as an institution. The Servants ascribed most of Parliament's ethical problems to the actions of the few dishonest individuals who inevitably must crop up in a basically honourable gathering. They admitted that some MPs were engaging in borderline improprieties, but asserted that this was primarily because they were not sufficiently acquainted with the standards of the House and suggested that at most a more concerted effort to convey those standards to the entire membership would curb most potential for abuse.

The Servants were not especially concerned about the register and definitely opposed attaching sanctions to it. Many thought the register somewhat superfluous given the traditional method of orally declaring one's interests on the floor of the House. The Servants were in no way interested in covering up misconduct – they favoured strong, perhaps even criminal penalties for genuine transgressions. The Servants expressed mild support for a register of lobbyists as long as it was an extension of the movement towards more openness in government. While they had concerns about the behaviour of some lobbyists, they did not assert, as did many Puritans, that the entire industry was dangerous, but accepted the activity of lobbyists and interest groups as an integral part of the British system of representation.

The Servants were not resistant to change per se, but they insisted that changes to Parliament's ethical framework be evolutionary modifications rather than revolutionary redesigns. The Puritans questioned the fundamental assumptions of honour and collegial resolution of problems; the Servants reaffirmed them, and found fault primarily with the depth of individual commitment to these assumptions. In many ways, though they share a mutual intolerance for conflict of interest, the Servants and Puritans held directly opposing views of the ethical ecology of the House. The Servants felt that the ethics of the House could best be improved by the election of candidates with stronger personal standards, and by better education of members as to the ethical expectations of the House.

CHAPTER FIVE

The Muddlers

The Muddlers were those MPs, twenty-one in number, who scored low tolerance for constituency service and high tolerance for conflict of interest. Like the Servants, the Muddlers displayed a mix of high and low tolerances. The Servants drew the line between corrupt and not corrupt in an essentially altruistic manner – they were willing to accept behaviour benefiting others that they would not accept were it purely self-serving. The Muddlers, in contrast, condemned ethically question-able acts that would benefit only constituents, yet condoned acts that would confer direct personal advantage on an MP himself.

The Muddlers were for the most part strong in their condemnation of the constituency service items. Many objected especially to the "Old Boy Network," which they saw as the central issue in the SCHOOL situation. They were opposed to the notions of privilege and tradition that such networks conjure up: "This sort of thing is established in England. It all depends on your name, your public school contacts and who you know. It is wrong and I refuse to write letters, nor do I appreciate finding out that my name has been used on a form at an institution." Other Muddlers thought MPs risked debasing their posi-tion by engaging in this sort of activity: "We must also be seen to be above board. This is a weakness which can be considered a form of corruption."

The CONTRACT scenario drew similar disapproval:

To my mind this is undoubtedly corrupt. While a Minister may be entitled to put forward his case, he must go through the appropriate channels.

While there is no direct personal financial gain here, this would advance a Minister's political career. There are political rewards at stake.

Whereas the Servants considered these constituency service acts as part and parcel of their representative function, the Muddlers saw them as incursions of political expediency into the realm of legislative deliberation. The Muddlers felt it important to shield their legislative autonomy from what they considered the inappropriate demands of their representative role.

On the other hand, the Muddlers seemed much less diligent in protecting their autonomy from personal considerations. In general, the Muddlers felt that the acts depicted in the conflict-of-interest scenarios were acceptable as long as the interests involved were declared. In a sense the Muddlers seemed to think that declaration actually resolved the conflict: "The whole point is public accountability. Full declaration is necessary. We must make known the influences at work on us, then I feel it is okay. With full declaration ethics is reasonably protected." This faith in declaration was especially clear in the RETAINER and ORDER PAPER scenarios:

Yes, this happens and there is nothing corrupt in it. Everyone knows about the interest. I do not like it personally, but I accept it.

Well isn't that what the company is paying him for? Everyone would know of the interest.

The Muddlers also justified the activities described by citing the absence of restrictions against them and the frequency with which such activities were practised in the House:

I would not regard this as corrupt – the rules of the House allow it.

This is unethical, but not corrupt. The rules allow it. We all advocate causes and arrange meetings between MPs and external pressure groups.

The Muddlers found it difficult to disapprove of behaviour if many of their colleagues engaged in it, or if there was not a specific prohibition against it.

The Muddlers seemed almost to defer to the ethical judgment of their fellow MPs – that many others were involved in certain activities was reason enough for the Muddlers to consider those activities acceptable. Unlike the Puritans and the Servants, many Muddlers were willing to accept as legitimate activities they found personally objectionable. Others made no mention of their own feelings, but simply remarked that "this happens all the time, and everyone does it." That the Muddlers apparently compromised their own principles for the sake of conformity, or substituted the observed standards of others for personal ethical convictions, suggested that the Muddlers were not sure of their own ethical standards and seemed to lack sufficient guidance. Either by admission or implication, they displayed, in contrast to the Puritans and Servants, weakly held ideas about ethics. The Muddlers seemed to lack an ethical compass.

Of all the interviews conducted, the Muddlers were the MPs who had the least amount of time to spend on the interview and in general were reluctant to expand on their numerical answers or talk about corruption in the abstract. In place of the Puritans' passionate ideological fervour, the Muddlers displayed a preoccupation with the instrumental details of acts of impropriety – they seemed almost fascinated with the intricate ways MPs could circumvent the existing regulatory framework. They were quick to point out violations of the letter of the House rules, but relatively unconcerned about the spirit. Whereas the Puritans viewed themselves as an island of rectitude amid a sea of indifference and impropriety, the Muddlers seemed content to drift along with the currents and prevailing winds.

MUDDLER PERCEPTIONS

Muddler Definitions of Political Corruption

By far, most Muddlers (67 per cent) defined corruption as an abuse of office. This type of definition, narrower in scope than those favoured by the Puritans and Servants, reduces corruption to an issue of conduct rather than ethics. Judgments based on this type of definition depend crucially on where and how the line between use and abuse of official powers is drawn, and not on abstract standards and principles of ethics. One Muddler was clear about what he felt constituted corruption: "Blatantly using your position for dubious financial gain." What was not so clear was how blatant an act had to be, or how dubious the gain, before he deemed it corrupt.

Many other Muddlers' definitions also reflected a preoccupation with money, and the influence it could buy:

Corruption is doing things for money, using your influence for money.

Political corruption is using the system for improper purposes – to line your own pocket.

Narrow definitions like these suggested that for many of the Muddlers, corruption was a synonym for bribery, or at best was a subtler, perhaps not explicitly illegal form of bribery. Even this lengthy and thoughtful response centred on money and influence:

Political corruption means a number of things: 1. using one's office or position to feather one's nest, or family, friend or business acquaintances. 2. to manipulate one's position to obtain a gain which one would not be able to obtain if it was open to the light of day. 3. to so use political power to be able to maintain yourself in power by the use of inter-locking relationships which might be on the face of it legal, but in reality are using the existing institutions for personal financial gain.

Only one Muddler defined corruption in terms of betrayal of the public interest and just 14 per cent offered inducement-oriented definitions. One other considered corruption to be a change of political allegiance – he saw only those who cross the floor of the House as corrupt. Many Puritans and Servants referred in their definitions to the public interest and how it was harmed or disregarded in corrupt acts. When the Muddlers included the public in their definitions, it was largely in terms of reluctance to have an interest or inducement made known: "Political corruption is thinking or acting under some kind of pressure or inducement in a way which you would not do otherwise. When you would not be happy to have an inducement known to voters, colleagues and the press." For this Muddler, the public good was irrelevant in identifying corruption; what identified an act as corrupt was that, for the official involved, it would not be good if the public found out about it.

The Muddlers' propensity for abuse-of-office definitions exemplified their conventionalist, almost minimalist approach to ethical determinations. They did not insist, as did the Puritans, on comparing behaviour to firm principles that might well be more restrictive than explicitly required; they did not, as did the Servants, impute a certain ethical wisdom to MPs and imply that corruption must involve an external corrupting influence. Additionally, unlike the Puritans and Servants, the Muddlers' tolerance scores seemed to contradict their explicit definitions of corruption. While many of them said they considered a direct personal financial benefit to an MP to be especially damning, they tended to judge conflict-of-interest activities – many of which involved such a benefit – as relatively acceptable. They were much harsher in their criticism of the constituency service acts, which involved no such personal monetary gain.

General Perceptual Profile

The statement "Political corruption is not a widespread problem" met with the overwhelming agreement (90 per cent) of the Muddler MPs (see table 8). The Muddlers did not perceive British society or the British political system as conducive to widespread political corruption. According to one: "I just do not think there is very much corruption in Britain. I feel that the standards of integrity are very high – if they were not the individuals would be ferreted out." Another added: "British society is much more closed than other societies, although I am not entirely convinced of this, as there might be some corruption which we just do not know about." This Muddler, while asserting that corruption is scarce, allowed that an accurate measure of corruption may be impossible because of its secretive nature.

A number of Muddlers, as many Servants, also cited the British political system as an inhibitor to widespread political corruption. Most Muddlers added a comparison with the American system, which they generally perceived as corruption-ridden: "Corruption is much more prone in America as they have no real system of checks and balances like here. The notion of the Opposition and Question Time are foreign. In our system there is accountability." Another claimed that "the British Prime Minister does not have the same powers as the American President. Thus Watergate could never happen in Britain. In Britain the Prime Minister would have been exposed much earlier." These cultural and systemic factors, according to the Muddlers, serve to limit the incidence of corruption in Britain.

Apparently, the Muddlers felt that corruption was much more of a problem in the realms of local government and business than in Parliament. Like the Servants, the Muddlers pointed to the greater power of individual local councillors, as compared with MPs. They felt this encouraged more frequent or serious impropriety. Like almost all the MPs surveyed, the Muddlers perceived parliamentarians to be more virtuous than individuals who operate in the world of business.

None of the types of MPs was significantly distinguishable by its response to the two societal statements (18 and 20), but the Muddlers were the group that insisted on elaborating their answers with disparaging remarks about the public. A few suggested that a large segment of the public could not even identify their own MP; such people, they insisted, not only did not understand politics, but did not care about it. Another proposed a theory: "Everyone needs someone to hate – a scapegoat. Politicians are good for that. In the public eye they are perceived as being one rung higher than estate agents." Thus the

Table 8
Muddler General Perceptual Profile

Statement	Text	Agree (%)	Disagree (%)	Mean	Std. Dev.	Median	Significance
15	Political corruption is not a widespread problem.	90	10	2.5	1.5	2	**F:** *p < .05*
		82	*15*	*2.5*	*1.6*	*2*	
16	In so far as citizens distrust elected officials it is because they do not understand what politics is all about.	76	19	2.8	1.9	2	
		66	*28*	*3.2*	*1.9*	*3*	
17	Dishonesty is more widespread in politics than in business.	5	90	6.2	1.1	7	
		4	*89*	*6.0*	*1.2*	*6*	
18	Political corruption is more widespread at the local than at the national level of government.	76	10	2.7	1.5	2	
		73	*12*	*2.7*	*1.6*	*2*	
19	No matter what we do, we can never eliminate political corruption.	90	0	2.1	1.0	2	
		80	*13*	*2.5*	*1.7*	*2*	
20	The corruption that exists in the political world simply reflects the standards of the rest of society.	48	38	3.8	1.9	4	
		55	*31*	*3.4*	*1.9*	*3*	
21	If it hadn't been for the Poulson scandal, we would hear a lot less about corruption in government.	15	85	5.9	1.6	6.5	**t:** p < .01
		29	*64*	*4.8*	*2.0*	*5*	**F:** p < .01
22	MPs are sufficiently well informed to act as the sole guarantors of acceptable conduct in the house.	57	38	3.6	2.2	3	
		52	*40*	*3.7*	*2.2*	*3*	**F:** p < .05
23	Once allegations of corruption are made, MPs in their parliamentary capacity should be brought within the ambit of criminal law	50	33	3.6	2.3	3.5	**t:** p < .05
		70	*23*	*2.7*	*2.1*	*2*	**F:** p < .01
24	Britain's libel laws inhibit the uncovering and reporting of political corruption.	19	67	5.2	1.6	6	**t:** p < .05
		37	*53*	*4.5*	*2.2*	*5*	**F:** *p < .001*

Key: Values in *italics* pertain to the entire sample of 100 MPs. "Agree" equals responses of 1, 2, or 3 (as a percentage of valid responses). "Disagree" equals responses of 5, 6, or 7 (as a percentage of valid responses). "Significance" equals significance levels for t-statistic (difference between Muddler and non-Muddler means) and F-ratio (analysis of variance across the four types of MPs).

public distrusts politicians because it is convenient and they do not know any better. This attitude towards the public's distrust of politicians will be reinforced by the Muddlers' comments on whether the public see MPs as trustworthy or untrustworthy: for the Muddlers, this distrust was seen as an inevitable consequence of political representation, and at the core was, apparently, this inevitable misunderstanding on the part of the public.

The Muddlers were again nearly unanimous in their belief that political corruption can never be completely eliminated. Ninety per cent agreed with this statement, and not one disagreed. But while the Muddlers believed corruption could not be eradicated, they did think that steps could be taken to control it: "we can make it better." Unlike the Servants, however, the Muddlers did not offer suggestions as to how this could be accomplished.

Of all the groups of MPs, the Muddlers were the least convinced of the importance of the Poulson scandal in uncovering and revealing corruption in government. Eighty-five per cent of the Muddlers disagreed with statement 21 (p < .01). In stark contrast to the Servants, the Muddlers were generally of the opinion that the activities of John Poulson were all but gone from memory. It was a case, they claimed, which was not much discussed nowadays. One Muddler thought that "many of the new members would not even know what the scandal was about." While they were willing to classify the affair as a classic case of corruption, they were quick to add that there have been and will always be scandals to replace it. The Muddlers thought that, had the Poulson affair never occurred or been uncovered, another incident would inevitably have shocked Britons into recognizing the existence of corruption within their political system.

The Muddlers were divided on whether MPs were sufficiently well informed to act as the sole guarantors of acceptable conduct. While most (57 per cent) agreed with statement 22, another 38 per cent disagreed. The Muddlers who supported this view thought that, as a collectivity, MPs were able to ensure acceptable conduct. They were none too certain that individuals were able to do so, but that, as an institution, it was Parliament's responsibility to act as the guarantor of conduct. The Muddlers cited recourse to parliamentary privilege, a subject not mentioned by the Servants or Puritans, as a method of ensuring acceptable conduct: "Parliamentary privilege helps to uncover acts of corruption. An MP can say or make whatever accusations they want in the chamber. We are not open to the libel laws, but they are very grave accusations to make." This remark suggests that fear of being named or accused of wrongdoing on the House floor acts as a deterrent against corruption. Yet the comments of many MPs indicated that such an accusation is extremely unlikely – MPS are extraordinarily reluctant to impugn their colleagues' ethical standards, especially when they have no formal criteria for their own. Given the collegial environment of the House, moreover, an accusation would be potentially more disastrous for the accuser than the accused.

The Muddlers who disagreed thought that MPS could not do the job alone, that as one member said: "I'm not so sure MPS are certain of their standards. Any activity which falls inside the grey area I would expect members to have a difficult time with." But once again the Muddlers did not offer suggestions as to who else should be involved in ethical regulation, or what could be done to help MPS with the ethical decisions they have to make.

The Muddlers, as a group, were clearly least in favour of bringing MPS within the ambit of criminal law once allegations of corruption have been made (p < .05). Not all the Muddlers were convinced that MPS should be subject to criminal investigation and penalties if implicated in a corrupt act. This could be related somewhat to the confidence they expressed in the ability and the responsibility of Parliament to guarantee the ethical conduct of its members. If punishment is warranted, then the Muddlers felt the House should issue an appropriate penalty. It is Parliament that should play the role of disciplinarian.

Finally, only 19 per cent of the Muddlers agreed that the libel laws inhibited the uncovering and reporting of political corruption. A full two-thirds (67 per cent) disagreed, in significant contrast to the Puritans, of whom 67 per cent agreed (p < .05). As noted previously, the Muddlers believed that parliamentary privilege, which was unfettered by libel statutes, could be used in the management of corruption. In addition, a number of the Muddlers expressed the view that libel laws did not stop the press from printing allegations and reports of scandal: "Today the press is not hushing up sex scandals or financial scandals." One Muddler thought that while the laws might inhibit the initiation of an inquiry, they need not prohibit the press from reporting developments in an ongoing scandal. Others thought the laws were necessary in order to prevent damage to the reputations of public persons, and that this benefit outweighed any restrictions they might place on the investigation of actual wrongdoing. The Muddlers viewed the libel laws as both necessary and effective, and not a major roadblock to exposing acts of political corruption.

In general, except for their belief that corruption was not widespread, the Muddlers' opinions were in sharp contrast to those of the Servants. This was not surprising, given that the tolerance levels of the two types were exact opposites. This disagreement was greatest over the importance of the Poulson scandal and the impact of existing legislation on the management of political corruption. Despite their essentially conservative outlook, the Servants were insistent that MPs be brought within the ambit of criminal law and that libel laws posed a problem to investigations. The Muddlers were not even in favour of these changes to the system.

WHO ARE THE MUDDLERS?

Political Characteristics

As in the case of the Servants, party affiliation can not be considered a reliable indicator of membership in the Muddler category (see figure 7). Muddler MPs were drawn from all of the parties: 62 per cent were Conservatives, 29 per cent Labour, and 9 per cent Alliance members. The Muddlers placed themselves slightly to the right of centre in the ideological spectrum within their respective parties. While the Servant category was predominantly made up of MPs who placed themselves in the ideological centre, the Muddlers, like the Puritans, claimed ideological positions across the spectrum. The Muddlers stood out somewhat more clearly from their fellows in their self-perceived degree of ethical liberalism. The Muddlers' mean response of 4.6 was the highest of the four groups, indicating that they saw themselves as fairly permissive, relative to other MPs, on questions of ethics.

The Muddlers were in general the most experienced members of parliament in the sample. Their mean length of parliamentary service was fourteen years (median value thirteen), as compared with a mean of twelve years (median nine) for the sample, and a mean of eleven years (median eight) for the Servants and Puritans. The median values indicate that the average Muddler had been in the House for a full term longer than the average MP. While many Puritans and Servants were found to have less than two terms' service in the House, two-thirds (67 per cent) of the Muddlers were in their third or later term, and 43 per cent had served for more than sixteen years. This finding tends to support the hypothesis that increasing parliamentary experience is correlated with increased tolerance of unethical behaviour. The more time one has spent in the House, the more cynical about and more able to indulge in conflicts of interest one can become. The Muddlers were the MPs who most often cited the absence of written rules to justify a number of the activities they themselves were willing to describe as questionable. This argument, in extreme, is that whatever is not expressly prohibited is permissible.

Though many had been MPs for several terms, relatively few Muddlers had experience in cabinet or the Whip's office. Only 29 per cent

Figure 7
Party Affiliation

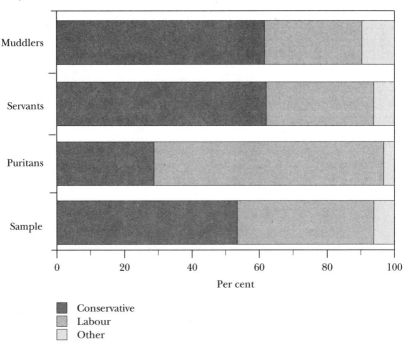

Muddlers

Servants

Puritans

Sample

0   20   40   60   80   100

Per cent

☐ Conservative
☐ Labour
☐ Other

of the Muddlers were former ministers or Whips. In contrast, 63 per cent of the Servants had such experience. This continues to support the assertion that prior experience with a formal code of conduct tends to be associated with more restrictive ethical standards.

The Muddlers' high tolerance levels for the conflict-of-interest scenarios, especially those like RETAINER, ORDER PAPER, and PASS that involved outside employment of MPs, might be partially accounted for by the large number of Muddlers (81 per cent) who held another occupation besides MP (see figure 8). The fraction of Muddlers employed outside the House was higher than that of the Servants and the Puritans (although still less than that of the Entrepreneurs). Additionally, a majority (59 per cent of those with outside employment) of the Muddlers' external occupations were either parliamentary consultancies or directorships. Such jobs were in the minority among the Servants, and quite rare in the Puritan category. The Muddlers did not express much concern over MPs accepting retainers from consultancy firms. In their opinion, outside employment was perfectly acceptable. and few Muddlers were worried about the relationship between the MP and these outside firms. Those few who did

Figure 8
Outside Employment Types

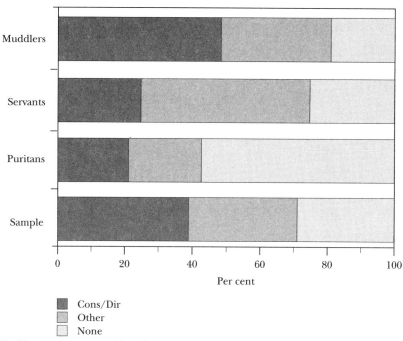

Key: "Cons/Dir" MPs engaged in parliamentary consultancies or corporate directorships.
      "Other" MPs engaged in other forms of outside employment.
      "None" MPs with no outside employment.

express concern centred their comments on the MP's lack of power
or influence:

Companies that hire MPs to act as consultant and advisers do not get their
money's worth. They are not worth any sort of representations they can make.

I think MPs have no power, therefore they are not worth buying. The point is
though that companies and firms don't know this. They are paying for something: the old boy network, personal contact with Ministers. There are large
sums of money involved, but it is difficult to know exactly how much.

The Puritans and Servants were troubled by, and in some cases bitterly
opposed to, outside employment of MPs because of the potential effect
upon legislative autonomy and the possible negative consequences on
the public interest. The Muddlers' concerns, in contrast, seemed to
be based on a fear that external employers were being taken in by

relatively powerless MPs, and that the victim in any corruption that might arise out of the relationship was not the public, but the employer.

Not one Muddler expressed the view that outside employment should be prohibited. Nor did they become engrossed in discussions of the full-time as opposed to the part-time legislator, as did many Servants and Puritans. Despite the number who engaged in outside employment and the responsibilities such employment must entail, 81 per cent of the Muddlers described themselves as full-time members of Parliament. Only one classified himself as a part-time legislator.

A number of the Muddlers asserted that the holding of outside employment and interests could be rendered much more acceptable by public disclosure: "Everything is above board as long as it is declared. It is secrecy which disturbs me and makes an act corrupt." But some of the Muddlers were even opposed to public disclosure and did not think it should be required of those holding additional employment: "I do not believe in disclosure as there is no need. I didn't sign the register myself until I was given a government position." Another said: "I just don't think disclosure is important." Whereas the Puritans believed declaration an insufficient means of ensuring ethical compliance, the Muddlers were quite happy with it, and some even considered it an excessive intrusion into a member's privacy.

The Muddlers justified the acceptance of retainers and outside employment by referring to their low salaries and poor facilities which, they argued, necessitated their securing additional income. In their opinion the inadequate salary and insufficient allowances and resources left them no other alternative: "I don't think MPs are furnished with adequate resources and staff, and I am surprised by the low intelligence of the people who work here. But we don't have the resources to attract better people. Nothing would entice me back into the business world more quickly than having spent a term as an MP." Another added: "We are not even paid enough to be corrupt. You have to be devoted to be an MP, as the pay and hours are crazy." Finally, one Muddler indicated that he "would prefer MPs to be paid a realistic salary, and then rules governing outside employment such as those that apply to government Ministers would apply throughout the House." Unlike the Servants and even the Puritans, the Muddlers did not seem to subscribe to the view that public service was its own reward and demanded sacrifice. While many MPs were clearly displeased with the remuneration they received, the Muddlers continually returned to low pay as a rationale for the types of outside involvements the Puritans and Servants found especially difficult to justify.

Politically, the Muddlers were distinguished by their relative willingness to serve on corporate boards of directors and as parliamentary consultants. While the Servants did not differ significantly in the number who pursued outside employment, they favoured the more traditional occupations of law and journalism. The Servants also viewed their outside employment as an extension of their representative function, whereas the Muddlers viewed it simply as a means of supplementing their income – an additional benefit to which they were entitled because of their low official salary.

Spatial Characteristics

Once again there proved to be no significant regional concentration among the Muddlers. Constituency type was the spatial factor that displayed significant association with MP type. As with the Puritans, most Muddlers represented predominantly urban constituencies. While the Puritans were concentrated in inner cities, most urban Muddlers represented smaller urban centres. Additionally, of the urban Muddlers, only a few had experience in local government. Almost all urban Puritans and Servants, in contrast, were found to have such experience. Such experience, and the code of conduct it would have exposed the MP to, could have played a part in shaping the stricter ethical standards of those groups.

Background Characteristics

As with the previous categories of MPs, a significant fraction of the Muddlers had a post-secondary education (75 per cent), although this was the lowest percentage of any of the groups. Nor were Muddlers significantly distinguishable from other MPs by their age, either chronological (mean fifty-one years), or at first election to the House (thirty-eight years). While the Muddlers in general had more parliamentary experience than their colleagues, no one age or age group seemed to dominate.

A number of the Muddlers (67 per cent) claimed membership in an organized religion. The majority (50 per cent) belonged to the Church of England. Fourteen per cent of the Muddlers professed to be agnostic. Unlike the Servants, the Muddlers were not particularly conscientious practitioners of their faith: only 23 per cent of the Muddlers who belonged to a religion claimed to attend services at least once a week. The same number attended services only a few times a year, and 15 per cent never did. It may be that the Muddler's lackadaisical approach to their faith mirrored their relatively lower concern for matters of ethics.

A typical Muddler has toiled on the backbenches for a suburban constituency for twelve years, but without capturing the eye of the prime minister or the party leadership. He came to the House from a moderately successful career in the City, and he has maintained close contacts with his former associates, serving as parliamentary consultant to two securities firms. The spacious office his clients provide him with reminds him that his MP's salary and benefits are much less than he could garner in the private sector, and he is glad of an opportunity to supplement them. He worries at times that his relationship with his clients might be seen as too close, but takes comfort in the fact that many other MPs maintain similar ties – if he is wrong, then at least he is not alone.

REFLECTIONS

While the Muddlers did not offer much additional information on the general statements put to them, they did have much to say with regard to the Register of Members' Interests, sanctions, discipline, and lobbying. Their views on these topics varied to some extent, but in most instances there was a consensus on the underlying principles at the heart of these questions of ethics and standards.

The Public's Image of MPs

The majority of Muddlers (58 per cent) thought the public perceived MPs as untrustworthy. This percentage was somewhat lower than that of the sample as a whole – it was the Servants and Muddlers who were most confident of their trustworthiness in the eyes of the public. Unlike the Servants, however, the Muddlers did not focus blame for the public's low opinion of politicians on the media. Rather, their responses indicated they felt that this perception was inherent in the position: MPs by the nature of their job are forced to deal in words. They make promises and speeches that they find increasingly difficult to uphold. The Muddlers thought that the core of the relationship between themselves and the public was the truth, and the problem was that the public did not always think MPs were playing straight and honestly:

The public tends not to believe the statements of politicians automatically, but this does not mean that they find them immoral.

The public views MPs as untrustworthy. MPs are perceived as not giving positive answers. They come across as people always leaving themselves gates to escape through. The public mistrust what MPs say and do.

The public have a healthy skepticism of MPs. They are wary of the politician's promise, but they don't see them as venal.

Thus, while the Muddlers were convinced that the public did not trust the "words" of MPs, they were quick to add that this did not necessarily mean that they thought of them as corrupt or unethical.

Even those Muddlers (33 per cent) who thought that the public perceived MPs as trustworthy qualified their responses: "The public see us as trustworthy, that we are honest and people of integrity. Sure they will accuse us of being evasive and of never talking straight, but not of corruption." Another added: "There is a strict code regarding the relationship with truth. By and large MPs are truthful. If they aren't and are found out, the consequences would be dire." Most Muddlers felt that, at the very least, they had the trust of their own constituents, no matter how they felt about MPs in general. One found this attitude rather amusing: "The British public have utter disregard and distaste for MPs as a group, but total and utter trust and respect for their own individual MPs. The things people come and ask me are amazing: advice on family planning matters, what baby clothes should be bought, where the best shops are. As if I should be an expert on such subjects, or at least I'm expected to be an expert."

In responding to this question about the public's perceptions, the Muddlers did not volunteer their own opinions about their own or their colleagues' trustworthiness, as did many Puritans and Servants. Nor did they make reference to the "rotten apple" theory to explain poor public perception. They deflected the public's generally negative perception of MPs by deeming it inevitable, but did not explicitly refute it. It may be that they saw little to gain in defending their behaviour, or indeed in ensuring that it conformed to high standards, when they felt that no matter what they do, they will be seen as shifty and perfidious.

The Register of Members' Interests

A large number of Muddlers (43 per cent) were dissatisfied with the operation of the Register of Members' Interests. But more so than the Puritans or the Servants, there were also a significant number of Muddlers (38 per cent) who were happy with the register. This was not necessarily because they were pleased with its operation, however. Like some Servants, these Muddlers did not want to see additional restrictions imposed on members: "The Register is all right as far as it goes and there is no need for it to go further. An elaborate Register of Interests would be unnecessary. It is misleading to the public and the press to whoop up the significance of the information disclosed." Others felt even the current register excessive:

I objected to the Register initially and refused to sign it. This caused great hue and cry. I view it as an invasion of privacy. It is an absurd device used to pander to public opinion.

It is not necessary to declare everything I receive. I don't really think there needs to be a Register of Members' Interests.

The Servants who offered similar views clearly based their opinion on trust in the honour of members and in the tradition of oral declaration. The Muddlers, in contrast, did not attempt to explain their position, but simply expressed a distaste for written inquiries into their private affairs.

Those Muddlers who claimed to be dissatisfied with the register indicated that they saw the register as a mechanism created to show the public that the House of Commons was concerned and doing something to address conflicts of interest. But as one Muddler put it: "The Register is nothing but a symbolic gesture. There is no inquiry, everyone is taken at their word." Another member spoke about the register's inadequacies: "I think the Register is a waste of time. All you have to do is declare defined interests. It is not an adequate measure. It does not measure relationships or fulfill anything. It is in fact, impertinent. The only possible benefit is that it reassures the public, but what it really is doing is providing a false sense of security." This cynical view of the register paralleled that of several Puritans. Only the Muddlers, however, added that they did not think the public was interested in the specifics and intricacies of the register: "The public does not read the Register of Members' Interests. People are not aware of who has a retainer and who doesn't." Members also added that the register does not generate much enthusiasm: "There is never a great rush to get copies of the Register the way there was to get copies of Andrew Roth's book on members' interests."[1] In the words of one Muddler: "After all, the Register is merely a guide, not the definitive book on members' interests."

The other suggestions offered by the Muddlers had to do with the basic structure of the register. A few seemed to think that much could be gained by revamping the general outline of the declaration forms. Their preference was for specific questions rather than a list of one's holdings under a number of categories. This they felt would help in ensuring that the same basic information would be provided by all members. Currently, they said, it was open to individual interpretation, and thus some MPs registered foreign trips while others did not. If specific questions were asked, such information would be clearly required to be disclosed.

The Muddlers seemed to view the register as an annoyance rather than a precautionary tool. Many objected to the public scrutiny of their private dealings that it embodied – not because they saw it as an assault on their reputations, but apparently because they felt it was none of the public's business. Others felt it was essentially ineffective for its stated purpose, and therefore not very useful. They also doubted whether the public was concerned enough about the issue to bother consulting the register.

Discipline and Sanctions

A majority of Muddlers (52 per cent) disagreed with the imposition of sanctions on members who fail to comply with the register. This was not quite as many as the Servants (67 per cent) but more than the Puritans (30 per cent) and the sample as a whole (44 per cent). A large number of Muddlers opposed to sanctions said they thought there were steps that should be taken before they could recommend the issuance of penalties. Such steps included making the register compulsory, and for some this meant the introduction of legislation. Others thought that registration should be made a condition of standing: "A law should be passed which indicates that individuals cannot stand unless they are prepared to sign the declaration."

Other Muddlers were opposed to sanctions on the grounds that there was only one individual who was violating the requirement to file a declaration. They were thus not willing to upset the *status quo.* They insisted that Enoch Powell was an honourable man and to punish him would have been an insult to him and the House as a whole. They felt that as long as it was Powell who defied the register, then it was not worth bothering about.

Only a few Muddlers opposed to sanctions based their reasons on underlying principles. Only one cited the principle of honour, a favourite of the Servants: "I am opposed to sanctions as I actually do believe that there should be personal freedom, that we should continue to rely on honour. Individuals are wary of their own activities. After awhile it becomes difficult to draw the line between public and private but that is a decision which should be left to each of us." A few others felt that Parliament-imposed sanctions usurped the prerogative of constituents to pass judgment on their MP's behaviour. Most other objections were of a more pragmatic nature: "Sanctions would be a complete waste of time. In this system you are always watching each other. MPs get away with things for awhile but eventually someone will expose them." These Muddlers felt that the system itself would punish those deserving of punishment. As one put it, "refusing to declare has its own impact."

Interestingly, the Muddlers, unlike the Servants, were reluctant to recommend severe punishment for non-compliance. They were satisfied with milder means of discipline such as reprimand, censure, the withholding of salary, and the imposition of a fine. In one member's words: "I would favour sanction if it were a referral to the Committee of Privileges or possible action by the Speaker – a rebuke." While a few were willing to recommend suspension, usually for only a few days, only two Muddlers even mentioned expulsion. In this instance, expulsion was thought to be appropriate only for the most serious infractions. As one indicated: "The ultimate penalty would be debarring someone from holding office."

The perceptions of the Muddler Whips with regard to disciplinary procedures were similar to those offered by the Servants and the Puritans. They too made use of the prefect analogy: "There is some truth in this analogy, although MPs are reluctant to admit it. As a Whip I am responsible for knowing what the MPs are up to and am responsible for speaking to those MPs I feel are misbehaving or participating in activities which are not in line with the standards the House is entitled to expect." Another Muddler Whip interpreted his role somewhat differently, portraying the Whip in a more managerial type of role: "As any manager of a team of people, discipline varies according to the person you are dealing with. If it is a young person with promotion prospects there would be a different approach. There are few sanctions at your disposal. I look after thirty-five MPs and some Ministers. I try to speak to them at least once a week whether there is a problem or not. I try to keep in constant touch, that way they will come to you if they have a problem, which they do." Another Whip summarized his role as follows: "As a Whip I am responsible for knowing what MPs are up to. I am responsible for speaking to those MPs I feel are misbehaving or participating in activities which are not in line with the standards the House is entitled to expect from its members."

According to the Muddler Whips, the key to being effective in matters of discipline was respect: "I don't think of myself as an example of standards. I think I can do a better job if the members respect me. The more they respect me, the more they will cooperate. You will not survive very long if you are not highly regarded as one of the boys." In order to earn this respect these Whips felt it important that the Whip's office be thought of as a place to seek advice, not as a judge and jury. A Whip put it this way: "MPs are independent people. You can advise and help them but in the end they have to make the decisions themselves." Advice was seen as particularly important for new MPs: "I always try to give advice. This is especially true for the new MPs. I give them general advice about what to do when in trouble, for example what to do if caught driving while intoxicated."

This is not to undermine the role of the Whip's office in disciplinary action. All the Whips indicated that in the instance of an act of impropriety they would be notified first. Then they would follow the expected chain of command, as alluded to by a number of the Whips interviewed. While no one respondent was too specific about this chain of command it undoubtedly leads to the Chief Government Whip and, ultimately, the prime minister. Their position at the beginning of the chain gave Whips significant influence: "If the Whip's office felt a particular individual did not reach the standards of behaviour expected of him, we would play an influential role. Especially with respect to promotion. Individual MPs have the ability to attain high office but not if they are out of favour with the Whip's office. The Whip's office discloses who are known rummies, what people are up to and what their standards of conduct are." More importantly, the Whips were fairly certain that the members themselves were aware of who was doing what. As one Whip indicated: "By and large people here know who the people are who step over the line. And they are penalized – slighted, avoided, ignored." Thus, in their opinion there were informal disciplinary procedures followed by members themselves to deal with colleagues perceived as behaving in an unacceptable manner.

Two-thirds of the Muddlers (66 per cent) admitted that they had known or suspected corruption in Parliament. A number of the Muddlers prefaced their comments about the prevalence of corruption by stating that the standards in Parliament had declined since they first entered the House. One put it this way: "I think corruption could be a growing trend on the edges. Things are not as clear cut as they used to be when I first entered the House. There has been a definite decline in standards. I think there are people taking advantage of their position." Another explained: "Compared to 40 years ago, the standards have been declining. There is a higher proportion of younger MPs on the make. Especially in the more crucial fields of defense and public works."

For the most part the Muddlers insisted that the corruption which occurred was of a minor nature and not cause for great concern. These infractions included such things as MPs who constantly accepted free hospitality, MPs who claimed allowances without necessarily giving detailed information of expenses, and the selling of small favours: "I have known of and suspected corruption in Parliament, but on a much smaller scale than I thought before I came to the House. MPs who work for lobbyists, take a fee for booking a dining room – this is only a minor offence." Others asserted that this sort of small-scale corruption did not affect anyone substantially and, as one Muddler indicated, "it has been dealt with in a moderately satisfactory way." These Muddlers insisted that corruption remained trivial because the "individual vote is very seldom decisive in the House of Commons." But one Muddler appreciated the need not to brush aside minor violations: "There is corruption in the grey areas and it is nothing large. But surely if you add up all the little or minor offences, it could conceivably lead to a greater scandal."

The Muddlers did not deny that corruption occurs in the House, but they apparently did not seem to think it much of a cause for concern. In this view, they resembled the Servants and opposed the Puritans. But while the Servants felt that the system would inevitably weed out cases of corruption, the Muddlers seemed to think that much of what went on was not worth worrying about – that it was easier to let the odd MP make a few extra occasional pounds than to mount an ethical offensive.

Lobbyists and Lobbying

Most Muddlers (62 per cent) favoured the introduction of a register of lobbyists. Whereas the Servants seemed to value such a register for the additional information it would supply, many Muddlers saw it as a means of controlling the access of lobbyists to the House of Commons: "I would approve of a register of lobbyists especially if special access is granted to that lobbyist – preferential access to Westminster in the form of a pass." The Muddlers were annoyed at how easily lobbyists were able to gain entry and obtain information, and felt they should be regulated. One pointed out that, despite what many lobbyists seemed to think, "Lobbyists have no rights here, unlike researchers." One Muddler in particular saw unregulated exposure to lobbyists as a danger to the autonomy of MPs: "The lobby system in Britain is wide open to corruption. Organizations lobby Parliament by holding dinners and parties for a number of MPs. What they are after is access to large numbers of members. Over a period of time MPs become conditioned to certain views that organizations put forward. I believe these dinners persuade MPs to vote the way they do. The lobby system needs to be severely curtailed." Interestingly, this Muddler was not willing to suggest, as did many Puritans, that the lobby system was in fact causing corruption, but remained worried about its potential for producing improprieties.

Other Muddlers were perturbed by the growing number of lobbyists penetrating Westminster, as well as the methods and techniques they employed: "Influence is not exercised through money. It is a moral, intellectual process. There is pressure from lobby organizations in the constituency. MPs are being intimidated. They are occasionally pressured too much. The growth of lobbying and the sophistication of techniques leads to the growth of intimidation. The lobbyists do not use money – they offer word processors, the use of cars ..." Another Muddler worried that lobbyists were attempting, and perhaps succeeding in the manipulation of members of parliament: "It is beginning to get like the American experience – I am concerned. I don't mind receiving letters, but it is the subterfuge methods of some PR firms I object to." Of the four types of MPs, only the Muddlers expressed concern over the methods used by lobbyists. This caution could be interpreted as stemming from the Muddlers' doubts about their own ability to withstand the pressures to which lobbyists subject them.

Many Muddlers also thought that a register would help them identify lobbyists and the interests they represent. These members admitted that they sometimes became confused in their dealings with lobbyists as to what interest was actually being represented, and what exactly they were being asked to do: "I have difficulty deciding what a lobbyist is and I can't see where they are leading me. Improper lobbying is taking place. People are being persuaded to do something improper on the basis of misleading information." Another offered this view: "The interests of a lobbyist are not always apparent. There are far too many asking for appointments and not always revealing who they represent. Also, most do not appreciate the virtue of brevity." One Muddler thought that some lobbyists were particularly successful at masking their actual intent: "I would support the introduction of a register of lobbyists ... I do not think most MPs are able to recognize a lobbyist when they are approached. I think they can recognize those from issue or charity groups, but it becomes much more difficult when it is a representative of a P.R. firm with a whole string of clients." Once again, only the Muddlers claimed to suffer from this insecurity and confusion. While the Puritans objected to many lobbyists' lack of candour, they nevertheless were not personally concerned, because for the most part they maintained an adversarial relationship with professional lobbyists. The Muddlers, in contrast, saw no overt problem in interacting with such individuals, but seemed to be bothered by the potential for being misled.

Only one Muddler expressed concern about MPs themselves acting as lobbyists from within the House of Commons: "The emergence of lobbyists is new in Britain. It has created new problems which must be dealt with. Paid political lobbying is spreading and the House must come to grips with it. For example, the standing committee on the aviation bill – the MPs serving on it are retained by aircraft manufacturers. This is a newly emerging problem." This problem was particularly distressing to the Puritans who objected to the possibility of members exploiting their elected position and influence by serving as "hired guns." This one Muddler was made uneasy by the process – he seemed to think it was problematic – but he did not appear to have come up with a solution to it.

Those Muddlers opposed to a register of lobbyists did not admit to sharing such concerns. They focused their comments on the positive aspects of the lobbying process and detailed the benefits MPs receive from their relationships with lobbyists:

I choose to decide whether to deal with a lobbyist or not. The lobbyist might help me to make contacts, or may be affiliated with an interest I personally feel strongly about. The relationship might just be a pleasurable one.

The influence of lobbyists here is grossly exaggerated. Occasionally I accept invitations, if it is a nice restaurant and if I would like to eat there. While the idea behind them is to change MP's minds, very few do.

I reject the common definition of lobbyist. They introduce you to clients and enable you to meet so and so. They are very well organized. The right group does not waste your time. They are not asking for anything. They explain their position which is usually well thought out. They provide advice and are not underhanded.

One Muddler insisted: "I know most of the PR people. I know the firms and the people who work for them. I like their hospitality." These Muddlers did not feel threatened or confused by the activities of lobbyists, and welcomed their efforts and presentations. But while the Servants' favourable attitude towards lobbying arose out of a conviction that it was a useful and necessary component of the representative process, the Muddlers appeared to be more impressed by the attention and entertainment shown them by lobbyists. The Muddlers were thus of two minds about lobbyists and lobbying: either vaguely worried about their own vulnerability to aggressive tactics, or pleasantly amused by ingratiating overtures. In neither case were the strong feelings displayed by the Puritans evoked.

ETHICAL STRATEGIES

Like the other types of MPs, the Muddlers offered a wide range of interpretations for the phrase "activity inconsistent with the standards the House is entitled to expect from its members." A few felt it was not a helpful source of guidance but rather an "elephant phrase, and individual examples actually do not define it." As one said: "This phrase is a catch-all, open to pretty broad interpretation. A violation of the phrase usually brings a rap across the knuckles." Another added: "This phrase covers a multitude of sins. Anything you would not want made public."

According to the Muddlers these sins included such violations as dishonesty, abuse of position, the acceptance of an inducement, unlawful sexual behaviour, disheveled appearance, and the fiddling of expenses. The only other defining characteristic the Muddlers agreed upon was that such activity was usually contrary to the public interest or the interests of the constituency. The following quotations are illustrative of the Muddlers perceptions of this phrase:

This phrase intimates a lack of candour. The reasons why one spoke or voted a particular way are concealed.

People not observing the conventions of the House. Abusing their position or the information they have obtained in that position.

This phrase implies that first MPs will behave as ordinary human beings and second, that they be truthful at least on the floor of the chamber or in committee or in activity that affects the House or its committees.

This phrase would cover where MPs begin to make representations or advocate facts or policies that they do not consider necessarily in the public interest, or interests of the constituency, but persist because of inducements offered to them.

This phrase covers a broad range of activities – dress, attitude, heckling, attention to the chair, to look like an MP. Some members are dressed like scruffs. It is an MP's duty to look reasonable, neat and tidy.

Thus, unlike the Servants, the Muddlers did not have any difficulty providing examples of activities that would fall within the purview of the phrase. One Muddler claimed: "MPs instinctively recognize this type of activity."

The majority of Muddlers (63 per cent) said they did not often encounter ethical dilemmas in the course of their work. But most of those who did thought that most of these dilemmas involved the clash between competing loyalties. As one member outlined: "I encounter dilemmas, but not really of the type in the questionnaire – not a conflict over a private, pecuniary interest. But there are grave ethical conflicts which are questions of conscience, such as the use of the frank. So much of politics is grey, not black-and-white. Another example would be the conflict between one's loyalty to party over your own personal opinion." One Muddler thought party discipline to be a source of dilemmas: "Ethical dilemmas occur when you have a political master with views different to your own political views. This causes certain problems." Another put the problem in another light: "Dilemmas occur when your own beliefs are contrary to the beliefs of your constituents. For example, what do you do on the issue of capital punishment when you are an abolitionist and your constituents are retentionists?" These comments raise traditional controversies in representational theory, such as whether legislators are expected to be trustees or delegates.

A few Muddlers offered more specific examples of dilemmas they had personally faced. One member related: "I was paid by a company to act as a liaison to offer information about how best to affect the process, but on questions of policy or on a piece of legislation I have voted contrary to the view of the company paying me. This gave me something to think about." One Muddler told of how he was offered a bribe to remove his private member's bill from the queue; another spoke about the dilemmas gifts caused him: "People out of the goodness of their heart give gifts. I refuse them anyway, but you have to explain if you accept them, things will grow."

If the Muddlers were particularly concerned about these dilemmas, they nevertheless did not think that a written code of conduct was a viable solution. Most (67 per cent) were opposed to such a code, and in fact thought one quite unnecessary. The Muddlers asserted that the current arrangements were satisfactory and emphasized the member's personal responsibility in resolving questions of ethics:

I think a written code of conduct unnecessary. It would be a lawyer's paradise. MPs are all big boys and girls and know about life. They should use their judgment just like ordinary citizens.

People look at situations in a different light. The answer to dilemmas come from inside, from the hearts.

Others felt a code would simply not make sense: "I doubt that a written code would be helpful. A special set of standards is not required. The same standards should apply here as throughout the rest of society. Common sense prevails."

These Muddlers thought that the ethical standards to be followed in the course of their parliamentary responsibilities should be no different from those expected of them in private life. They did not perceive a need for a separate or special set of standards. The rules and values that governed their lives before entry into the House should remain applicable and sufficient. One Muddler suggested that, when in doubt, "you can rely on the example set by colleagues whom you respect and the experiences they are prepared to share." Another viewed ethical education as an accretionary process: "MPs don't receive formal ethical training, we pick it up as we go along." This view of legislative ethics as at most a series of *ad hoc* additions to ordinary common sense sharply contrasted with the sense of a special public responsibility held by the Puritans and Servants.

The other main objections to a written code of conduct centred around the Muddlers' doubts that a code could be constructed to encompass all the ethical situations MPs face. One member suggested: "It would be impossible to cover all possibilities. It would be narrow in scope. In the end it would be a source of irritation rather than helpful." Another seemed to think "we wouldn't know how to frame it, or how to enforce it. There will be rebels who ignore all codes, written or not." One was concerned that a written code would limit the flexibility of the House: "We are reluctant in the U.K. to lay things down in tablets of stone. Parliament is living and changing all the time. Parliaments differ from one to another. We ought not to bind the next Parliament or create inflexibility." Another appealed to the traditional view of parliamentarians: "Honour is a state of mind – it can't be encapsulated within a code of conduct." Finally, one Muddler suggested that a code might exacerbate the problems it was intended to solve: "A written code could have funny effects. It suggests and encourages types of behaviour many MPs had not thought of."

Even those Muddlers who favoured a code thought it would be more helpful than actually necessary. Many thought a set of guidelines would be preferable, especially for new members who would appreciate some rough rules of thumb. The type of code they envisaged would be broad in scope so as not to lose the flexibility of the present system: "I would support the introduction of a code of conduct as long as it was very broad in its terms and that the spirit of the code was to be followed as well as its letter." Such a wider code would make expectations clear and would enable members to decide which activities were in obvious violation of the rules. According to one member, "if a written code existed then MPs would be aware that they were breaching certain standards."

This would be quite different from the current situation. The Muddlers indicated that as they saw it, if no specific rule existed to prohibit an activity, then it was permissible. The Muddlers were strong proponents of this point of view. While they objected to some of the activities described to them in their interviews, they would not call them corrupt or condemn them since there was no rule that indicated they were activities to be avoided. In the words of one Muddler: "Some of the activities I would view as unethical and I don't like them but I can't call them corrupt, as they are permitted by the rules. Anything goes as long as it is not strictly prohibited by the rules." Once again the Muddlers were willing to tolerate behaviour that made them uneasy, simply because they did not have a strong enough reason to reject it.

One Muddler indicated that this "negative logic" of assuming that what was not prohibited was acceptable ran throughout the procedures of Parliament: "If there exist no rules which expressly forbid certain kinds of activities then they are allowed. That's the way the House handles things. It takes a long time for them to come around and address questions at hand. This is very true for example, in the case of research assistants. The House as an institution has not come to a decision about the role of research assistants and the rules which should be implemented to govern their employ. The same holds true for ethical standards. Eventually we will come around to studying the issue, but it takes time." And in the opinion of the Muddlers, until such rules are implemented they will tolerate activities – even those they personally consider unethical – which are made legitimate by practice. As one Muddler put it: "If over time a certain activity becomes known as acceptable behaviour to the House, then it is acceptable." The Muddlers may have observed this tendency, but they did not follow it to a conclusion. If the Muddlers are right, however, then the House of Commons is vulnerable to a progressive decay in the standards of behaviour adhered to by its members.

CONCLUSION

To an observer of British legislative ethics, the Muddlers present a series of conundrums. They admitted that members were engaging in activities they found personally unethical, yet they continued to condone them because they were widespread. They feared the approaches and tactics of lobbyists, yet they continued to seek out opportunities to enjoy their hospitality and attention. They discussed numerous ethical dilemmas that were endemic to Parliament, yet they rejected the notion that parliamentarians should be held to specialized ethical standards. Indeed, their defining characteristic – their tolerance levels – depicted them as essentially "muddled." That they should tolerate a wide range of activities that might result in an MP enriching himself, while at the same time denouncing acts that benefit the constituency but provide no direct personal reward, seemed to indicate a particularly topsy-turvy set of ethical priorities.

Where the Puritans and the Servants indicated concern, the Muddlers were content, or at most vaguely troubled, with ethical developments in the legislative environment. Many balked at the suggestion that MPs be required to divulge more detailed information in the Register of Members' Interests. On the contrary, they felt that even as it currently operated, the register bordered on invasion of privacy. At the same time they belittled its effectiveness and worth as an investigative tool. They supported a register of lobbyists, but as a means of identification rather than regulation. Whereas the Servants viewed lobbying as an important component of representation, the Muddlers appreciated the efforts of lobbyists to provide them with information and other services primarily because these efforts made their jobs as legislators easier and more enjoyable. Again, while the Servants viewed outside employment as a tool for sharpening parliamentary debate, the Muddlers endorsed it as a way to top up their parliamentary salaries.

The Muddlers were satisfied with the ethical status quo in the House of Commons, not out of any strong conviction that things are as they ought to be, but rather out of recognition that things are as they are, and a lack of incentive for wishing them to be any other way. Their resistance to changes, such as an expanded register or a codification of rules, was based more on a desire to avoid the loss of opportunities now available than on belief in the ethical system's current strength. The Muddlers occasionally tacitly acknowledged that the system was not in perfect shape, but that they preferred it that way – it made up for the sacrifices they endured as MPs – and so, they perceived, did everyone else. The Muddlers were easily influenced by the actions of those around them. Currently, this means that they must occasionally suppress pangs of conscience about the activities they observe and engage in. It may be that they can be led in the direction of reform by a sufficiently numerous and strong-willed contingent.

CHAPTER SIX

The Entrepreneurs

The thirty-five Entrepreneurs formed the largest category in the sample. Respondents of this type displayed high tolerance for both constituency service and conflict-of-interest scenarios. In their eyes, almost anything goes, and they were in most instances willing to give MPs the benefit of the doubt. Some were even able to rationalize and justify the activity in the scenarios that the sample found overwhelmingly to be corrupt, such as DRIVEWAY; one asked rhetorically, "Is it ever done any other way?" Another added that the activity described was acceptable since the chairman was probably paying "less than retail" for the paving. Perhaps the most revealing comment was this one: "Relative to his status in society and the job he performs this is not corrupt. Certain perks come with elected office and this is just another one. The chairman is entitled to have his driveway paved."

This notion that public officials performed difficult and demanding tasks, and were therefore deserving of occasional "considerations," seemed to be a basic tenet of the Entrepreneur outlook. One Entrepreneur saw the TRAVEL scenario as a perfect example of this process: "This is not corrupt because we must accept an austere standard of living. Therefore, we take benefits in other ways." A colleague concurred: "I think people make great sacrifices to run for office in Britain. There is a lower standard of living, we don't have the best resources, and we tend to make up for it with small perks." The Entrepreneurs, more than any of the other types of MPs, were insistent that certain perquisites and advantages inhere to the position of member of parliament: "There are certain perks that are accorded to one's position or status in society. This is to be expected. Everyone has perks of some sort. MPs just have more than their share." The Entrepreneurs had obviously rejected the traditional view, espoused wholeheartedly by the Servants, and even by the Puritans, that being a member of parliament was in itself a reward that demanded a measure of personal sacrifice. The Entrepreneurs opted instead for tangible, bankable rewards.

The Entrepreneurs were more outspoken defenders of the ethical status quo than even the Servants. The Servants expressed confidence in the existing system of honour and trust in individual discretion – they thought it succeeded in curtailing impropriety. The Entrepreneurs, in contrast, did not express an opinion about the functionality of the system, but were merely appreciative of the latitude granted them as individual members. The Servants stressed the positive aspects of Parliament's ethical framework; the Entrepreneurs minimized the negative. Indeed, in most ethical determinations the Entrepreneurs seemed to take a materialist approach – as opposed to the ideological one followed by the Servants and Puritans – replacing adherence to ideal virtues with calculated cost-benefit analysis. In this sense, the Entrepreneurs apparently felt that the benefits and opportunities provided them by the largely informal ethical regulations of the House clearly outweighed the costs of occasional scandals.

Unlike the Servants, the Entrepreneurs did not attempt to rationalize their higher tolerance for the constituency service scenarios by invoking a sense of responsibility to their constituents. Instead, like the Puritans – the other group that scored constituency service and conflict-of-interest items relatively similarly – they seemed not to draw any conceptual distinction between the two types of activities. For the Puritans and Entrepreneurs, legislative ethics seemed to be an all-or-nothing proposition, without grey areas or gradations between different kinds of behaviour.

The Entrepreneurs overwhelmingly favoured the reductionist, legalistic interpretation of ethical rules previously put forth by many Muddlers. Most MPs in this sample, therefore, appeared to consider that activities not particularly restricted were, by default, acceptable. The Entrepreneurs were in fact the most ardent proponents of this view. By basing their ethical determinations on this criterion, the Entrepreneurs were largely able to avoid the ethical introspection that other types of MPs engaged in. A simple perusal of the existing regulations was all the Entrepreneurs needed to do to satisfy their ethical requirements. Thus the Entrepreneurs have chosen to rely on external standards of behaviour, shunning the use of internal standards which were essential to the judgments of the Servants and Puritans. If the Muddlers have lost their ethical compass, the Entrepreneurs have thrown theirs overboard.

ENTREPRENEUR PERCEPTIONS

Entrepreneur Definitions of Political Corruption

The Entrepreneurs' definitions of political corruption were similar to those offered by the Muddlers. Once again, money or a financial inducement of some kind was central. The abuse-of-office type of definition was most popular (54 per cent), followed by the inducement type (23 per cent). Only 6 per cent felt corruption was essentially a matter of betrayal. As did the Muddlers, the Entrepreneurs favoured the narrowest of these three types of definition.

But unlike any other group, a number of Entrepreneurs (12 per cent) advanced an even more restricted, purely legalistic definition: they asserted that the definition of corruption could be found in the criminal law. An act was only corrupt if it was illegal. For the Entrepreneurs using this definition, "corruption" was virtually synonymous with "bribery": "I operate from a strictly legal definition of corruption and thus would not be able to call a lot of these activities 'corrupt' because they are not 'sinister' or 'evil.'" Another offered: "Political corruption is surrounded by the taint of illegality – bribery – members being bought." Only one non-Entrepreneur MP offered such a strictly legal definition: a Servant and part-time solicitor.

Those definitions that did not specifically mention bribery referred to the acceptance of money by an elected official. Usually the definition was characterized by a *quid pro quo*. As one put it: "Political corruption involves the receipt of money in return for information and assistance." Along the same lines, one member thought corruption to be "obviously using government or parliamentary office or status to further illicit deals – insider dealing." A few Entrepreneurs characterized it as "feathering one's nest" or "lining one's pocket." Two Entrepreneurs thought the term defied definition. According to one: "I don't know what it means. Corruption is an emotional word. What is dishonest/honest?" The other MP felt that he would ask "anyone who uses it to define it. It means many different things to different people."

Like the Muddlers, the Entrepreneurs seemed to focus on the money involved in corrupt activities. These two types of MPs shared a similar preference for abuse over inducement definitions, implying that they have little difficulty imagining MPs as the instigators of unethical acts. Finally, the emergence of a purely legalistic definition from the Entrepreneurs – a definition even more narrow and anti-philosophical than the abuse definition – showed how completely some members were devoted to a minimalist view of ethical matters.

General Perceptual Profile

The Entrepreneurs agreed with the other groups, especially the Servants and Muddlers, that "political corruption is not a widespread problem" (see table 9). Eighty-five per cent of the Entrepreneurs supported this statement, 41 per cent strongly. Many echoed the common opinion that individual MPs were simply not in the position to commit seriously corrupt acts: "I just don't think the British system is open to much corruption. There is not much opportunity and the average backbencher cannot exert much influence. I don't even think a Minister exercises much influence." Some Entrepreneurs dismissed corruption as a problem by defining it away: "Corruption is not a problem here in the U.K. Scandal here is sex-related rather than financial." This MP tacitly implied that corruption was limited to scandal, and thus that only acts which unleash public uproar were deserving of the term "corrupt." Other Entrepreneurs emphasized that societal standards kept corruption in check: "This country since the Civil War has quite properly set high standards and expectations. But this has not stopped the public from denigrating us as frail politicians, which we doubtless all are." Unlike the Muddlers, the Entrepreneurs did not draw comparisons between the United Kingdom and the United States. Nor did they suggest institutional features, such as Question Time or the Opposition, to account for the absence of widespread political corruption. They simply denied its existence.

Seventy-six per cent of the Entrepreneurs agreed that there was a higher incidence of corruption at the local than the national level of government. This conviction was more or less shared across the typology – in all four categories from two-thirds to three-quarters of the MPs agreed with statement 18. One Entrepreneur displayed a typical attitude: "I do not think corruption is a problem especially in the Central Government. At the local level things are happening." Others said that this view was supported by the evidence available. One Entrepreneur, again equating scandal with corruption, said: "While I do not have personal evidence to prove this assertion, there is the public record. There simply have been more scandals at the local level." A few of the Entrepreneurs begged off on this question, explaining that while they expected this to be the case, since they had never been in local government it would be difficult for them to say with any certainty. Clearly, to these Entrepreneurs at least, instances of ethical impropriety were not of great concern.

Nearly all the Entrepreneurs (88 per cent) also disagreed with the notion that dishonesty was more widespread in politics than in business. Once again a large number of the respondents (53 per cent)

Table 9
Entrepreneur General Perceptual Profile

Statement	Text	Agree (%)	Disagree (%)	Mean	Std. Dev.	Median	Significance
15	Political corruption is not a widespread problem.	85 / *82*	15 / *15*	2.2 / *2.5*	1.6 / *1.6*	2 / *2*	**F**: *p < .05*
16	In so far as citizens distrust elected officials it is because they do not understand what politics is all about.	68 / *66*	26 / *28*	3.2 / *3.2*	1.8 / *1.9*	3 / *3*	
17	Dishonesty is more widespread in politics than in business.	6 / *4*	88 / *89*	6.0 / *6.0*	1.5 / *1.2*	7 / *6*	
18	Political corruption is more widespread at the local than at the national level of government.	76 / *73*	12 / *12*	2.6 / *2.7*	1.5 / *1.6*	2 / *2*	
19	No matter what we do, we can never eliminate political corruption.	82 / *80*	12 / *13*	2.3 / *2.5*	1.6 / *1.7*	2 / *2*	
20	The corruption that exists in the political world simply reflects the standards of the rest of society.	62 / *55*	26 / *31*	3.2 / *3.4*	2.1 / *1.9*	2 / *3*	
21	If it hadn't been for the Poulson scandal, we would hear a lot less about corruption in government.	18 / *29*	73 / *64*	5.1 / *4.8*	1.8 / *2.0*	5 / *5*	**F**: *p < .01*
22	MPs are sufficiently well informed to act as the sole guarantors of acceptable conduct in the house.	53 / *52*	38 / *40*	3.7 / *3.7*	2.3 / *2.2*	3 / *3*	**F**: *p < .05*
23	Once allegations of corruption are made, MPs in their parliamentary capacity should be brought within the ambit of criminal law	61 / *70*	36 / *23*	3.2 / *2.7*	2.3 / *2.1*	2 / *2*	**t**: p < .10 / **F**: *p < .01*
24	Britain's libel laws inhibit the uncovering and reporting of political corruption.	18 / *37*	74 / *53*	5.3 / *4.5*	2.0 / *2.2*	6 / *5*	**t**: p < .005 / **F**: *p < .001*

Key: Values in *italics* pertain to the entire sample of 100 MPs. "Agree" equals responses of 1, 2, or 3 (as a percentage of valid responses). "Disagree" equals responses of 5, 6, or 7 (as a percentage of valid responses). "Significance" equals significance levels for t-statistic (difference between Entrepreneur and non-Entrepreneur means) and F-ratio (analysis of variance across the four types of MPs).

strongly disagreed. This was another statement that all four categories of MPs emphatically agreed upon. MPs obviously felt that they were more trustworthy than businesspeople.

Unlike the Muddlers, the Entrepreneurs did not respond to the societal statements by criticizing the public's political awareness. The Entrepreneurs asserted repeatedly that all politicians had a unflattering public image and that this was undeserved, though they seemed not to be especially concerned about this negativity. Rather than faulting the public, however, they found this distrust somewhat understandable: "On the one hand there is some truth in this statement – the public distrusts us – but on the other hand they understand us all too well." On the whole they considered a poor public image an inevitable consequence of political life.

The Entrepreneurs did evince a certain feeling of ethical superiority over the public: "MPs are a reflection of society. In a crude way they reflect the society at large. But expectations and standards are higher in the political world. There is a strong code of public service." Others asserted that politicians lead the nation in ethical probity: "Politicians set the standards for the public to follow." Unlike the Muddlers, the Entrepreneurs acknowledged that politicians employed different ethical standards than average citizens. And while other types of MPs tended to retreat to the "rotten apple" notion in discussing this issue, the Entrepreneurs clearly expressed a perception of holding the ethical high ground in society. Because of their higher standards, the Entrepreneurs claimed that politicians must make great sacrifices, which others in society were not required or willing to make.

Still, the Entrepreneurs were quite pessimistic about whether corruption could ever be entirely eliminated. Eighty-two per cent of them did not think so. Unlike the Puritans and the Servants, only one or two Entrepreneurs added that while they doubted that corruption could be eradicated, it might in effect be controlled. One member said: "We will never eliminate it, as corruption is a sin and there will always be sin, but we can curtail it." Interestingly, only the Entrepreneurs and the Muddlers referred to corruption as "sin." The Servants, by far the most religious of the types, avoided using such terminology.

The Entrepreneurs agreed with the Muddlers that the Poulson affair had been overrated. While the Puritans and Servants were generally willing to accredit Poulson with raising the ethical consciousness of MPs and the British citizenry, the Muddlers and Entrepreneurs were not convinced of any crucial importance. A number of the Entrepreneurs insisted that they really couldn't remember the details of the incident, and some were not certain that corruption had been involved, especially in the case of Reginald Maudling. While they were willing to concede that the scandal might have caused attitudes towards corruption to coalesce, in the Entrepreneurs' opinion a similar scandal was inevitable; had Poulson acted differently or escaped detection, someone else would have drawn attention to the potential for impropriety. As one remarked, "other incidents have already happened to replace the memory of the Poulson allegations."

The Entrepreneurs were non-committal as to whether MPS are sufficiently well informed to act as the sole guarantors of acceptable conduct in the House. The Entrepreneurs and Muddlers formed a distinctive middle ground with respect to this statement, between the Puritans, who strongly doubted the wisdom of MPS policing themselves, and the Servants, who overwhelmingly supported the practice. Many Entrepreneurs insisted that they were not in fact solely responsible for ensuring ethical conduct; a number mentioned the importance of the Speaker in this regard, and others pointed out that MPS were accountable to public opinion and their constituents. In addition, they suggested that this self-regulation derived from the fact that no one else was in a position to regulate MPS. Only one Entrepreneur suggested the need for, or possibility of, an outside guarantor. The others were willing to rely on the traditions of the House and the system of parliamentary checks and balances.

Most Entrepreneurs (61 per cent) agreed that charges of corruption in the House should lead to criminal proceedings, but their support for such a measure was weaker than that of the Puritans and Servants. One Entrepreneur insisted that MPS were already within the ambit of criminal law. A few were willing to support the extension of criminal law to cover MPS, but added that they still thought Parliament the most appropriate and effective court for parliamentary transgressions. Only one pointed out that parliamentary privilege permitted MPS to circumvent and avoid criminal charges.

It was on the issue of Britain's libel laws that the Entrepreneurs finally took a polarized position. Seventy-four per cent disagreed (38 per cent strongly) that libel laws inhibited the uncovering and reporting of political corruption. This significant (p < .01) refusal to view libel legislation as an obstacle to ethical investigation placed the Entrepreneurs in conflict with the opinions of their peers. The Entrepreneurs in fact supported the current libel laws as essential to ensuring a responsible press. They claimed that the laws protected them from gossip, rumours, and unsubstantiated stories and allegations. The Entrepreneurs objection to this statement, however, seemed to consist only of tributes to the beneficial aspects of the legislation; they did not deny that the laws interfered with investigations. The Entrepreneurs once again appeared to have decided this ethical question on the basis of cost versus benefit.

Compared to the other types of MPs, the Entrepreneurs were not especially distinctive in most of their general perceptions. While they shared many sentiments with the Muddlers, the Muddlers were usually the more extreme of the two types. This lack of passionately held positions suggested that the Entrepreneurs were the least ideologically driven of the MPs. Rather than deriving their ethical opinions from basic convictions, the Entrepreneurs seemed to weigh the pros and cons, with an eye to maximizing the discretionary latitude granted to them as individual MPs. Additionally, in their elaborations, the Entrepreneurs displayed a distinct tendency to equate corruption with scandal. If this tendency was consistent, it could help account for their high tolerances for the hypothetical situations, as none involved public revelations of wrongdoing or negative repercussions. It also suggests that the Entrepreneurs may have been genuinely willing to tolerate a wide range of activities as long as they avoided attracting public attention.

WHO ARE THE ENTREPRENEURS?

Political Characteristics

Two-thirds (66 per cent) of the Entrepreneurs – more than in any of the other types – belonged to the Conservative party (figure 9). Twenty-nine per cent were Labour members. The association (p < .10) between Conservatives and Entrepreneurs can be partially accounted for by the proximity-to-power argument (see chapter 2). These Conservative Entrepreneurs were the ones who could occupy the positions of power from which the Labour Puritans were excluded. As government backbenchers, these MPs had the opportunity to be elevated to ministerial position and, as has been pointed out by a number of Whips, were the members companies and PR firms tried to secure on retainer, as they were seen to be in a better position to influence ministers and the direction of policy.

The ideology of the Labour Party is a contributing factor towards a more "puritanical" ethical outlook (see chapter 3). While more traditional Conservative ideology might seem to be most consonant with the attitudes expressed by the Servants (who especially propounded the idea of MPs as an enlightened, altruistic elite), the behaviour of the Conservative Party under the tutelage of Margaret Thatcher led some to identify in it new ideological principles. In rejecting the paternalism of government interventionism, and in its place emphasizing the societal value of unfettered self-interest, the Conservative Party espoused views similar to that of a typical Entrepreneur: that

Figure 9
Party Affiliation

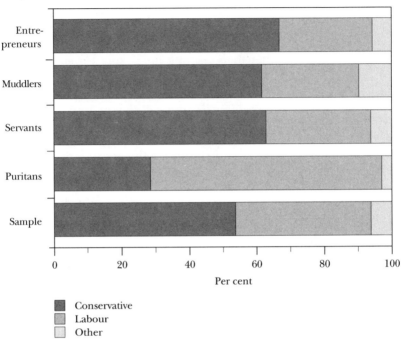

Per cent

Conservative
Labour
Other

which is not explicitly prohibited is acceptable, and creativity in interpreting the restrictions that do exist is not necessarily penalized.

The Conservative Entrepreneurs did indeed appear to be drawn
largely from the more fervently Thatcherite wing of their party: self-
described "drys" outnumbered "wets" by more than three to one (in
contrast, not one Conservative Servant described himself as "dry").
While the Entrepreneurs as a whole displayed only a minimal right-
ward lean in their responses to the question "Where do you think most
people would place you on the ideological spectrum?" (mean response
4.2), the Conservative Entrepreneurs averaged 4.8, a firmly right-of-
centre position offset by the Labour Entrepreneurs' mean response
of 2.7. The Entrepreneurs' self-perceived degree of ethical liberalism
identified another trend, this time within the Labour Party. The
Labour Entrepreneurs (mean response 5.0) identified themselves as
the most liberal MPS in their party (mean response for all forty Labour
MPS was 4.4).

As with the Muddlers, the Entrepreneurs tended to be more experienced in the House than the average MP in the sample. Parliamentary experience of the Entrepreneurs ranged from three to thirty-three

years. Twenty-six per cent of the Entrepreneurs were in their first term in the House, 23 per cent in their second term, and the remaining 51 per cent had nine or more years of parliamentary experience. Whereas the Puritan and Servant groups featured a relative abundance of freshman MPs, the Entrepreneurs and Muddlers were made up of somewhat more senior MPs. Relatively few Entrepreneurs (20 per cent) were former ministers or Whips, and only 17 per cent had previous local government experience. Thus 63 per cent of the Entrepreneurs – more than in any other type – had no experience with a formal code of conduct.

The Entrepreneurs' high tolerance levels for the conflict-of-interest situations might be partially explained by the significant ($p < .05$) number of them who currently engaged in outside employment (see figure 10). Eighty-six per cent of the Entrepreneurs had another occupation, more than in any of the other groups. As was the case with the Muddlers, these other jobs were primarily consultancies and directorships (63 per cent of those Entrepreneurs claiming an outside occupation held one of these types of positions, the highest ratio of all the types of MPs). Despite the fact that only five Entrepreneurs (14 per cent) did not claim another job in addition to their representative responsibilities, virtually all (89 per cent) of the Entrepreneurs considered themselves full-time MPs. Only four thought of themselves as part-time legislators.

The consensus among the Entrepreneurs was that outside employment was perfectly acceptable and, in the opinion of some, to be encouraged. Endorsing the same notion of functional representation that the Servants used to justify the practice, one Entrepreneur explained: "I am all for the representation of outside interests. This makes for informed debate." Another concurred: "MPs should be permitted to have outside interests and to speak on these interests, especially if they are so-called experts. This only makes Parliament a better place." The only qualification offered by some was that such employment be declared. As did the Muddlers, the Entrepreneurs asserted that "anything goes as long as it is declared" – public declaration was seen to legitimize any outside interests a member may be paid to represent.

The Entrepreneurs also echoed the Muddlers' contention that outside employment was necessary because of the poor salary and resources allocated to an MP. One said somewhat resentfully: "If you want to make a fortune, Westminster is not the place." Another provided more detail: "This is a very precarious way of life. I feel strongly that if the facilities were better and the resources for MPs increased, there would be less temptation and pressure. The workload

Figure 10
Outside Employment Types

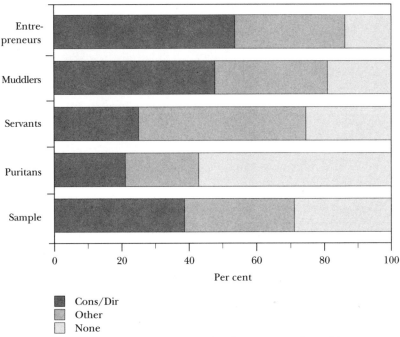

Key: "Cons/Dir" MPS engaged in parliamentary consultancies or corporate directorships.
      "Other" MPS engaged in other forms of outside employment.
      "None" MPS with no outside employment.

is very heavy and there are practices I do not care for which stem from the inadequacy of the support system for MPS." Another went even further: "The whole notion of corruption in Parliament is related to the poor pay and allowances MPS are forced to live with. We all could be making more in the private sector. £18,000 is all right for a bachelor to live on, but it is a bit dodgy when you add a wife and family." Whereas the Muddlers seemed most disturbed by the poor opinion the public have of MPS' trustworthiness, what most rankled the Entrepreneurs was the low pay and inadequate resources they were expected to put up with.

Finally, the Entrepreneurs insisted that the ease with which consultancies and directorships were obtained make them attractive to MPS. There did not seem to be a rigorous procedure involved in securing a retainer. Rather, as one Entrepreneur claimed, "It is very easy to get a consultancy; you don't have to be clever to get a retainer." A seat in Parliament would seem to be the only prerequisite of interest to employers. Of course, the attractiveness of the retainee increases if he happens to be a government member, a former minister or shadow cabinet member, a vocal booster of an interest pertinent to the company, or an MP who has a high public recognition factor.

The tendency, observed in the general perceptual profile, for the Muddlers to be more extreme than the Entrepreneurs seemed to be reversed when it came to actual political traits and activities. The Entrepreneurs were like the Muddlers, only more so – more Conservative, more involved in parliamentary consultancy, more upset by the inadequacy of their official salary and benefits, and more unacquainted with formal codes of conduct.

Spatial Characteristics

Entrepreneur constituencies were evenly distributed across the country, although a certain excess over the sample average was found in the Southeast region. Sixty per cent of the Entrepreneurs represented urban areas. Unlike the previous three types of MPs, however, the Entrepreneurs did not show any statistically significant distribution pattern with respect to constituency urbanization level. Aside from the general tendency towards urban constituencies, the Entrepreneurs were not concentrated in particular constituency classifications. Interestingly, while most of the urban Puritans had prior experience in local government, less than one-fourth of the urban Entrepreneurs (24 per cent) were former councillors.

Background Characteristics

As was the case with the other types of MPs, the majority (91 per cent) of the Entrepreneurs attended college or university, making them second only to the Servants in this regard. These two groups were also those with the highest concentrations of Oxbridge-educated MPs (34 per cent and 63 per cent for the Entrepreneurs and Servants, respectively, versus 18 per cent and 14 per cent for the Puritans and Muddlers).

Except for the finding that the two youngest Entrepreneurs were both members of a third party (and they were the only third-party Entrepreneurs), the type was not in any significant way different from the sample in terms of mean age (fifty-one years), mean age at first election (thirty-nine years), or age distribution. As this was the case with all the four categories, it can be concluded that these chronological variables neither add to the composite picture of each category nor help to explain the observed variance in ethical tolerances among the groups.

Most Entrepreneurs (57 per cent) claimed membership in an organized religion, with the greatest number (56 per cent of those specifying an organized religion) belonging to the Church of England. Three Entrepreneurs were agnostic and another two were atheist. For the most part the Entrepreneurs can be described as infrequent churchgoers. The greatest number said they attended church several times a year, normally at holidays. Only 17 per cent of those specifying an organized religion said they went every Sunday. Thus, as was the case with the Muddlers, most Entrepreneurs professed to an organized religion but were casual practitioners.

A former Lloyd's underwriter and currently parliamentary consultant to an insurance-industry group, the archetypal Entrepreneur is a vociferous supporter of the prime minister, although this has not yet been translated into a position in the ministry. He enjoys travel and has accompanied several parliamentary friendship groups on trips to the Middle East. He has seats on the boards of directors of several diversified holding companies. He is known for a tendency to complain about the high pressures and low rewards he endures in public service, although many of these pressures seem self-inflicted, as he is constantly involved in enterprising ventures of one kind or another in the public relations field. He occasionally considers leaving the House to resume his higher-paying career in the private sector, but has grown accustomed to the various perquisites available to him as a member of parliament.

REFLECTIONS

The Public's Image of MPS

Most Entrepreneurs (65 per cent) thought the public viewed MPS as basically untrustworthy. This was the same percentage as for the Puritans, making these two groups, in opposite camps on most other issues, equally pessimistic about the public's trust in MPS. As did the Muddlers, the Entrepreneurs indicated that this distrust was largely inherent in the position of MP and in the relationship MPS have with the public. One noted that MPS dealt in words and that "the MP's business is making promises. Often circumstances conspire to make them unfulfilled." A number of Entrepreneurs believed that, as a group, MPS were perceived to be untruthful, and thus could not be taken at their word: "The public view all MPS as bloody liars, they cannot believe them. I think they have a right to be cynical. Politicians tend to take voters for granted." The Entrepreneurs felt that the general tendency was for the public to say that MPs were all crooks and that "when they speak about politics they are not to be trusted."

The Entrepreneurs characterized the public's perceptions as flip and cynical. A number were quick to point out that the public tended to view the position of MP as a particularly low-caste pursuit: "As a group they rank us at the bottom of all professions. This is understandable and unavoidable. We have to live with it. People's eyebrows go up at the very mention of the word 'politician.'" Another added: "As a collectivity we are regarded as shifty, unreliable, self-centred womanizers, who rank lower than estate agents, journalists and car salesmen." Several also asserted that the public did not think them intelligent enough to become involved in corrupt activity: "The public view us as fools rather than knaves. Or more accurately, they view us as knavish fools."

Like the Muddlers, the Entrepreneurs did not blame any particular institution for the public's dim view of their virtue. To the Servants and Puritans, misrepresentation by the media – sensationalism and scandal-mongering – was a key factor in the public distrust of politicians, but the Entrepreneurs merely accepted that, no matter what they did or how they were described, the public will see MPs as a bunch of "knavish fools." The Entrepreneurs in particular seemed the least offended by this perception. They tended to acknowledge the public's distrust, but to ignore it as unimportant and inevitable – an occupational hazard – certainly not worth attempting to rectify. Moreover, there was a sense that they should not risk disillusioning the public by behaving with exemplary ethical restraint: if the public wished to see MPs as an untrustworthy bunch, then the Entrepreneurs at least felt no compunction to act otherwise.

The Register of Members' Interests

The Entrepreneurs were nearly evenly divided over the operation of the Register of Members' Interests. Forty per cent said they were entirely satisfied with the register, while 46 per cent indicated they were not. One Entrepreneur admitted he had never even looked at the register and could not offer an opinion. In general, those Entrepreneurs who indicated that they were satisfied with the register would support the maintenance of the status quo. They saw no need for further restrictions and were advocates of the "honourable members" argument: "Yes, I am satisfied with the Register. It is voluntary and open to public scrutiny. It is adequate as is. It is always suggested that there be more detail, but I think there is enough now. We must rely on members' goodwill, that they are filling in the declaration forms honestly." The Entrepreneurs seemed to view this very inefficiency of the register – that it still relied on an honest willingness to declare all information – as one of its better features: "I think it works very well. In no way are we forced to declare. We are all still presumed to be honourable members." Apparently, to these MPs the function of the register was not to assist in the identification of improprieties, but to reinforce the perception that MPs were above reproach. This closely paralleled the cynical suggestions of several Puritans that the register was a useless device enacted to lull the public into a false sense of security about the behaviour of their representatives.

Any effort to strengthen the register would be viewed by these Entrepreneurs as a further invasion of privacy and discouraging to prospective candidates. A member put it this way: "I do not want sums of money included. This is an undue invasion of privacy. If a financial or pecuniary interest is known this does not invalidate our role as MP." Another MP argued that "The Register is perfectly adequate, although I would be willing to go the distance with disclosed tax returns. But people come to Parliament with solid business credentials – professionals, academics – we can't be too purist or people will be discouraged from running." These Entrepreneurs were not supportive of additional information being included in the register or of the declaration principle being extended to include spouses and dependent children. In addition, these Entrepreneurs felt that the public was simply not interested in the register or its operation. A few insisted that "no one pays attention" to the publication of the register and, as one member said, "there is never a great hoo-hah over it."

Those Entrepreneurs who were dissatisfied asserted that MPs were able to manipulate the register to suit their own needs. These members were convinced that MPs were able to declare only what they wanted revealed – if a member did not want one of his activities to become public knowledge, he would just leave it out of his declaration. A Entrepreneur offered this analogy: "People approach the Register like they do a customs declaration form. They try and get away with saying that they have nothing to declare. They only tell what they want known." A colleague added: "If someone was up to something they wouldn't register it. What there is, is what they want people to know. It is not an absolute declaration, it is a P.R. device." Another pointedly doubted the register's effectiveness: "It does not flush out the odd crooked person and I'm willing to believe that there are one or two crooked people around here." These Entrepreneurs thought that it was all too easy to fool the Register. The implication was that those who depended on the Register to identify misconduct would be all the more quickly fooled by it.

The Entrepreneurs' attitudes towards the register were strangely skewed: those who were satisfied with it trivialized its motivation; those who were dissatisfied trivialized its operation. Neither subgroup appeared to endorse wholeheartedly its goal of identifying outside involvements that might compromise a member's legislative autonomy. Many felt that as a tool it produced little useful information and served only to invade MPs' privacy.

Discipline and Sanctions

Despite the Entrepreneurs' willingness to acknowledge the possibility for abuse of the register, they were not all convinced that members who fail to comply with it should be punished. Only 45 per cent were in favour of sanctions. Another 9 per cent insisted that members were already subject to sanction. They were the only MPs in the sample to espouse such a view. Unlike the other types of MPs, notably the Servants, the Entrepreneurs did not even question whether the prerogative to sanction belonged to Parliament or to a member's constituents. As one member said, "this is certainly a matter for the House." Not one of the Entrepreneurs suggested that electoral retribution was a more appropriate means of discipline.

Many of those Entrepreneurs who were opposed to sanctions adopted this position because it was only Enoch Powell who had not registered. A number insisted that if more members had defied the resolution, or if it had been anyone other than Powell, the House would have taken action: "It is only Enoch who does not comply and he's different. If there were more people, then the House would change the rules." Another Entrepreneur put it this way: "People should comply and only Enoch doesn't. He was born in the wrong century. He is a 16th Century man, whose vocation would have been to burn at the stake. No one will burn him at the stake here. He is totally uncorrupted." To the Entrepreneurs, a major drawback of consistent sanctions would have been the loss of Powell from the House. Given that Powell was defeated in the 1987 election it would seem that the problem has dissipated. But it is important to understand Powell's reasons for refusal and the Entrepreneur's reasons for supporting his refusal.

Like many of the MPs surveyed, the Entrepreneurs agreed with Powell that the register would first have to be made compulsory and a condition of standing, before any type of sanction for non-compliance could be imposed. But the Entrepreneurs were not necessarily in favour of this regularization. They felt that informal pressures were doing a effective job: "The embarrassment of exposure and the publicity which follows is sanction enough." Another added: "Members who fail to put things in the Register are censured – there is eyebrow raising and journalists get involved. You become a marked man from then on. It is no good not to declare." These Entrepreneurs felt that refusing to register only focused more attention on one's interests: "If a member does not sign then people will draw their own conclusions. If members do not sign they will be ferreted out. You can go too far with rules and regulations. Conventions and external pressure are enough."

Many Entrepreneurs also suggested that it would be impossible to impose sanctions for any violation other than blatantly failing to submit a declaration form, since there existed no established procedure for examining the forms' veracity and completeness. Without a means of investigation there would be no way to substantiate allegations: "At the present time members lean over backwards to be honourable members. We can't impose sanctions. We don't even know if violations have occurred – there is no investigation. Given the existing structures we can't do more." This was further complicated by the unwillingness of MPS to question the declaration form of a colleague: "When you have suspicions or even proof of scandal or misbehaviour, MPS are very reluctant to make accusations or name a member. This is the gravest accusation one can make. It is all very difficult." Even if they felt sanctions were desirable, these Entrepreneurs doubted whether they could be applied fairly and effectively.

Those Entrepreneurs who were in favour of sanctions were also not sure about how they could be operationalized. As one MP remarked: "I don't know what the sanction could be. To fling him out would be silly." Others suggested the same sort of informal sanctions that their colleagues argued already exist: "Well they should be dressed down in some way. Called before the Committee of Privileges, but the individual should be given due warning." Only two Entrepreneurs suggested the formal sanction of suspension, and none went so far as to recommend expulsion. Thus even those Entrepreneurs who said they supported sanctions tended to prefer collegial pressures to formal punishment.

Only one Entrepreneur discussed his experience in the Whip's office. His views on disciplinary procedures were somewhat different from those of the other Whips in the sample. In his perception, disciplinary action was not an important part of the Whip's job. It was his responsibility only by default – there was no one else to do it. In his words: "The Whip is the only means of discipline available to the party leader if a supporter misbehaves. And the only form of sanction available is to dismiss the chap from the party. The Chief Whip would do this under the authority of the Leader. As a Whip I would try to talk to a member before the rumours circulate, but talk is cheap." The Entrepreneur Whip, in contrast to the other Whips, did not attach much importance to his duties as disciplinarian and seemed to convey the feeling that they were a waste of time. He felt he had only one means of keeping errant members in line – expulsion from the party – and did not seem to believe that more subtle messages could be given to MPs by denying them advancement through the ranks.

Forty-four per cent of the Entrepreneurs said that they had definite knowledge of some kind of corrupt activity involving members of parliament. But 38 per cent insisted they had not even suspected corruption at the parliamentary level. Several stated they would know if there was corruption occurring: "No I've never seen corruption in Parliament and I've looked under every plate at all the luncheons I attend, and there has never been any money." Others based their opinion on personal experience: "No one has tried to bribe me." But many of these Entrepreneurs appeared to be having difficulty with the word "corruption" itself. As evidenced by their tolerances and their definitions, the Entrepreneurs were reluctant to apply such a label to behaviour that did not blatantly violate a rule: "I don't think there is much corruption at the parliamentary level in Great Britain, but there is a high incidence of unethical behaviour. Corruption is a very strong word. I think MPs are not really in a position to engage in corruption. They do not have any power or authority – this comes into play where the individual has the ability to exercise discretion." Another member summarized this point of view: "I think MPs are basically not corrupt; some are undesirable, but not corrupt. It is not really the word that bothers me, it's just that I would go pretty far in terms of determining what is ethical behaviour." Apparently, the activities known to this last Entrepreneur did not go far enough to earn the designation "corrupt."

Those Entrepreneurs who conceded that some corruption did occur in Parliament, asserted that it was almost entirely of a marginal nature. They used a number of words to characterize the examples of corruption they referred to, including minor, petty, cheating, and dishonesty. As one Entrepreneur said: "They are not the type of things that merit jail." For the most part the activities they described centred on an MP receiving a "favour" in return for services rendered. As to what these services were, the Entrepreneurs suggested a number of possibilities: the advancement of an interest in the House, attempts to influence a minister, and speaking in the House at the hire of a foreign embassy. One downplayed these activities: "MPs do use their status –

the title of MP – to get benefits. But members are not being paid off."
To this member at least, active exploitation of the opportunities available to holders of a seat in the House was acceptable; actual corruption only occurred when an MP was paid to do something grossly contrary to his duties.

Another Entrepreneur, while prepared to acknowledge that "there is more going on in the political arena than most are prepared to concede without proof," related MPs' behaviour to general trends in society as a whole: "There is more happening especially in the area of fiddling. There are persistent rumours of MPs misusing their car allowances: travelling in one car – say all the MPs from the North – but all of them putting in for travel claims. This is a reflection of what is happening in society. People are more dishonest than they used to be." Another concluded that "a lot of what occurs is petty corruption. This goes on all the time, everywhere, in all jobs and companies, it is a way of life. Everyone would not put 50p in a parking metre if they could get away with it." Others allowed that rotten apples will always manifest themselves: "No matter what you do, or where you are, there will be crooked people who abuse their position."

It would seem that the Entrepreneurs were not particularly upset by the improprieties going on around them. They saw Parliament as a microcosm of society, and any decline in standards within the House as a mere reflection of a broader societal trend towards acceptance of minor misdeeds. The traditional notion, so important to the Servants, of public officials as models of exemplary conduct held no sway with the Entrepreneurs. To some, it may have once been an important ethical tenet, but as one Entrepreneur described, forces within the House served to erode the ethical standards of its members: "Charges of corruption are always being made. The place becomes more and more comfortable as time goes on. It is like a piece of cotton – it absorbs you. There is a definite club-like atmosphere, you get to know other members, officers, staff and you are lulled into a state of tolerance." While the Puritans complained bitterly of the consequences of this overly collegial environment, the Entrepreneurs merely observed it as an inevitable state of affairs.

Lobbying and Lobbyists

Like most of their colleagues in the other three categories, the Entrepreneur MPs favoured the introduction of a register of lobbyists. While their support was not as high as that of the Puritans, the majority of them (70 per cent) would like to see some type of regulation imposed on the lobbyists who operate at Westminster. Once again it was the

Puritans and the Entrepreneurs who clustered together in their agreement. The Entrepreneurs' chief reason for supporting a register, however, was quite different from that of the Puritans. The Puritans were genuinely concerned about lobbyists as a potentially large-scale threat to the independence of MPs and the ethical values of Parliament. Many Entrepreneurs, in contrast, primarily wished to curb the physical abuse of space at Westminster by lobbyists: "I'm a little unhappy about the influx of lobbyists and the risk of abuse. Physically the place is not designed for lobbying. It squeezes out the MPs." Others mentioned that lobbyists tended to take up the dining rooms and thus made it difficult to take constituents to lunch in Westminster. These Entrepreneurs viewed lobbyists as more an inconvenience or annoyance than a threat.

One reason seemed to be that the Entrepreneurs did not think much of lobbyists and their abilities. They argued that the professionalization of lobbying had not reached the same level as in the United States. They depicted British lobbyists as crude amateurs: "I started off believing that a register would confer an aura of acceptability. But lobbyists here are not very good. I wouldn't pay £5 to have them represent me." Another referred to them as "appalling amateur companies." While they acknowledged that the number and expertise of lobbyists was increasing, for the moment they remained confident that a register would be useful but not essential.

Only two Entrepreneurs indicated that they felt uneasy about lobbyists and thus would support the introduction of a register as a positive measure. One member confessed: "I am uneasy about the lobbying situation. It is all rather dubious behaviour – lunches, cocktail parties, trips abroad, gifts, entertainment of various kinds." The other admitted, "I am constantly approached but I usually turn them down. There is just something about them which makes me feel uneasy." But for the most part, the Entrepreneurs were confident they were able to adeptly handle the lobbyists who approached them and they willingly accepted the hospitality, information, and briefings offered. As one Entrepreneur stated: "There are no moral qualms. The lobbyists are just putting their case."

Those Entrepreneurs opposed to a register of lobbyists were doubtful about how such a register would function. One member claimed that "such a register would be infinite as all my constituents are lobbyists." A few wondered how "lobbyist" would actually be defined. For the most part these members did not see anything to be gained by formalizing the relationship: "Once you start to give them privileges, then regulation is required." In the end, they felt that any decisions about lobbying and lobbyists should be left to the individual member's judgment. One Entrepreneur put it this way: "MPS know who the lobbyists are and how they operate. We would not feel the protection of a register. If an MP cannot identify a lobbyist then he shouldn't be here."

The impression conveyed by these Entrepreneurs was that they felt they had a grip on lobbying, that they were in control, and that they could not be induced or pressured by lobbyists' tactics. The Entrepreneurs insisted that, unlike the Muddlers, they were readily able to recognize lobbyists and that MPS were neither the targets of, or vulnerable to, intimidation or coercion: "Hospitality from lobbyists is not intended to corrupt your judgment in any way. It is thought to create a relaxed meeting place." Another member explained: "Lobbyists will write and ask your consideration on a bill. They tell you their clients are x and y. They offer to brief you on their point of view over a few drinks, lunch or dinner. But they are not buying you with a meal – everyone has to eat." One MP glibly responded: "PR companies are widely known among my colleagues. It is not very difficult – they are transparent, everyone knows what they do. The freebie circuit is well known. Jokes abound about free trips and meals."

Like the Muddlers, the Entrepreneurs were more concerned with the hospitality lobbyists offered them than with the reciprocal nature of lobbying. Not one Entrepreneur suggested that lobbyists were seeking more than an opportunity to present their views and to "bend the ear" of an MP. Unlike the other types, the Entrepreneurs seemed unfazed by lobbyists' attempts to gain access to the halls of Westminster – as long as such access did not interfere with an MP's needs for space – nor were they concerned about the willingness of MPS to accept retainers from lobbying firms. Better logistical management seemed to be the most important reason why they would support a register of lobbyists.

ETHICAL STRATEGIES

Like their colleagues, the Entrepreneurs did not really have many positive things to say about the guiding phrase "activity inconsistent with the standards the House is entitled to expect from it's members." As might be expected, they too regarded the phrase as a catch-all, intended to cover every imaginable type of indiscretion: "This phrase covers a multitude of things – behaviour procedurally within the precincts of the House, the common stages of a bill, social behaviour, habits – a lot of things. Once you enter public life you become public property. We have to watch our step all the time and be discreet about our weaknesses." Another added: "This is a catch phrase. It could mean an MP using his position in such a way as to reflect badly on the Parliamentary system, or the divulging of information of a highly confidential nature. The position of MP gives access. It is a matter of judgment as to what is proper and how long an activity continues."

The specific themes mentioned most often by the Entrepreneurs were those of dishonesty, lying, or concealment. In their opinion, these were the activities the phrase was intended to prohibit: "The phrase covers a great many sins, the chief one being dishonesty, whether it is legal or financial dishonesty." Another member agreed: "Carrying out acts which are fundamentally dishonest – not upholding honesty and integrity – most people know when they are not behaving in a manner expected of them." One Entrepreneur thought the phrase addressed openness in debate: "The phrase implies the concealment of an interest which would affect the reasonable utterances and conduct of an MP."

Other Entrepreneurs said the phrase would cover any activity that would be damaging to the reputation of Parliament: "The 11th Commandment here is to avoid doing something that you should not be engaging in – bringing Parliament into disrepute by your activities. If you are going to let your hair down, do it behind closed doors." Others interpreted the phrase as an injunction to avoid conduct "unbecoming to an officer and a gentleman," and to endeavour to act like "honourable gentlemen." Of the four groups of MPs, the Entrepreneurs were the members who provided the most consistent interpretations of the phrase.

The Entrepreneurs also identified ethical dilemmas MPs face which arise from their representative duties. As did other members, they complained of being pulled in different directions by different groups: "There are the conflicts between instinct, party, constituency – which do you follow? The best politicians never loose sleep over them though, they are all part of the job." Most Entrepreneurs pointed to the dilemma inherent in party discipline: "Frequently I am asked to vote in favour of legislation with which I have reservations. Occasionally I don't vote, but I can't do this all the time." Another member agreed: "I usually vote according to my conscience but frequently I vote for the party on a policy which is not strictly consonant with my views." The Entrepreneurs recognized that in the course of their parliamentary responsibilities they were asked to play a multiplicity of roles, and that some of the most difficult choices they had to make arose from situations in which they had to play two or more roles simultaneously.

Other situations the Entrepreneurs suggested cause dilemmas were gifts, patronage appointments, and the clash between religion and politics. These sources of dilemmas for MPs are illustrated by the words of the Entrepreneurs:

Gallup sends you their latest questionnaire along with a pen to fill it out. Do you put both into the bin?

There are small dilemmas such as whether to offer colleagues money to get an honour for a friend or constituent, and the receipt of gifts from ethnic groups.

If one believes you should act according to Christian teaching, but then find yourself wondering whether a particular decision is in line with the Christian teaching.

The Entrepreneurs did not, however, provide any actual personal accounts of specific dilemmas they had faced.

As did the Muddlers, the Entrepreneurs believed that these sorts of ethical decisions must be resolved by the individual member. Given this attitude, it was not surprising that an overwhelming number of Entrepreneurs (71 per cent) were opposed to the introduction of a code of conduct. This was the highest percentage of MPs disagreeing with a code. The Entrepreneurs believed a code unnecessary and felt that MPs in matters of ethics had to rely upon their own sense of judgment and common sense to distinguish between right and wrong. As this member put it: "It is all a matter of your own broad good sense. If a person is elected to Parliament void of basic integrity or unable to distinguish between right and wrong, then God help us!" Another Entrepreneur explained: "If you get here you have to make up your own mind. There are already too many codes. They are a halfway house between doing nothing and legislation – who enforces it? And the quality of people enforcing it. In the end, good people will abide by it and bad people will not." The Entrepreneurs suggested that prior to election to Parliament, MPs would somehow have come to know the proper ethical course to follow in the situations which arise. They would have to draw on their values and personal standards which should already be firmly established: "If you don't have an inherent sense of propriety and probity then we are all in trouble."

The Entrepreneurs objected very strongly to the idea of an external authority imposing a set of standards or rules on them. In the words of one member: "I don't need someone else telling me how to behave." Another clearly felt MPs had to be trusted to do the right thing: "I take great exception to anyone writing guidelines. I'm not here as a delegate. I was sent here to use my judgment. To rely on my interpretation of things on a day-to-day basis. I would be terribly upset if anyone imposed preconceived guidelines." The Entrepreneurs argued that a written code would be superfluous as well, since MPS were already guided by an informal network of norms and conventions. And as they suggested, "an unwritten code is the right way." One Entrepreneur explained: "Codes don't solve anything. There are already too many rules in existence. Britain is a rule-oriented society. We have conventions and they are much stronger than rules could ever be." Another emphasized the cultural importance of unwritten conventions: "It is just typically British to have no formal, written rules in Parliament." In addition to this unwritten, understood set of standards, the Entrepreneurs suggested that members could rely on one another for examples of appropriate behaviour and that rules could not change people's ethical motivations: "A code is not necessary. You can rely on your colleagues as well as your own personal standards. An honest man equals an honest MP. A crooked man equals a crooked MP. No rules of conduct will make him honest."

Like the Muddlers, the Entrepreneurs also objected to the implication, which they felt was inherent in a code of conduct, that elected officials should be held to standards different from that of society as a whole. The Entrepreneurs contended that they should be expected to follow the same rules as everyone else, and that additional or unique rules were not welcome: "There is no need for a separate set of behavioural standards – one's moral principles should guide one's conduct. This place is no different than other institutions." Another observed: "There are a lot of written codes generally applicable in all walks of life. It does not help to define particular ethical rules or codes." One Entrepreneur clearly objected: "We don't require our constituents to abide by a written ethics code." Despite their recognition of the various dilemmas involved in representation, the Entrepreneurs apparently wished to project the view that Parliament was simply a gathering of people who happened to be MPs, and that it did not pose any particular ethical problems to, nor make any particular ethical demands on its members. They would consider a written code an affront to their honour and personal ethics.

Those few Entrepreneurs who favoured a written code felt that rules could be helpful, especially with respect to gifts. They pointed to the effectiveness of the ministerial code of conduct, the ethical guidelines observed in local government, and the Bar Association's code. As one member admitted: "I've been in local government and we had Standing Orders which were far more extensive than what we have here. Such a code would be useful for the new members of the House, especially those with no prior government experience." Another claimed a code would be helpful because "disparate standards are being employed. Whose standards are supreme?" This is one question which Parliament has yet to resolve, with or without a code of conduct.

The Entrepreneurs' objections to a code resembled those of the Servants, and tended to invoke the idea that members of parliament should be trusted to use their discretion wisely and properly to resolve the ethical situations they confront. But the Entrepreneurs were also the MPs who otherwise seemed, in their ethical decisions, to fall back on the minimalist idea that whatever was not restricted was acceptable. In other words, when asked to determine the propriety of an act, the Entrepreneurs in fact tended to ignore principles of discretion and norms of aspiration, and instead simply compared the act with existing rules.

In general, the Entrepreneurs felt that the House of Commons adopted a fairly relaxed, informal approach to ethics and standards. A Entrepreneur described it as follows: "There is a great sense of honour which surrounds the place. Jeffrey Archer broke the club rules. The club is very tolerant until you get caught. The House is fairly relaxed about standards. We rely on one's own perception of what is right. Fairly loose parliamentary standards exist. There are sanctions of an informal and formal kind which can be employed if the rules are broken. The ultimate sanction is expulsion. There is large room for manoeuvre. If you move outside the broad parametres the roof falls in." Another Entrepreneur reiterated that "MPs are basically an honest group who rely on, and have a great respect for, the traditions of the House, the Speaker and the Mace." In the end the Entrepreneurs conceded that there may be some people given to overstepping the boundaries, but they do not perceive themselves to be doing anything wrong. Unless steps are taken to establish that the activities they are engaging in are manifestly unethical, the Entrepreneurs will continue to tolerate whatever is not explicitly disallowed, and thus encourage the progressive enlargement of the boundaries of acceptable behaviour.

CONCLUSION

If the Servants exemplified the "old guard" in the House of Commons, at least with respect to ethical attitudes, the Entrepreneurs represented a new breed of MP. Unfettered by old-fashioned, patrician considerations, but still willing to call upon the rhetoric of honour, the Entrepreneurs reduced questions of behaviour and conduct to measures of cost, benefit, and compliance with explicit regulations. Situations that led the Puritans and the Servants to deep ethical introspection, and the Muddlers to at least self-doubt, were easily digested by the Entrepreneurs' economic analysis. For these professionalized politicians, their seat in the House was like a seat on the stock exchange – a business asset convertible into contacts, contracts, opportunities, and additional remuneration.

Like the Muddlers, the Entrepreneurs displayed few overt qualms about Parliament's potential for ethical imbroglios. They too doubted the effectiveness of the Register of Members' Interests and added a cynical assertion that it could be easily circumvented and manipulated by unscrupulous individuals. They felt that the balance between the public's right to know and an MP's right to privacy was already weighted dangerously against them, and that any further elaboration of the register would be an unjustifiable slight on their character. The Entrepreneurs felt that lobbying needed to be controlled just as pests need to be controlled – to keep them from getting in the way. They disparaged the skills and professionalism of most lobbyists and dismissed the Muddlers' fears that MPs were vulnerable to manipulation at their hands.

As the largest group of MPs, the Entrepreneurs were the ethical trend-setters that the Muddlers mimic. Unlike those following their lead, the Entrepreneurs' minds were made up – they were not swayed by doubts as to the validity of their course. And it was quite obvious to them that any significant reform was not in their interest. If they were to support changes in the ethical framework of Parliament, it would be because all other avenues had been blockaded. The Puritans could be motivated, the Servants convinced, and the Muddlers won over to the reformist cause. But they will have to contend with the Entrepreneurs, who can be counted on to defend their perquisites and their reductionist ethics with vigour.

CHAPTER SEVEN

The Dynamics of Reform

The views of the Puritans, Servants, Muddlers, and Entrepreneurs have been discussed with respect to political corruption, legislative ethics, and the establishment of rules to prescribe the parametres of public and private morality. The issue that remains to be discussed is that of reform. Based on the MPs' perceptions and attitudes, how viable are ethical reform efforts in the British House of Commons? From which groups will the initiatives for reform come and what kind of reform proposals are the MPs willing to support?

Not all legislatures manage ethical improprieties in the same manner. In the last twenty-five years, legislatures in Western democracies have moved away from sole reliance on norms, conventions, and folkways towards a more formal network of codes, legislation, and regulation in managing impropriety. The United States, Germany, Canada, and Australia have all introduced legislation, codes, or guidelines to aid legislators in their ethical decision-making. The British House of Commons, however, remains reluctant to outline explicit behavioural expectations and boundaries, and continues to resist the institutionalization of ethics and the trend towards ethical micromanagement. Westminster increasingly risks becoming an isolated curiosity as far as ethical matters are concerned.

One reason that may account for the British insistence on clinging to their traditional method of managing ethical problems is that the incidence of scandal has not been of the same scope and magnitude as it has elsewhere, most notably in the United States. Scandal creates a demand for reform that can seldom be completely assuaged by polite reassurances. Scandal affects the speed of change and encourages experimentation with regulatory mechanisms. The relatively low historical incidence of scandal in Britain does not, however, imply that the House of Commons has somehow managed to solve problems of legislative ethics that still elude other legislatures. Additionally, in the last decade, Britain has faced an increasing number of allegations of impropriety involving parliamentarians and other political figures (see chapter 1). Thus, the pretence that unwritten codes are effective or that the prime minister can manage all the problems that arise by exacting political retribution is losing credibility.

At the same time, the changing character of representation in Britain and the continuing evolution of the parliamentary career hold out the prospect that legislative ethics will become an increasingly important problem. Anthony King suggests that there are a growing number of MPs who view themselves as committed "career" politicians.[1] Given the demands of their parliamentary responsibilities and their heightened constituency expectations, it is becoming less feasible to combine a parliamentary career with an outside profession, such as law or medicine.[2] But this does not mean that MPs are giving up outside employment altogether. While they may be forsaking active legal and medical practices, they are accepting remunerated appointments to corporate boards of directors and acting as paid parliamentary consultants and salaried advisers to various interest groups. The rapid growth of these alternative forms of employment is placing additional stress on the British system.[3]

A LETHARGIC HOUSE OF COMMONS?

Britain has traditionally relied on legislative norms and conventions to define ethical conduct. As the MPs have indicated, their behaviour is constrained only by a vague, almost entirely unwritten code, consisting of accumulated resolutions, recommendations, and rulings. But these pertinent determinations are not contained in any one source and thus the parametres of ethical conduct in the legislature remain hazy and blurred.

The guidance they can glean from this unwritten code is narrow in scope and conforms to what Bruce Jennings terms "minimalist ethics."[4] Concern is focused almost exclusively on the identification of financial conflicts of interest. The House does not question the propriety of the outside interests held by its members, only the means and timing in which they are declared and made public. Accordingly, although ministers have been subject to certain restrictions, no backbench or opposition frontbench MP has been required to divest himself of interests that might conceivably prejudice his public duties.

While provisions exist for the declaration of conflicts, no mechanisms exist for their resolution or avoidance – such matters must be dealt with by individual MPs according to their own judgment.

In this system, where important ethical decisions are left to the discretion of the individual MP, personal attitudes and perceptions are especially crucial. The British Parliament, by providing its members with only the bare outlines of ethical expectations, gives to each MP much of the responsibility for determining what is and what is not acceptable behaviour, and trusts that common principles of honour and integrity will lead each member to form essentially similar judgments. The results of this study suggest, however, that this trust is largely belied. Not only was there a significant lack of consensus among MPs as to what constitutes ethically acceptable conduct, but MPs were, in general, inconsistent in applying their own standards to situations involving ethically questionable behaviour.

This lack of consensus extended to MPs' attitudes towards the need for reform and the shape reform should take. Many MPs supported the abstract idea of reform and could identify particular abuses that disturbed them, but few could be expected to muster the will to support actual reform measures that would do more than tinker with the existing system. Many others admitted that the system was more vulnerable than it should be, but were unwilling to accept the restrictions on their activities that measures designed to strengthen the system would necessarily impose.

Nevertheless, the system guarantees that only MPs can change the rules to which they are themselves subject. From time to time, various proposals for reform have been put forward, by MPs as well as outside observers, but for nearly two decades after the introduction of the Register of Members' Interests in 1975 the ethical world of Westminster evolved only slightly. Finally, in 1992, in response to the first direct challenge to the operation of the register, the Select Committee on Members' Interests published the results of a review of the registration system. In the course of their assessment, the committee heard testimony from members, professional parliamentary consultants, and academics. What it did not have at its disposal was systematic information on the attitudes of MPs towards some of the key issues of legislative ethics.

THE DIRECTION OF REFORM

In the course of the interviews, the MPs identified five basic areas of prospective ethical reform: the requirements and operation of the Register of Members' Interests; the employment of MPs outside the

House; parliamentary salaries, allowances, and support staff; lobbying and lobbyists; and various cosmetic or "House-keeping" measures. Each of these areas will be discussed in the context of the typology and it will be shown which MPs can be relied upon to work together to support various reform proposals. MPs of different types will occasionally back the same initiatives, but they will do so for different reasons, as each type will be operating from its own agenda. The key to a successful reform effort may well be a structure that allows a proposal to draw support from more than one type of MP.

The Register of Members' Interests

As has been discussed, the register is the one formal mechanism employed by the House in the management of ethical conduct. It would seem that there was enough support among the Puritans and the Servants, and even from a number of the Muddlers and the Entrepreneurs, for efforts to make registration more truly compulsory. The MPs supporting this reform generally proposed incorporating the register into statute. This would also appease those MPs, primarily Servants, who echoed Enoch Powell's contention that the requirement to register should be made a precondition of standing for office before it could be effective or enforced. These MPs argued that candidates should be made aware that they will, if elected, be asked to declare their assets and holdings. In addition, it was also felt that enshrinement in legislation would change the general perception of the register from a voluntary nicety to a legal imperative, and thus heighten awareness of the conflicts the register is designed to help resolve.

As to the specifics of the register, it was the Puritans and the Servants who favoured additional restrictions. The Puritans believed declaration alone to be insufficient. They wanted to restructure and tighten up the register as well as the registration process and requirements. Most Puritans supported a requirement for members to disclose value amounts of outside earned income, assets, shares, and any remuneration received from directorships. Perhaps additional support for such a measure could be secured if the American example was followed. In the United States the value amounts need not be precise but must fall within a specified range. Thus, for example, a Congressman can claim that his outside income was between $2500 and $3000. Such a measure would at a minimum provide a clearer estimation of the scope of a member's interest.

In addition, the Puritans favoured the inclusion of names of clients on the declaration form. Currently, members are required only to list the name of the company they are employed by and must list specific clients only if the member has a direct personal interest. Thus MPs who act as parliamentary consultants need only reveal a corporate name, and it remains uncertain what kind of interests they are advancing. If the actual clients represented by the MP were disclosed, the Puritans felt that a clearer indication of the member's outside interests would be ascertained.

The Servants supported these restrictions and added the suggestion that MPs be required to include in their registrations the interests of their spouses and dependent children. Many Servants also thought a greater effort should be made to keep the register up to date and some even suggested publishing it more often than once a year. Finally, both the Puritans and the Servants supported the establishment of a procedure for investigation and verification of members' registrations. They wished to ensure that all MPs followed the same standards in filling out their forms so that they were a consistently accurate and complete reflection of the outside interests of their fellow members. In the absence of specific complaints, the registrar only checks that each MP has complied with the requirement to register and that each form is properly filled out.

While the Muddlers were opposed to any further restrictions being introduced, such as the disclosure of value amounts and clients, a number of them would be receptive to a change in the format of the register. They felt that not much information was gained by asking members to declare their holdings and interests under categories. Instead, these Muddlers would prefer that specific questions be asked, such as: "How much income did you earn last year from outside employment?" They felt this format would reduce the number of generalizations that the forms contain and would ensure that all members were answering the same questions.

The only group of MPs that did not support any type of reform of the existing register was the Entrepreneurs. While a few of them would have liked to see the register compulsory, they did not favour the disclosure of additional information and they did not feel that verification of declarations was desirable. The Entrepreneurs felt that members must be taken at their word that the information disclosed was truthful and complete. To insinuate otherwise they saw as a direct threat to the honour of MPs and to the trust that imbues legislative life.

The Puritans and the Servants were the MPs who displayed the lowest tolerances for conflict of interest. It is thus not surprising that they wished to see the register – Parliament's primary means of regulating conflict of interest – expanded and fortified. Their concern over the loopholes that exist in the current system reflected their distaste for the activities depicted in the conflict-of-interest scenarios. At the same time, the Puritans and Servants were significantly less involved with the outside interests the register seeks to identify than their Muddler and Entrepreneur colleagues. They had less sympathy with such activity, as well as less to lose by any restrictions that might be introduced. The other two groups displayed considerably less enthusiasm for reform of the register. The Muddlers' contention that the register should be clarified, although not necessarily overhauled or strengthened, could reflect the ethical confusion with which they have been identified. The Muddlers might benefit from, if not actually appreciate, the additional guidance provided by a clarified or more explicit register.

Outside Employment

The nature of the British parliamentary career has traditionally permitted MPs to secure employment outside Parliament even after they are elected. This tradition of the MP as public-spirited amateur is reinforced by a level of salary and support services that makes additional sources of income highly attractive, or even, as some would argue, essential. That many MPs maintain their previous positions, at least in part, after election has always been the case. More recently, however, members have been taking advantage of new opportunities that are available to them primarily, if not solely, because of their parliamentary position.

None of the MPs surveyed thought members who also practice as barristers or doctors presented a problem. What did raise objections were those MPs who accept retainers from consultancy firms and act as salaried parliamentary advisers to outsiders. This distinction between types of outside employment is important because it is obvious that an MP who maintains a medical practice has an interest in legislation affecting health care, regardless of whether this interest is explicitly declared. The declaration of a parliamentary consultancy, however, provides little insight into the actual interests that may affect an MP's judgments. A parliamentary consultancy also allows an MP to be involved with a greater number of more varied interests, and thus presents a greater risk of conflict, than does an active professional practice.

The 1987 Register of Members' Interests revealed that 183 MPs held corporate directorships and that 100 of these members held more than one such position. The Rt.-Hon. Geoffrey Rippon sat on the greatest number of boards of directors (forty-seven, on thirty-three of which he was the chairman). Both Sir Peter Emery and Thomas Arnold served as directors for ten companies, and a number of members held as many as five directorships. One hundred and seventy-one members reported serving as parliamentary consultants and advisers, with sixty-two being employed by more than one company. Michael Grylls registered ten different consultancies. The 1992–3 register shows a slight reduction in directorships (141 MPs, with 70 holding more than one), but an increase in consultancies (181 MPs, with 91 multiple consultancies). The most worrisome trend, especially according to the Puritans, was represented by MPs like Patrick Cormack and Dudley Smith who have established their own parliamentary consultancy firms. There was concern that permitting MPs to operate their own companies, based on the information, experience, and access they were able to secure because of their position, was an open invitation to compromise of legislative independence.

Fred Silvester, a former MP who went to work for the public relations firm Advocacy Partnership Ltd, submitted a written memorandum to the Select Committee on Members' Interests to accompany his testimony during the committee's inquiry into lobbying. In this memorandum he provided figures on the number of MPs who register outside employment:

Only 15 per cent of MPs who are not members of the Government make a return which is nil or nearly nil (such as overseas visits or occasional articles). Nineteen per cent register sponsorship by a Trades Union only. Two-thirds register some other job and approximately half of these (one third of the House) register some kind of Parliamentary consultancy.[5]

In his oral testimony, Silvester also spoke at some length on the assets MPs have which make them desirable to consultancy firms, companies or corporations:

There are privileges which exist for MPs which will always be attractive to outsiders whatever the limitations. His letters are answered. He can insist on meetings. If he is persistent he can make waves which may be better avoided by compromise. It is illuminating to try and obtain the simplest information from a Government as a member of the public or a company ... Until attitudes change within Government, the pressure to "go through a member" will continue.[6]

The rise and increase of these new types of outside employment represent a threat that the British parliamentary system is not equipped to defend itself against. While the possibility of MPs pursuing careers outside the House has always been a feature of the system, it has always been assumed that, by allowing members to keep one foot in the outside world, a higher level of practical expertise and knowledge would be brought to parliamentary debate, and thus Parliament itself would benefit from such employment. MPs who set up parliamentary consultancies, and even those who merely allow themselves to be used as consultants, however, are not contributing practical experience to parliamentary proceedings, but instead are exploiting their position in Parliament for their own benefit.

The strongest supporters for a movement to curtail MPs' outside employment as consultants and directors were the Puritans, many of whom would welcome a blanket ban on this practice. They contended that members simply could not effectively execute their representative responsibilities if they were on the boards of directors of several companies and acting as paid parliamentary consultants to public relations firms. The Puritans disliked the apparent ease with which MPs were able to trade on their name. They claimed that vast sums of money were involved and that it had become increasingly difficult to determine whether a member was speaking in the Chamber out of conviction or because he was being paid to advance a particular position or point of view. This attitude was not surprising, given that the Puritans were significantly less involved with outside interests than their colleagues. Not only were they less likely to be employed outside Parliament, but those who did have an outside occupation were less likely to be involved in the more problematic areas of parliamentary consultancy or corporate directorship.

The Servants were not easily distinguished from the Muddlers and Entrepreneurs with respect to the fraction employed outside the House, but they were far more "puritanical" with respect to the nature of employment they accepted. While the Servants' traditional outlook accommodated the practice of MPs representing outside interests – in fact they recognized this as part and parcel of a member's representative responsibilities – they would appreciate restrictions on the type of services MPs provide. The Servants felt that the acceptance of retainers was not in itself wrong, but that there needed to be limits on what services could be expected in return. The Servants felt that a retainer should purchase no more than the informed counsel of a parliamentarian, and experienced advice on how interested parties might best affect the legislative process. Actual assistance to outsiders in affecting that process was considered beyond the parametres of legitimate parliamentary conduct.

Both the Muddlers and the Entrepreneurs cannot be relied upon to support any reforms in the area of outside employment. The majority of MPs in both of these groups currently held outside occupations – many of them as consultants or directors – and they defended this additional employment as a necessity in order to make ends meet. Unlike the Servants and Puritans, they were not concerned about the type of employment MPs couple with parliamentary careers. Perhaps if members' salaries were adjusted and support provisions enhanced, these MPs might discard their outside endeavours. But for the time being, since retainers were profitable and easy to come by, the Muddlers and Entrepreneurs were reluctant to alter the status quo.

An outright ban on outside employment and involvements is not feasible, even with the support of many Puritans, without a major restructuring of the British system. One milder but potentially more palatable reform possibility that would address the concerns of the Puritans and Servants is the adoption of an outside income ceiling, as is imposed on members of the US Congress. Such a limitation might help to establish some boundaries for MPs in the area of outside employment. The imposition of a ceiling would also assist in making public the value of retainers and thus the magnitude of a member's financial relationship with outside groups, corporations, and firms. Finally, such action would focus reformist attention on the issue of parliamentary salaries, and on exactly who is paying the full amount of an MP's compensation, just as occurred in the US House of Representatives, where lowering the outside income ceiling to nil (eventually) became the political precondition of a Congressional pay raise.[7]

One reform possibility that has been suggested to address concerns over the growing influence of outsiders on parliamentary debate is the adoption of recusal provisions. In the British House of Commons, members are permitted to continue in active debate and to vote on matters in which they have a direct personal pecuniary interest as long as the interest has been declared. Allowing and encouraging recusal, as in the US Congress, would help prevent the appearance of conflict in such cases – MPs may presume that their colleagues' honour will prevent them from exploiting such a conflict, but the electorate may remain unconvinced. On the other hand, since party discipline ensures that actual "vote-buying" in the House is impractical and prohibitively expensive, voting on a conflicted interest, while questionable in appearance, does not present as severe a problem in Britain as it does in the United States.

The Servants and especially the Puritans were more concerned with the possibility of members using their far less restrained powers in debate to obtain information for outsiders by submitting written or oral questions for the order paper. This "information-buying," and the related "access-buying," are where the opportunities lie for outside interests to exploit parliamentary contacts. More significant reforms that would help curtail these activities would be the indication on the order paper of those questions in which a member has a direct personal interest, or even the barring of such questions. Better regulation of the granting of research passes would also find support from Servants and Puritans, who complained of MPs who provide these passes – intended only for staff – to their clients or representatives of interest groups.

The nature of the parliamentary career has undergone significant change in the recent past, as the traditionally amateur avocation of MP has become increasingly professionalized and as the "occasional MP" is replaced by the career politician.[8] The development of professional lobbying – lobbyists for hire rather than citizens, activist groups, or industry spokesmen petitioning Parliament on behalf of their own interests – indicates that the House is no longer merely a gathering of gentlemen, but has become a resource that can support an entire industry designed to exploit it. These changes may contain an inherent reform, in that as members increasingly come to perceive their parliamentary position as a profession rather than a part-time hobby, tolerance of additional outside work may decline.

On the other hand, Bruce Cain has suggested that the volume of constituency casework – always a large part of an MP's job – and the expectations of constituents for personal attention from their MP have increased significantly in recent years.[9] This could explain why so many MPs find parliamentary consultancy an attractive option. Unlike professional practices, or other occupations unrelated to their position, consultancies can easily be combined with parliamentary duties, without subtracting from the time an MP has available to spend on his constituents.

Salaries, Allowances, and Staff

Significant reform of outside employment will inevitably come up against the issue of members' salaries and facilities. Of the types in the sample, only the Servants did not rationalize the pursuit of ethically questionable outside interests by the low salary and poor support provisions available to MPs.[10] The Entrepreneurs and Muddlers were understandably more insistent on this point – many tended to point out how much more money they could be making in the private sector – but even some Puritans recognized that, while they themselves did not subscribe to this argument, they understood how it motivated others to seek additional remuneration. The previously identified trend of the Servants to possess more traditional attitudes towards their office was supported here, as they were the least likely to characterize salaries and allowances as "inadequate" rather than simply "low," and did not feel the need to justify the time-honoured practice of MPS holding other positions.

Several Muddlers and Entrepreneurs envied the salary and facilities of members of other legislatures, notably the US Congress. It has been argued that comparing the salary and service of British and American legislators is inherently difficult and potentially misleading, because of the constitutional differences between the countries and the divergence in how allowances and facilities are structured and allocated.[11] Still, comparative studies of parliamentary systems have revealed that British MPS are paid less than legislators in Australia, Canada, Germany, France, Italy, and New Zealand. In addition, only Italian and New Zealand legislators have access to support that is judged inferior to that available in the British House.[12] Canadian MPS are eligible for a fully indexed pension, which they may begin to draw upon leaving the House at any age, after only six years in Parliament; British MPS can receive their pension before the age of sixty-five only in case of disability, and the amount tops out at two-thirds of salary only after thirty-three years of parliamentary service.

A comprehensive study of MPS' views and opinions on staffing and resources was conducted by the All Party Reform Group in 1984. Austin Mitchell, MP, reported several of the main findings of the survey and revealed that most British MPS operated with the assistance of, or at least access to, a secretary in Westminster.[13] On the other hand, not all MPS had their own office, and many that did were housed outside Westminster's gates. In their constituencies, only 38 per cent of the MPS polled had a secretary and only 24 per cent had their own private office – most tended instead to operate out of the local party headquarters. No parliamentary provisions existed to cover expenditures incurred in the operation of a constituency office: MPS had to defray costs such as postage, telephone, stationery, rent, and office equipment out of their own pocket[14] and with whatever assistance the constituency party association was able to provide. Only 30 per cent of the respondents had a word processor. Examination of the Register of Members' Interests reveals that many members now accept from outside sources office space and equipment – sometimes on loan – research assistance, and even the use of a car. While a British MP's office is certainly not the high tech, plush, spacious offices occupied by many in the private sector and in other legislatures, these outside contributions have made working conditions more pleasant.

MPS are provided with an office costs allowance, to be allocated at their discretion.[15] The number of staff to be hired is not specified, nor are guidelines provided, and according to Mitchell's findings the majority of members preferred it this way. The bulk of this money was used to secure secretarial help. Only 7 per cent of the MPs employed a full-time research assistant (47 per cent secured part-time research help).[16] Most MPs – some of the senior ones by choice, and the newer ones by circumstance – did their own research. A number accepted the free assistance offered by American students participating in internship programs, but there were several concerns about such assistants, primarily as to their familiarity with the British parliamentary system. The British House might capitalize on the principle of free assistance to MPs by establishing a parliamentary internship program similar to that operating in the Canadian House of Commons. British university students or recent graduates could be given the opportunity to assist members in their Westminster or constituency offices in return for a stipend or academic credit. While there would be spatial considerations, the students could conceivably conduct research for members on a number of topical issues from their university libraries.

In addition to their salaries and staff allowances, MPs can call upon a number of other official sources for financial assistance. Travel reimbursements are available for the use of personal automobiles, as well as warrants to cover rail, air, or sea travel within the triangle of home, constituency, and Westminster. A limited number of special travel warrants are made available to members for use by spouses and dependent children. The other major allowance available to MPs is the London supplement, intended to help cover additional expenses incurred in the maintenance of two residences.[17] There are also pension provisions, winding-up allowances, and resettlement grants that are paid to defeated MPs under the age of sixty-five.

Yet many MPs still feel forced to supplement their direct income, and they find that interest groups are only too willing to help provide computer equipment, office space, and research assistance. An MP may be denied an office in Westminster, but as a corporate director he may be given one far better appointed in a nearby area. And any MP may find the offer of a research assistant – paid for not out of his strained staff allowance, but by a sympathetic interest or lobby group – too tempting to refuse. Some MPs eventually discover that their ability to secure passes to Westminster for such researchers – passes that confer uninhibited access to the Vote Office, telephones, the catering services, and of course other MPs – is valuable in itself to outside organizations. Some MPs surveyed suspected that there were MPs engaged in effectively selling research passes, and thus access to the corridors of the House, to outsiders.[18]

Such questionable activity is difficult to gauge. Technically, only researchers who are paid out of an MP's staff allowance are eligible for a pass. A separate register of interests of secretaries and researchers is maintained by the Registrar of Members' Interests, but it is a private document, made available only to MPs. As of February 1988, however, there were 330 secretaries and research assistants registered as in possession of a House of Commons pass and having additional outside occupations to which that pass was relevant.[19] It has been suggested that this register be made public – thereby helping to open up the lobbying system and making it easier to identify the firms that have an employee working on the inside – but the House has thus far resisted making such a change.

Reforms could be implemented to relieve some of the pressures on MPs and to diminish the temptation to accept assistance from outside sources that might ultimately be a threat to their legislative independence. Members accept the information and briefing papers given to them by special interest groups and lobby firms because they do not have the time or the staff to gather the relevant facts themselves. An increase in salary and allowances is one reform that all types of MPs could be counted on to support. One Muddler even hinted that, were he to receive a significant increase in pay, he would support the extension of ministerial restrictions on outside employment to all MPs. A pay increase has often been touted as a cure-all for various parliamentary ills, but it remains to be seen whether low pay is at the root of the problems or is only an excuse or rationalization for them.

House-keeping Reforms

Changes to the register, salary, or outside employment would involve major restructuring of Parliament's ethical framework. A number of other, smaller-scale reform proposals, related to but separate from these larger issues, were also suggested by the MPs in the study. These "House-keeping" reforms have to do with the legitimacy of gifts from constituents and interested parties, foreign travel by MPs, and the manipulation or "fiddling" of allowances and reimbursements.

Each group of MPs had members within it who would welcome the introduction of some kind of value ceiling on the acceptance of gifts, with the Servants and Muddlers perhaps the most fervent proponents. Such a rule would aid MPs in determining what can be accepted and what should be returned. A public rule would also be helpful to grateful constituents, intent on presenting their MP with some sort of token of appreciation. A number of members from all four groups mentioned the rule prohibiting ministers from accepting a gift in excess of £50. Such a rule of thumb, if extended to MPs, would not only disallow a not-so-subtle form of bribery, but also offer MPs a way of refusing – on the grounds that they exceed the proscribed limits – extravagant gifts that might be presented with strings attached, without offending the donor. Such a rule would further protect the independent judgment of individual MPs.

Both the Servants and the Puritans favoured additional regulations on foreign travel by individual MPs. While they were satisfied with the current method in which travel was undertaken by parliamentary committees, delegations, and even friendship groups, they were worried about the increasing frequency with which individual members were invited to visit foreign countries. While the majority of members enjoyed these junkets and viewed them as just another perk that came with the job, a few were suspicious of the motivations of a foreign government in issuing invitations to British backbenchers. While members were expected to register foreign trips, it was clear that some Puritans and Servants thought there were trips that remained off the record. These MPs recommended prohibiting individual members from travelling to foreign countries except as part of a parliamentary group.

A final area of potential for reform is discretionary expenditure. The Muddlers supported some type of measure intended to limit "fiddling" and the abuse of MPs' allowances. According to these MPs, the easiest areas in which to fiddle allowances were travel expenses, primarily those allocated to cover travel between one's constituency and Westminster, and the reimbursement of food and living expenses. The most common abuse reported was to claim the allowance limit whether it was fully used or used for its intended purposes. According to one Muddler: "There are members who pay their wives the entire £20,000 salary allowance; there are members whose wives are put down as secretaries – they collect the salaries but do not do the work; [they] fiddle their allowances, abuse mileage and living provisions. Everything is claimed to the limit." Most MPs, however, did not advocate major changes in this area. The common belief seemed to be that any additional compensation that might occasionally result from a less than perfectly accurate expense statement was not considered worth recovering, given the low salary and poor facilities provided to MPs. Many MPs felt that the demands of their position and the hardships they endured entitled them to "supplement" their meagre incomes in this manner. Once again the Muddlers stood out by their tendency to harp upon details and technicalities of ethical misbehaviour and their fuzziness as to actual solutions.

These types of reforms would require less effort to implement than, for example, significantly restricting outside employment of MPs, and they could be expected to generate less resistance from those who feel they are unnecessary or who oppose them. On the other hand, they cannot be expected to generate dedicated support and excitement, as they are at most a way of tinkering and tuning the existing system. Cracking down on fiddling would help keep wayward MPS in line, but it does not address the larger issue of defining the ethical standards that Parliament can expect of its members.

Lobbyists and Lobbying

In recent years, pressure groups, interest groups, and voluntary associations have increasingly tended to hire professional public relations firms to engage in lobbying as an intermediary on their behalf, rather than attempting to influence the legislative process directly. These professional firms act as a liaison between group and government. They are able to attract clients because they profess to have expertise in the area of government relations – qualified staff, strategic planning, and, in some instances, access to ministers, civil servants, and MPS. The involvement of these firms in the lobbying process has created problems for parliamentarians.

According to a number of the MPS interviewed for this book, the growing number of professional lobbyists in Westminster was becoming disturbing. Most felt that the frequency with which they were approached by lobbyists – usually by mail or phone, with an invitation to lunch or dinner – had increased in recent years. MPS mostly welcomed such opportunities to be in contact with interested parties, especially given their own limited time and research resources. At the same time, while they insisted that they could not be bought for the price of a meal, they feared that the interest groups, and more importantly the public, might think they were somehow compromising their independence by accepting such free lunches.

Many MPS, especially the Muddlers, admitted they were not always able to recognize lobbyists as such, nor were they always certain of the interest an individual lobbyist was representing, even when they knew which public relations or consultancy firm employed the lobbyist. According to the Rt.-Hon. Stan Orme, former chairman of the Parliamentary Labour Party, these professional firms have adopted tactics that some MPS found objectionable: "I think members have found that where another firm would not press us if you resisted an invitation to go to some organization or some presentation, you might find that the pressure increases with these rather professional organizations and it gets, at times, very close to what I call even a form of corruption."[20] For the moment, most MPS felt that they were still in control of the situation, but there was concern for further proliferation and professionalization of the lobbying industry.

The Study of Parliament Group has conducted research into the means by which organizations outside government seek to influence public policy through Parliament.[21] Nearly 75 per cent of the organizations admitted to extensive contact with Parliament, and 59 per cent claimed regular or frequent communication with MPs. Almost half the organizations ranked backbench MPs as the most important source of parliamentary influence, and 57 per cent said they kept in touch with what was happening in Parliament through personal contact with backbench MPs. More than half the organizations revealed they were represented in Parliament by one or more MPs.[22] In return, many organizations offered to MPs factual information they did not have the time or staff to collect for themselves. A representative from one organization explained: "We provide information, case histories, parliamentary questions, parts of speeches and full briefs."

The organizations were also asked whether they knew of any abuses of the lobby system. The biggest complaint came from those – mostly smaller, single-issue groups – who felt unable to compete for parliamentary attention with professional lobby groups and public relations firms owing to their relative lack of resources and contacts. One spokesperson cautioned: "There is cause for concern ... in the level of resources which professional P.R. firms and commercial organizations are able to deploy, which gives them preferential access to Parliament and government, relative to the private citizen." This same concern for access was evident with respect to the employment of MPs as parliamentary consultants: "Paid consultant MPs are a general abuse of the system, favouring the rich and casting a potential doubt on vested interests." Many organizations also contended that the system of passes designated for MPs' research assistants was being abused by MPs who provided these passes to lobbyists, perhaps for a fee, and by organizations who provided and paid for researchers to serve particular MPs.[23]

All types of MPs, especially the Puritans and Entrepreneurs, could be expected to support some sort of official identification of lobbyists. Over two-thirds of the MPs surveyed in this study favoured the registration of lobbyists, along the lines of the Register of Members' Interests. But just as the existing register facilitates, at least in theory, the identification of conflict-of-interest cases, without providing a means of resolving them, so the registration of lobbyists was seen primarily as a way of identifying lobbyists, but not as a means of controlling or managing their activities. Support for actual restrictions on lobbying beyond registration was harder to find among MPs, and was largely limited to the Puritans.

Interestingly, support for the registration of lobbyists was almost as high among Entrepreneurs as among Puritans, but the Entrepreneurs'

support was primarily motivated by concern for the lobbyists' impinge-
ment upon the space and facilities of Westminster, rather than out of
any suspicion of ethical impropriety. Many Entrepreneurs objected to
the tendency for lobbyists to take up space in the dining rooms, thus
making it difficult for MPs to bring constituents for lunch at Westminster. The Entrepreneurs rejected the suggestion that lobbying subjects
them to ethical risks and claimed that lobbyists were in general too
obvious and incompetent to be able to influence MPs effectively. While
the Entrepreneurs felt that formalization of the relationship between
MPs and lobbyists would have some benefit, they were also confident
that MPs were capable and should be left to control that relationship
by themselves.

For the Muddlers, however, the problem of identifying lobbyists was
a primary reason for supporting registration. The Muddlers were
especially worried about lobbyists exploiting their preferential access
to Westminster and felt this access needed to be restricted, not
because lobbyists were taking up valuable space, but because they were
genuinely worried about MPs being influenced by them: "What they
are after is access to large numbers of members. Over a period of
time MPs become conditioned to certain views that organizations put
forward."

Whereas the Entrepreneurs viewed lobbyists as a pesky annoyance,
the Muddlers saw them as a threat and worried that their methods
were insidious. Of all the types of MPs, it was the Muddlers who were
most worried about the techniques used by lobbyists. As with the
problem of "fiddling" allowances, the Muddlers were very aware of the
means, but not so sure about the ends. Many of them admitted to
exploiting the hospitality of lobbyists, despite their concerns. It could
be that the Muddlers' fears arose out of a sense of their own vulnerability – reflected in their high tolerance for conflict of interest – to
this process of "intimidation."

The Servants echoed the confidence of the Entrepreneurs in the
ability of MPs to manage the pressures applied to them by lobbyists.
The Servants felt that registration of lobbyists made sense as an obvious extension of the declaration principle, and would welcome it as a
source of additional information for MPs, especially new MPs who, they
believed, were not as adept at recognizing lobbyists. The Servants
accepted lobbying as a useful process that could be improved by
making it more orderly and more open. At the same time, the Servants
were wary of providing, via a separate register, a perceived parliamentary stamp of approval to lobbyists which might then be exploited to
procure clients. Once again, the Servants' faith in the power of informal traditions, and their reluctance to suspect MPs of ethical turpitude

or even weakness, seemed to guide them in their perspective towards reform.

The Puritans were, predictably, the MPs most perturbed by the activities of the lobbyists among them. They reiterated many of the concerns raised by the Muddlers, but added a clear belief that lobbying was causing serious problems. In addition, the Puritans were concerned that the growing number of MPs on retainer as parliamentary consultants were beginning to act as a lobby from within – a "fifth column" promoting outside interests to other MPs inside Westminster. The Puritans feared that this phenomenon of MP-lobbyists only added to the difficulty members faced in trying to identify who was representing whom and for what purpose. The Puritans, already none too sure about the motivations and forthrightness of their colleagues, saw this process as yet another threat to the autonomy and independence of Parliament, and felt that registration would be only a first step.

THE PROCESS OF REFORM

The interviews with the MPs took place during a period of relative quiescence in ethics regulation in the House of Commons. Not much had happened since the introduction of the register in 1975, in the wake of the Poulson affair. Over the next several years scandals continued to occur, and, as the interviews revealed, MPs were accumulating a lengthy, if unexpressed, "wish list" of ethics reforms. The Select Committee was kept busy with various inquiries, but little came of their efforts until 1992. Once again the reform effort was prompted by the flare-up of scandal – the case of Conservative MP John Browne.

In March 1990 the House suspended Browne without pay for twenty sitting days for failing to disclose fully his business interests and involvements.[24] Essentially, he was caught out with an incomplete registration form. The Browne case represents the first serious inquiry into the affairs of an MP that the select committee has undertaken. Given the absence of a precedent, the committee was unsure how far their power extended in such a matter and thus did not recommend whether disciplinary action should be taken against Browne. The decision of the House to suspend Browne was reached without clear division along party lines – in fact, the penalty was proposed by Sir Geoffrey Howe. Perhaps the departure of Enoch Powell allowed the House to begin enforcing its own rules without offending respected members. As for Browne, he continued to fight the decision and protest his grievances against the committee and Howe. In the 1992 election he stood as an Independent Conservative, having been deselected by the party, and lost his seat.

After the flurry of attention generated by the Browne case, the House requested that the select committee re-examine the issues of registration, declaration, outside interest, and enforcement procedures. The select committee's response, contained in a series of reports to the House beginning in March 1992, was to recommend a number of reforms and attempt to clarify the principles it felt were central to the ethical milieu of the House. Essentially, the committee reaffirmed the two distinct requirements of registration and declaration as the cornerstones of ethical probity. Rejecting the arguments of some MPs, notably Tony Benn, who called for more stringent requirements, the committee clearly limited a member's ethical duty to the identification of potential sources of bias – on paper in the register, and orally, before participating in any debate or vote affecting a financial interest. Unlike members of many other legislatures, such as the US Congress, who must either divest themselves of sources of conflict of interest or recuse themselves from the affected legislative business, British MPs remain free to mix their private and public responsibilities as long as the House is fully informed of the potential for collision.

The actual changes recommended by the committee primarily pertained to the format and organization of the register. In a move that the Muddlers would certainly approve of, each category of the registration form now begins with a question. For example, under the first category of Directorships, the questions is: "Do you have any remunerated directorships in any public or private company?" MPs are then instructed to circle "Yes" or "No," and to provide the appropriate details in the adjacent column. The actual number of registration categories remains the same (nine, excluding a *pro forma* Miscellaneous category), but two ("Remunerated employments or offices" and "Remunerated trades, professions and vocations") were amalgamated, and the "Financial sponsorship" category was divided to separate regular sponsorship from occasional gifts, hospitality, and domestically derived benefits (the new form is reproduced in table 10).

In addition, the notion of sponsorship was extended to include any regular and reoccurring payments or benefits – not only cash, but also paid research or secretarial assistance and accommodation – totalling £500 or more per year. The committee took at least a step towards satisfying the Puritans' wishes by insisting that MPs list, with respect to their parliamentary consultancies, the specific clients they provide service to, and not merely the consultancy firm with which they are associated. And the scope of registration was extended for member's spouses and dependent children to cover not only shareholdings but

Table 10
Revised Members' Interests Registration Form

The main purpose of the Register of Member's Interests is to provide information of any pecuniary interest or other material benefit which a Member receives which might reasonably be thought by others to influence his or her actions, speeches, or votes in Parliament, or actions taken in his or her capacity as a member of parliament.

Registrable Interest	*Details*

DIRECTORSHIPS

1 Do you have any remunerated directorships in any public or private company? YES/NO
If so, please list opposite (briefly stating the nature of the business of the company in each case).
Notes: (i) You should include directorships which are individually unremunerated but where remuneration is paid through another company in the same group.
  (ii) In this category and category 2 below, "remunerated" should be read as including taxable expenses, allowances, or benefits.

REMUNERATED EMPLOYMENT, OFFICE, PROFESSION, ETC.

2 Do you have any employment, office, trade, profession, or vocation (apart from membership of the House or ministerial office) for which you are remunerated or in which you have any pecuniary interest? YES/NO
If so, please list opposite. When a firm is named, please briefly indicate the nature of the firm's business.
Note: Membership of Lloyd's should be registered under this category. If you register membership of Lloyd's, you should also list your syndicate numbers for the current year and your membership of any syndicates which remain unclosed.

CLIENTS

3 Does any of the paid employment registered in categories 1 or 2 above entail the provision to clients of services which depend essentially upon or arise out of your position as a member of parliament (see note (i) below)? YES/NO
If so, please list opposite all clients to whom you personally provide such services. Please also state in each case the nature of the client's business.
Notes: (i) The services covered by this category include action connected with any parliamentary proceeding, sponsoring meetings, or functions in the parliamentary buildings, making representations to ministers, fellow members, or public servants, accompanying delegations to ministers, and the provision of advice on parliamentary or public affairs.

Table 10
(continued)

Registrable Interest	Details

(ii) Where you receive remuneration from a company or partnership engaged in consultancy business which itself has clients, you should list any of those clients to whom you personally provide such services or advice, directly or indirectly.

SPONSORSHIP (REGULAR OR CONTINUING SUPPORT IN MONEY OR KIND)

4 (a) Did you benefit from any sponsorship before your election, where to your knowledge the financial support in any case exceeded 25 per cent of your election expenses at that election?   YES/NO
If so, please give details opposite. Where a company is named as sponsor, please indicate briefly the nature of its business.

(b) Do you benefit from any other form of sponsorship or financial or material support as a member of parliament?   YES/NO
If so, please give details opposite, including the name of the organization or company providing the support. Where a company is named, please indicate briefly the nature of its business.

(c) Do the arrangements registered under category 4(b) above involve any payment to you or any material benefit or advantage which you personally receive?   YES/NO
Notes: (i) You should register under this section any source of regular or continuing support from which you receive any financial or material benefit, directly or indirectly; for example, the provision of free or subsidized accommodation, or the provision of the services of a research assistant free or at a subsidized salary rate.

(ii) You should not register sponsorship by your constituency party. But you **should** register, under category 4(b), any regular donations made by companies or organizations to your constituency party in excess of £500 per annum which are linked directly to your candidacy in the constituency or for which you yourself acted as an intermediary between the donor and the constituency party.

GIFTS, BENEFITS, AND HOSPITALITY (UK)

5 Have you or your spouse received any gift of a value greater than £125, or any material advantage of a value greater than 0.5 per cent of the current parliamentary salary, from any company, organization, or person within the United Kingdom which in any way relates to your membership of the House?   YES/NO
If so, please give the details opposite.

.

Table 10
(continued)

Registrable Interest	*Details*

Notes: (i) You should include any hospitality given and services or facilities offered *gratis* or at a price below that generally available to members of the public, **except that** where the advantage is known to be available to all members of parliament, it need not be registered.

(ii) You should include not only gifts and material advantages received personally by you and your spouse, but also those received by any company or organization in which you (or you and your spouse jointly) have a controlling interest.

OVERSEAS VISITS

6 Have you or your spouse made any overseas visits relating to or in any way arising out of your membership of the House where the cost was not wholly borne by yourself or by United Kingdom public funds?   YES/NO
If so, please list opposite, in chronological order, countries visited, dates of visits, and who paid for the visit.
Note: You are not required to register visits undertaken on behalf of the Commonwealth Parliamentary Association, the Inter-Parliamentary Union, the Council of Europe, the Western European Union, the North Atlantic Assembly, or the CSCE Parliamentary Assembly. Other categories of overseas visits which are exempt from the requirement to register are listed in the guidance pamphlet on Registration and Declaration of Members' Interests.

Countries Visited   Dates of Visit   Who Paid?

OVERSEAS BENEFITS AND GIFTS

7 Have you or your spouse received any gift of a value greater than £125, or any material advantage of a value greater than 0.5 per cent of the current parliamentary salary, from or on behalf of any foreign government, organization, or person which in any way relates to your membership of the House?   YES/NO
If so, please give the details opposite.
Note: Overseas hospitality and travel facilities should be registered under category 6. Otherwise the notes under category 5 apply here also.

LAND AND PROPERTY

8 Do you have any land or property, other than any home used solely for the personal residential purposes of you or your spouse, which has a substantial value or from which you derive a substantial income?   YES/NO
If so, please indicate opposite the nature of the property (eg, estate, farm, smallholding, woodland, residential rented/leasehold property, commercial rented/leasehold property), and give the general location of the property in each case.

Nature of Property   Location

Table 10
(continued)

Registrable Interest	Details

SHAREHOLDINGS
9 Do you have (either yourself or with or on behalf of your
spouse or dependent children) interests in shareholdings in
any public or private company or other body which have a
nominal value (a) greater than £25,000, or (b) less than
£25,000, but greater than 1 per cent of the issued share capital of the company or body?   YES/NO
If so, please list each company or body opposite, indicating
in each case the nature of its business and whether your
holding falls under subcategory (a) or (b) above.

MISCELLANEOUS
10 If, bearing in mind the definition of purpose set out in
the introduction to this form, you have any relevant interests
which you consider should be disclosed but which do not fall
within the nine categories set out above, please list them
opposite.

Source: Select Committee on Members' Interests, *First Report*, Session 1991–2. The first register prepared under these headings was published in January 1994.

also gifts and overseas visits, although complete spousal registration
was explicitly rejected.

In other respects, however, the concerns raised by the interviewed
MPS remain unresolved. The committee discussed but ultimately chose
to avoid further reforms that would have significant ramifications for
the operation of the current system. As long as those over £125 are
registered, MPS can continue to accept gifts given to them in their
parliamentary capacity of any value. The complaints procedure, considered cumbersome and discouraging by the Puritans, was determined to be sufficiently effective and was left unchanged. While Early
Day Motions in which members have a pecuniary interest are now to
be marked on the Notice Paper, written questions for the Order Paper
do not have to be similarly noted.[25] No further restrictions or registration requirements were placed on foreign travel by MPS.

Unfortunately for the House, this very loophole in the rules was
subsequently exploited by two MPS in July 1994. A *Sunday Times* "sting"
operation offered twenty members £1,000 to place a question on the
Order Paper. Graham Riddick (C. Colne Valley) and David Tredinnick
(C. Bosworth) appeared to accept the offer. The ensuing scandal
forced the government to suspend both men from their positions as
parliamentary private secretaries. In response the House has requested

the Committee on Privileges to investigate not only the specifics of this incident but also the wider issue of MPs serving as paid parliamentary advisers and consultants. In debate, many Conservative members blamed the *Times* for the scandal, and accused it of unethical behaviour in seeking to entrap the MPs. The Committee was therefore directed to examine this aspect of the case as well.

Puritans and Servants in the House will no doubt also remain frustrated by the continued absence of restrictions on outside employment. No outright ban on extracurricular jobs was adopted, and even the increasingly common practice of MPs acting as parliamentary consultants was not curbed. Nor did the committee, despite its obsession with reinforcing the registration principle, require MPs to reveal the amount of their outside remuneration – on which there is no ceiling – even in the less explicit format of income ranges. The determination of the committee to avoid income revelation is almost ostrich-like:

As Mr. Speaker succinctly put it, "it is the nature of the interest not the actual sum of money, that is important." Nor is it necessarily the case that amounts of remuneration would be a reliable guide to the degree of influence which an interest might exert on a Member of Parliament: this could depend at least as much on the personal circumstances of the individual member and on other, non-pecuniary, considerations. To require the disclosure of amounts would represent a significant intrusion into the privacy and personal affairs of a Member of Parliament, and we can find no substantial justification for recommending such a step.[26]

Certainly, the difference between interests of £50 and £50,000 is indeed quantitative, but at some pecuniary scale the difference becomes qualitative as well.

The committee has begun attempts to address the problematic issue of lobbying, beginning in 1988 with an initial inquiry. To aid them in their deliberations the committee looked to other legislatures for examples of lobbyist registration. The US Congress instituted lobby legislation in 1946 and the Canadian Parliament in 1989. The Canadian example addresses one of the concerns of some of the British members, in that a distinction is made between individuals whose clients pay them to lobby the government (first-tier lobbyists) and representatives of organizations whose responsibilities may include lobbying the government (second-tier lobbyists). Far more information is required in the registration of first-tier lobbyists.[27] The British Select Committee visited Canada in April 1990 to study this new system in operation.

The discussions of the committee indicated, however, that it was not sure whether a distinction should be made between professional lobbyists-for-hire and others whose job may occasionally include, but is not limited to, lobbying. In addition, Fred Silvester offered an observation about how a register of lobbyists would serve as a check on MPs' declarations of private interests:

The current Register of Members' Interests within its limits has been successful. It does however rely on Members to make their own declaration. Proposals for a Register of Lobbyists rest on the proposition that this is not enough. It supposes that there are financial benefits conferred on members which are not declared by them but which would be exposed if the responsibility of declaration were passed to the lobbyist. This is a fundamental change in the traditional view that an Honourable Member will police his own conduct subject to the control of the House.[28]

This connection was not made by the MPs in the sample, even those who felt that more scrutiny of members' interests was warranted. The main objection to a register of lobbyists raised by witnesses and members of the committee was one that was emphasized by the Servants: they did not want the register to be perceived as a form of parliamentary accreditation that could be used by registered firms to increase their fees or volume of business.

In 1991 the committee finally proposed that the House establish a register of professional lobbyists and a companion code of conduct, and offered draft versions of each document for further discussion with interested parties. A short, preliminary debate was held in the House in June 1993, but no decisions were taken. In December 1993 the committee began to hear more testimony from expert witnesses, and it may or may not publish a further report. The issue thus remains unresolved and, despite the fears expressed in the interviews, there appears to be no great commitment on the part of the House to pursue it.

Another major area which the committee examined was the relationship between parliamentary consultants and MPs. The ethical propriety of an MP serving on retainer to a PR company and lobbying from within was questioned by a number of committee members and witnesses. Concern was raised over the increasing number of members who are heading their own consultancy firms while still active members of the House. Even more alarming were revelations that there are chairmen of House committees who are also directors of PR companies. The House approved without debate two of the committee's recommendations – that the financial interests of select committee members be circulated prior to the selection of a chairman, and that it be recognized that there are occasions when it is prudent for the chair to excuse himself altogether from the proceedings.[29] Beyond these familiar admonishments to disclose one's interests, however, the House has not taken any steps to help address the conflicts that result.

The Members' Interests Committee has also sought to elucidate the parameters of what organizations expect from the MPs they retain. According to a representative of the all-party disablement group: "MPs are used in various ways such as arranging within the House presentations, lunches, dinners, the use of facilities. If these are used by P.R. firms to enhance their own position with a client, to enhance the fees it can charge for example, and MPs are not fully aware of how it is they are being used, in my mind this becomes quite dangerous."[30] The concerns voiced by various witnesses echoed those of the Puritans and some Servants. Apparently, the committee has implicitly recognized that not all MPs are able to resolve the conflicts caused by outside interests in a monolithic way.

Related to this discussion of the relationship between MPs and lobbyist is the question of whether trade union sponsorship is different from MPs accepting consultancy retainers. Representatives from the trade unions definitely thought so and this view was put forward most ardently by James Knapp, general secretary of the National Union of Railwaymen, who went to great lengths to explain the historical roots of sponsorship and how any money given by the unions went directly to the constituency party and not to the personal coffers of the sponsored MP.[31] But some members were interested in determining whether in this day and age it was still necessary for unions to sponsor individual members and whether in fact sponsorship should only be bestowed upon Labour members of parliament. As with consultancies, the advice of the committee is that proper and complete registration and declaration is sufficient to forestall any difficulties that might arise.

Perhaps the most useful change introduced by the committee is the publication of an advisory and interpretative guide to declaration and registration. This document, compiled by the Registrar of Members' Interests, gathers together for the first time many of the rulings and directives that pertain to financial interests.[32] The guide also provides step-by-step assistance to MPs in filling out their annual registration form. All four types of MPs can be expected to appreciate this source of guidance, though perhaps for different reasons. The Entrepreneurs may welcome this more explicit definition of the rules as a more exact delineation of loopholes, while the Muddlers might actually become less "muddled." The Puritans, of course, will find it insufficient, but a step towards improving the conduct of their colleagues. Finally, the Servants might resent somewhat the implication that they are not aware of the relevant requirements, but they also might find the clarifications contained in the guide reassuring. The compilation of the guide seems to be as far as the committee is willing to go towards ethical codification: "To attempt to define, on a much wider and hypothetical basis, the types of conduct which the House might in particular circumstances judge to be contempts, would be a far more hazardous enterprise and one doomed to almost certain failure."[33]

This guide is one response to the perceived weaknesses in the ethical framework of the House. The committee and the House explicitly rejected the alternative response: the codification of the rules in statute. Throughout its many reports the committee has consistently opposed such a move as inappropriate to the small scale and minor nature of the ethical violations that have occurred. It considers statutory regulation a fundamental challenge to the basic philosophy and autonomy of Parliament and therefore unwarranted, barring an outbreak of extreme and otherwise uncontrollable corruption. The committee continues to trust in the ethical intuition and discretion of the individual member – and the ability of the House to regulate itself without outside interference – as the best safeguards against unethical behaviour. On the other hand, in recognition of the number of other legislatures that have moved towards more formal regulation and the continued complaints of "puritanical" MPs, the committee admitted that the matter is not permanently settled. The House may only have set this decision aside temporarily.

In fact, the series of scandals that erupted in the winter of 1994 may yet presage a return of ethical issues to the foreground in British politics. Most of the attention has focused on a series of juicy sex scandals – made worse by the involvement of several leading spokesmen for the Conservative government's "Back-to-Basics" family-values theme. But there have also surfaced in the press allegations of financial impropriety on the part of at least one parliamentary secretary, and the involvement of Conservative MPs and party officials in a scheme to gerrymander close London constituencies by manipulating council housing sales.

The recent reforms do nothing to change the fact that the House of Commons remains committed to registration and declaration as the twin pillars of its regulatory edifice. The select committee has cautioned members against assuming that proper registration and declaration fulfil their entire ethical responsibility and has reminded them of their duty to avoid activities that bring the House into disrepute. Yet even as it has aided MPs in the technicalities of making their interests public, the committee has done nothing to identify the types of conduct the House considers disreputable. They have rejected the adoption of a more comprehensive code of conduct as unnecessary, misguided, and ultimately unfeasible. Unlike the US Congress, whose regulatory framework acknowledges that legislators are periodically elected who choose to enrich their private coffers at public expense, the committee admits that none of its provisions will "deter the member who has a calculated determination to use his position for personal financial gain."[34] As always, the House counts on individual members to be motivated by the ideal of public service, and to distinguish for themselves between acceptable and unacceptable behaviour. But as this book has revealed, ethical dissensus amongst members is a hallmark of the contemporary House of Commons.

THE DYNAMICS OF REFORM

The potential areas of reform that have been examined thus far are all responses to specific mechanical problems or institutional vulnerabilities. Changes in the operation of the Register of Members' Interests, limits on outside employment, and even improvements in salary and support all amount to modifications of the ethical rules of Parliament. It was clear to at least some MPs – most Puritans and a number of Servants – that these modifications were desirable, if not necessary. But mechanical changes in the rules do not address the more fundamental issue of how those rules are understood, interpreted, and applied. And particular changes in the rules are ultimately irrelevant when there exist MPs who are not sure what the rules are, or what they actually mean.

The question of how the rules are to be applied is especially important, given the prevalence among surveyed MPs of the attitude that whatever is not explicitly prohibited is tacitly approved. Most Entrepreneurs and Muddlers indicated, directly or indirectly, that they ascribe to this view. As one put it: "I find some of these activities distasteful and in my book they would be corrupt but the rules of the House permit them – they are viewed as acceptable practices – people are doing it, so it must be so." Jennings's term "minimalist ethics" has already been used to describe the narrow scope of formal restrictions placed on its members by the British system of legislative ethics, but this attitude of the Entrepreneurs and Muddlers is an ethical minimalism of a different sort – a perceptive rather than a prescriptive minimalism.

Parliament does in fact place few formal restrictions on the behaviour of its members, but expects that informal norms and standards will be a more important force in guiding MPs' ethical decisions. Parliament assumes that between the processes of selection as representatives and socialization as members of the legislature, MPs will develop a common ethical intuition that will allow the flexible application of standards to situations of conflict. An oft-cited explanation for occasional scandals is the failure of the selection process in a particular instance – the "rotten-apple" syndrome. But the prevalence of perceptive ethical minimalists suggests that the socialization process may be inadequate to assure ethical consensus. The wide diversity of ethical attitudes discovered by this study certainly tends to support this conclusion. One Servant stated: "No one tells you what is expected of you. There is no guidance. You are pretty much left on your own." Or as an exasperated Albert Roberts asked during the Poulson investigation: "What standards do I take? One can read Beaverbrook by Taylor. Do I take my standards from there? From where do I take my standards? I have no do's and don'ts of Parliament."[35] The minimalists, similarly abandoned by the system and lacking guidance, have either chosen to abandon the informal component of the "rules" or have never managed to fully understand and apprehend the standards they are expected to uphold and have thus fallen back on a strict constructionist interpretation of the few clear prohibitions in force.

And yet the fundamental ethical assumptions of the system remain in the background – that MPs are all honourable gentlemen who would not knowingly bring dishonour upon themselves or the House. This presumption of honour, in the absence of the underlying ethical consensus it relies upon, leads to a progressive legitimization of behaviour that is more and more removed from the original boundaries of probity. Members, especially new MPs, see their colleagues engaged in activities they might at first question (such as selling access to the parliamentary dining room for clients), but the fact that such behaviour is neither sanctioned nor infrequent leads them to conclude that it is generally accepted and is therefore acceptable. A different kind of socialization process thus usurps the intended one: even MPs who attempt to adhere to the informal standards learn not what is expected of them, but that if others are doing it, it must be legitimate. The result is what can be called "legitimized corruption." That is, once the institution's basic ethical assumptions desynchronize with the attitudes of its members, positive feedback can cause once exceptional and questionable practices to become routine and unremarkable.

It is to avoid these consequences of ethical minimalism that the select committee has argued against ethical codification. Their fear is that a rule-based system would precipitate a loophole-based mentality – with members forsaking their broad, normative ethical responsibilities for the narrow, legalistic path of avoiding conflict with the rules. The committee's outlook in this respect is similar to that of the Servants. Yet the interviews showed that Servants are the least common type, and they are far outnumbered by Muddlers and Entrepreneurs – MPs who have already made the transition from aspirational ethics to violation-avoidance. The traditional view of Parliament provides little guidance for MPs and does little to address the problems caused by members who have already rejected the basic assumptions of that view.

MPs of all four types expressed the opinion that Parliament is experiencing this sort of ethical deterioration, although some types were more concerned than others and each placed a different emphasis on the problem. The Puritans were for the most part harsh in their condemnation of the activities of many of their colleagues and felt that the collegiality of the House only accentuated the tendency to ignore or overlook transgressions. Many Puritans felt that the existing system was outdated and inefficient, that the rules could be ignored and were not enforced, and were convinced that significant structural change – the use of restrictions and penalties, rather than just declaration – was needed. They suggested that MPs were on the whole more interested in safeguarding the name and reputation of Parliament than in sincerely pursuing allegations of misconduct. Having found the attitudes of their fellow MPs to be a significant barrier to ethical reform, many of the Puritans have fallen back into a position of ethical isolationism: they will maintain their own high standards, but were unable or reluctant to impose them on others, and could only watch as those around them engaged in activities they considered inappropriate.

The Servants, in contrast, felt that the system was basically sound and that most MPs were in fact honourable members. They felt strongly that ethical decisions were a personal matter and that rules were no substitute for common sense and sound judgment. The Servants saw possibilities for improvement in the way the existing provisions for ethical management were applied – expectations could be made clearer, more guidance could be offered to MPs who are unsure of how to resolve dilemmas. Thus, what the Servants saw as the most productive type of reform the Puritans viewed as mere tinkering. Whereas the Puritans saw themselves as significantly different from their colleagues, the Servants believed themselves to be typical MPs and expected that their own level of ethical commitment would be mirrored in the judgments of the rest of the House.

The Muddlers turned this interpretation on its head. They saw "typical MPs" all around them engaging in activities they might at first have considered questionable, and concluded that such behaviour was in fact acceptable and above reproach. While they may be troubled by their conscience when participating in such "acceptable" activities, they felt they had no incentive for listening to it and ultimately fell back on the minimalist attitude that they were not doing anything wrong if they were not contravening any explicit rules. Like the Servants, the Muddlers believed ethics to belong to the personal sphere, but unlike the Servants they did not think that MPs should be held to a standard of behaviour that is higher, or even different, from that applicable to society as a whole. The Muddlers thus rejected the notion that membership in Parliament does or should confer any special ethical awareness, even though it offers the possibility of ethical entanglements unavailable to the general public.

Finally, the Entrepreneurs took ethical minimalism to the extreme and essentially removed ethical matters from the realm of valid or worthwhile considerations. The Entrepreneurs' reliance on a strict legalistic definition of corruption freed them from the responsibility of examining the ethics of their behaviour for compliance with nebulous standards. They needed only determine whether they were breaking any rules (and perhaps the likelihood of being caught doing so). In this sense they have rejected the fundamental ethical assumptions of the House. Whereas the Muddlers could be seen as the victims of the trend towards ethical minimalism – their uncertainty led them to follow the practice of those around them – the Entrepreneurs were more the perpetrators of the trend. By excluding ethics from all but the most simplistic consideration, they guaranteed its marginalization in their activities. Their preference for the application of fixed rules over discretionary judgment, however, did not lead them to call for more extensive or more explicit rules. The Entrepreneurs felt, as did many Puritans, that more rules were what would be needed to curb ethical misconduct, but the Entrepreneurs, rather hypocritically, were definitely not in favour of more rules.

Despite the existence of legitimized corruption, the MPs overwhelmingly did not think written rules the answer. The Entrepreneurs and the Muddlers resented the possibility of outsiders imposing standards on them. Nor did they want to curb the flexibility they claimed the current system allows. The Servants agreed that too much stock was placed in the value of written rules. Even the Puritans, while they would welcome additional rules in the guise of a stronger framework, were reluctant to put rules of ethics down in formal codes of conduct. The MPs admitted that they could use assistance in making decisions, especially in the areas of gifts, hospitality, and foreign travel, and a number would welcome more explicit and detailed guidelines. Such guidelines would make it easier for MPs to evaluate their own behaviour, and would assist outsiders (such as the public) attempting to judge the activities of MPs. None but the most puritanical MPs, however, favoured actual written rules, even though that was what many of them said would be required to prohibit activities they regarded as unethical or even corrupt.

Given the MPs' apprehension for a code of conduct, it is unlikely that there would be much support in Britain for legislation similar to the Ethics in Government Act, which has been in operation in the United States since 1978. The act regulates the behaviour of all elected representatives as well as individuals serving the government in an official capacity, and created the Office of Government Ethics to monitor compliance. The legislation is thus administered by an external, non-legislative body and carries with it both criminal and civil penalties, in particular the imposition of fines. While some MPs might favour the institutionalization of sanctions for violators, the idea of an external body interfering in Parliament's affairs by monitoring and disciplining its members would be anathema to virtually all of them.

Perhaps efforts will thus have to focus on strengthening or expanding Parliament's internal regulatory mechanisms. As the Rt.-Hon. Cranley Onslow testified before the select committee:

Your whole Committee is evidence of the need to monitor the rules which are laid down, because laying down rules is one thing, seeing they are maintained is another. We do, I think, know that in areas of this kind it is unwise to take things for granted. It would be unwise to presume that the existence of the registers is widely known to my colleagues. I am not even sure all my colleagues could recite by heart the various categories of beneficial interest which they are required to declare when they complete their own registration. Therefore it is right that you should maintain a close and continuous watch.

If MPs are reluctant to share the responsibility of enforcement and investigation with an external agent, they may well be compelled to become more vigilant in monitoring one another's behaviour.

CONCLUSION

The ethical framework of the British House of Commons is based on the assumption that all members will approach questions of ethics in the same manner. As this book has demonstrated, however, there appear to be distinct subpopulations of MPs with different, perhaps even directly competing, attitudes towards ethical misconduct and management. At one extreme lie the Puritans, who saw themselves as lone voices crying out in an ethical wilderness. They felt that the ethical framework of the House has potentially dangerous structural defects and that it is open to abuse by the rapacious tendencies of their colleagues, whom they saw as a disappointing lot. They felt additional formal rules were needed to rid the House of legitimized corruption and to elevate the rest of the membership to the high standards the Puritans set for themselves. But the Puritans were not optimistic about the institution of effective rules. They were grimly aware of the disincentives imposed on those who would question the ethics of honourable members, even when they have proof of inappropriate behaviour.

At the other extreme were the Entrepreneurs, for whom ethics was not a preoccupation or even a concern. Unethical behaviour was in their minds merely a synonym for illegal behaviour, and since few activities available to an MP were actually restricted by law or parliamentary rules they felt free to indulge in behaviour that the Puritans condemned, and that even they themselves considered questionable. Were the rules to change, the Entrepreneurs would have to alter their behaviour accordingly, but they cannot be counted on to support change. They valued the current system for its simplicity and flexibility, and especially for its faith in the discretion of the individual MP. They did not appear to realize that their application of the system involves a reduction of that discretion to a mere legalistic rationalization.

The other two groups fell somewhere in between these extremes, though not along a linear continuum. The Servants shared many of the ethical concerns of the Puritans, but were almost as reluctant to advocate reform as the Entrepreneurs. For the Servants, however, trust in the system and its soundness was a matter of honest faith, not convenient rationalization. The Puritans saw as needed the revolutionary reconstruction, perhaps from the ground up, of a rickety and unsafe ethical framework; the Servants, conservative and traditionalist, favoured the evolutionary adaptation of a basically sound structure to new challenges – strengthening here, extending there, but always in line with the existing plan. The Servants were believers in the "rotten-apple" explanation of ethical misconduct, and even those who were alarmed at the prevalence of rotten apples felt that their numbers were primarily attributable to the lack of ethical leadership in the House. They felt that the current norms were adequate and they just needed to be more openly and more consistently promulgated throughout the House by those in positions of responsibility, and especially by the government.

Perhaps the most interesting MPs were the Muddlers, who were as involved in questionable activities as the Entrepreneurs, but managed to question their involvement. The Muddlers appeared to be nagged by their consciences and doubts about the propriety of their actions, but their doubts were appeased by their observation that these actions were common and unremarkable among their colleagues. Just as the Puritans had no incentive to identify violations, the Muddlers had no incentive to follow their consciences – the "if I don't do it, somebody else will" mentality. This mindset can be seen as an implicit call for more explicit guidance in ethical matters. The Muddlers' concentration on the particulars of ethical misconduct also suggested that they would benefit from stronger and more concrete specifications of the standards they are expected to uphold. Of all the types, it was the Muddlers who were the most unsure of their own ethical position, and therefore the most pliable in their ethical attitude.

The Muddlers and Servants both held to their own brands of conformitarianism. The Servants attempted to align themselves with what they saw as the traditional ideal MP. The Muddlers, perhaps for lack of a preconceived model, attempted to fashion themselves after what they saw in the real MPs sitting beside them. The Puritans, in contrast, rejected both their colleagues and their traditional ideas as a source of ethical guidance, and, lacking faith in the capability of the established system to withstand misconduct, instead turned inward to establish a personally derived, restrictive, nonconformist set of standards. Lastly, the Entrepreneurs rejected all sources of ethical inspiration and conformed only to a minimal, rigidly legalistic interpretation of the few explicit regulatory provisions in effect. In doing so, they were the MPs seen as rotten apples by the Servants, as colleagues to emulate by the Muddlers, and as unredeemable examples of the failure of Parliament's ethical system by the Puritans.

The discussion of legitimized corruption suggested that change in ethical attitudes is the foundation upon which significant reform of legislative behaviour must be built. In this view, it may be the Muddlers who are the key. The Entrepreneurs will likely continue to resist any changes that limit the range of opportunity available to them. The Servants may support some limits, but will oppose change to the fundamental nature of the system and its dependence on individual discretion. It is not clear, however, that effective reform can proceed without some shift of emphasis from individual to institutional responsibility for monitoring and regulating behaviour. The Puritans will probably support any and all reforms – they feel that any change is probably for the better – but are not a group that can be counted on to spearhead a reform effort. Their ethical isolationism leads them to doubt the utility of trying to reform a fundamentally corrupt system, unless they can be guaranteed support from other groups. The Muddlers could go the way of the Entrepreneurs and ignore impulses towards change, but their comments revealed that their doubts about many current practices in the House could be turned to the reformist cause, if sparked by a major scandal or nudged by an extraparliamentary player. Their ethical uncertainty would only be increased were attention focused, by a scandal or heightened public interest, on the range of borderline activities that currently persists. In such a situation, the voice of conscience could break through the ethical apathy that currently rules their behaviour and lead them to champion reform.

Conclusion:
The View from Westminster

The truth is that some honourable members have
allowed inducements to influence their judgment, and
increasingly we are hiding behind the term "honourable
gentlemen" to disguise what is in reality an erosion of the
standards expected of us.[1]

D.N. Campbell-Savours, MP

The legislative ethics of the British House of Commons is a fragile
and subtle construct. Parliament presumes that all MPs can be counted
on to apply uniform principles of honour and good judgment to the
situations they face, and thus it grants considerable discretion to
individuals in the resolution of ethical dilemmas. The result is that
the House is dependent for the maintenance of probity on the con-
gruence of multiple individual attitudes with a single indistinct ideal.
The basic premise is that those elected are by nature "honourable
gentlemen," and that collegial experiences within the halls of Westminster ensure that MPs remain "honourable members." This system
based on individual attitudes is preferred by the House for its flexibility and economy: no need is seen for the creation of sets of specific
rules or a bureaucracy of ethical watchdogs when members can be
counted on to ensure that their own behaviour remains above
reproach.

Chapter 1 identified the inherent vulnerabilities of this approach
to ethical management. Standards of behaviour exist, but they are
informal, imprecise, and incohesive, and the House has no direct way
of ensuring that members abide by them or are even aware of their
basic content. Nor can the House affirm that the presumed ethical
consensus is in fact achieved or maintained. If members are applying
their own divergent standards of conduct, then a whole range of
activities that some might consider improper or even corrupt can go
unrestricted. Examination of the data in chapters 2 through 7 indicated that this is indeed the case: on many important issues there is
stark dissensus among MPs as to what constitutes acceptable behaviour,
and many MPs are engaging in activities that many others find reprehensible. Mr Campbell-Savours's impression is corroborated by the
responses and remarks of the MPs surveyed.

Chapter 1 also addressed the perception that the parametres of the British parliamentary system restrict the opportunities available to MPs who might venture into impropriety. Deprived by party discipline of the chance to sell their vote or tailor legislation to financial benefactors, it is sometimes thought that MPs can at worst get into mischief, none of which poses a serious threat to the integrity of government. Indeed, many surveyed MPs commented on the relative "powerlessness" of the backbencher and were confident that large-scale bribery and misappropriation of public funds were not afflicting the House. On the other hand, most of the complaints (from the Puritans) and rationalizations (from the Entrepreneurs) offered in the interviews referred to practices on the fringe of political activity, particularly the sale by MPs of privileged information, access, and contacts. These sorts of activities are especially problematic. In "conventional" corruption, such as bribery, it is clear what those involved are obtaining by their transaction, but when a corporation is able to retain the "services" of a member of parliament directly, it is not certain what range of benefits the company expects in return for the retainer.

The increasing popularity of these arrangements, however, attests to their desirability for those entities that seek better information about and access to the governing process. It is to managing these sorts of fringe activities that the ethical system of the House is, paradoxically, at once well-suited and completely incapable. Because it has failed to achieve an ethical consensus, and at the same time does not provide clear direction, the informal norms of the House are powerless to restrict activities that are thought by many MPs to be clear violations of parliamentary standards. The much-vaunted flexibility of the system has not allowed it to adapt to the proliferation of opportunities caused by the professionalization of politics and the commoditization of the office of member of parliament.

These are the ethical challenges currently facing the House of Commons. This study seems to support the contention that changes are taking place in Parliament and that a "new breed" of MP is asserting its presence. The traditional outlook expected of all MPs is in fact exemplified only by the Servants – the least numerous of the four types. Apparently taking its place is an attitude entirely decoupled from institutional expectations – the legalistic minimalism of the Entrepreneurs. The Muddlers represent a faction that has lost touch with the informal standards, or else has decided that common practice is a more convenient source of guidance. Other MPs still cling to strong personal standards, but the Puritans do so despite their lack of faith in the system, rather than out of a belief in its efficacy.

Parliament has three alternatives. One would be to attempt to work within its existing ethical paradigm by strengthening the promulgation of its informal norms and standards. As many Servants suggested, Parliament could pay more attention to the ethical education of MPs, so that all would be completely informed as to the standards they are expected to uphold. A greater willingness to punish those who violate these standards might also assist in fortifying the ethical framework of the House.

Another option would be to abandon sole reliance on an informal schema and to move to a formal network of regulations and codes, with attendant investigative and disciplinary bodies. While they were not great supporters of formal codes, the Puritans could be expected to favour more rigidity in exchange for better overall compliance. Even some Muddlers would appreciate more explicit ethical guidance. One example of such a formalized system is found in the US Congress, although experience in Washington has shown that formal regulatory machinery is no cure-all for legislative impropriety. The Canadian House of Commons, until recently similar to Westminster in its ethical approach, has been introducing more formal components and represents a legislature in an interesting phase of transition.

The final option – and the one most palatable to the Entrepreneurs – is to maintain the status quo, at least until a scandal of sufficient gravity jolts the House into taking action. The House has in the past suffered bouts of concern over the ethics of its members, has appointed tribunals of inquiry, has produced voluminous reports on the cases, and has quietly allowed their recommendations to slip unimplemented into obscurity. This scenario may be the most likely, if we can judge from past performance, but will only cause the underlying ethical problems and tensions to fester.

If the House should choose to take action, it must be clear that the goal will be a change in the ethical attitudes and perceptions of many MPs. Such a realignment cannot be accomplished without determined ethical leadership. Behaviour this leadership feels is inappropriate must be firmly curtailed, and those involved must be advised of the consequences of recidivism. MPs whose personal standards are more restrictive should not be made to feel that they are ethical oddities. Whether formally or informally, the House of Commons will need to ensure, by actual knowledge rather than presumption, that its MPs are in fact "honourable members."

Interview Schedule: MPs and Their Attitudes towards Political Corruption

SECTION A: GENERAL QUESTIONS CONCERNING CORRUPTION

1. How do you think the public see MPs? Trustworthy or untrustworthy?
2. Do you think significant political corruption exists in Britain? What do you understand the term "political corruption" to mean?
3. If a committee was appointed to investigate corruption in government, in your opinion where should it begin to look?
4. Do you think there is much scope for abuse in the way political parties raise money? Anything on the other side?
5. Are you satisfied with the operation of the Register of Members' Interests?
   a) Are there important things not covered?
   b) Are the categories too stringent?
   c) Not enough financial information?
   d) Published often enough?
   e) Have you received any feedback about your own declaration?
6. Do you approve of the recent extension of the declaration principle, requiring the registration of interests of lobby journalists, researchers, and secretaries?
7. Should there be a separate register of lobbyists? Do you get many personal approaches from professional lobbyists? Can you describe a typical one for me?
8. Should members who fail to comply with the register be subject to sanction? What should it be?
9. What do you understand by the key phrase "activity inconsistent with the standards the House is entitled to expect from its Members"?
10. As an MP, do you often encounter ethical dilemmas? What sort of thing?

11. Do you think a written code of conduct would be helpful in solving the ethical dilemmas MPs face?
12. To what extent today do you think an MP's career would be affected by a sex scandal?
13. Have you ever known of or suspected corruption in Parliament? What is the most serious case you have heard of?
14. On the left-right, wet-dry spectrum within your own party, where do you think most people would place you?
    On a seven-point ethical scale ranging from puritanical to liberal, where would you place yourself?

SECTION B: GENERAL STATEMENTS ON CORRUPTION

Please indicate your agreement or disagreement with the following statements:

Strongly agree							Strongly disagree
	1	2	3	4	5	6	7	

If you agree completely, you would pick position number 1.
If you disagree completely, you would pick position number 7.
Of course, you can pick any of the numbered positions in between.
Here is the first statement:

15. Political corruption is not a widespread problem.
16. In so far as citizens distrust elected persons it is because they do not understand what politics is all about.
17. Dishonesty is more widespread in politics than in business.
18. Political corruption is more widespread at the local than at the national level of government.
19. No matter what we do, we can never eliminate political corruption.
20. The corruption that exists in the political world simply reflects the standards of the rest of society.
21. If it hadn't been for the Poulson scandal, we would hear a lot less about corruption in the government.
22. MPs are sufficiently well informed to act as the sole guarantors of acceptable conduct in the House.
23. Once allegations of corruption have been made, MPs in their parliamentary capacity should be brought within the ambit of criminal law.
24. Britain's libel laws inhibit the uncovering and reporting of political corruption.

SECTION C: CORRUPTION SCENARIOS

Recently, publicity has been given to a few politicians who have engaged in activities that some would call corrupt, others not. I would like your opinion on the following hypothetical situations:

We will use the following response card:

Corrupt								Not
	1	2	3	4	5	6	7	corrupt
a) Probably								Probably
	1	2	3	4	5	6	7	not
b) Probably								Probably
	1	2	3	4	5	6	7	not
c) Definitely								Definitely
yes	1	2	3	4	5	6	7	not

25. A cabinet minister promises an appointed position in exchange for campaign contributions.

Corrupt								Not
	1	2	3	4	5	6	7	corrupt

   a) Most citizens would condemn this activity.
   b) Most of your colleagues would condemn this activity.
   c) Would you yourself engage in this activity?

26. An MP uses his influence to get a friend or relative admitted to Oxford or Cambridge, or some other prestigious institution.

Corrupt								Not
	1	2	3	4	5	6	7	corrupt

   a)   b)   c)

27. The driveway of the chairman of the City Council's private home is paved by the council's District Works Department.

Corrupt								Not
	1	2	3	4	5	6	7	corrupt

   a)   b)   c)

28. A cabinet minister uses his influence to obtain a contract for a firm in his constituency.

Corrupt								Not
	1	2	3	4	5	6	7	corrupt

   a)   b)   c)

29. An MP is retained by a major company to arrange meetings and dinners in the House at which its executives can meet parliamentarians.

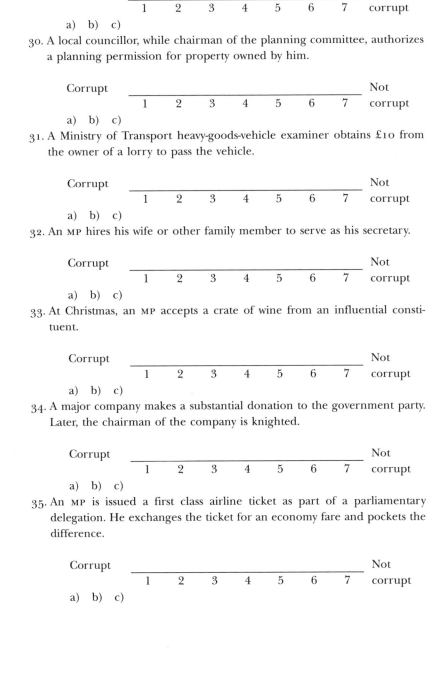

Corrupt _____ Not

       1   2   3   4   5   6   7   corrupt

a) b) c)

30. A local councillor, while chairman of the planning committee, authorizes a planning permission for property owned by him.

Corrupt _____ Not

       1   2   3   4   5   6   7   corrupt

a) b) c)

31. A Ministry of Transport heavy-goods-vehicle examiner obtains £10 from the owner of a lorry to pass the vehicle.

Corrupt _____ Not

       1   2   3   4   5   6   7   corrupt

a) b) c)

32. An MP hires his wife or other family member to serve as his secretary.

Corrupt _____ Not

       1   2   3   4   5   6   7   corrupt

a) b) c)

33. At Christmas, an MP accepts a crate of wine from an influential constituent.

Corrupt _____ Not

       1   2   3   4   5   6   7   corrupt

a) b) c)

34. A major company makes a substantial donation to the government party. Later, the chairman of the company is knighted.

Corrupt _____ Not

       1   2   3   4   5   6   7   corrupt

a) b) c)

35. An MP is issued a first class airline ticket as part of a parliamentary delegation. He exchanges the ticket for an economy fare and pockets the difference.

Corrupt _____ Not

       1   2   3   4   5   6   7   corrupt

a) b) c)

36. An all-party group on the aged secures the services of a full-time research assistant at the expense of Age Concern.

Corrupt   _____   Not
        1   2   3   4   5   6   7   corrupt

a)   b)   c)

37. A member on retainer to a PR company representing a foreign government submits several written questions for the Order Paper on British industrial development in that country.

Corrupt   _____   Not
        1   2   3   4   5   6   7   corrupt

a)   b)   c)

39. An MP requests and receives a House pass for a lobbyist to act as a research assistant, although his services are paid for by an outside source.

Corrupt   _____   Not
        1   2   3   4   5   6   7   corrupt

a)   b)   c)

SECTION D: IN CONCLUSION, I WONDER WHETHER I MIGHT GO OVER A LITTLE PERSONAL INFORMATION:

40. Are you happy with your job as MP?
   a) Yes, a lot
   b) Yes, some
   c) Yes, but only very occasionally
   d) No

41. How efficacious do you feel as part of the parliamentary process?
   a) a great deal
   b) a little
   c) a very little
   d) not at all
   e) don't know

42. How much of your time would you say you devote to your duties as MP?

43. What is the population size of your constituency?

44. In general, which description best fits your constituency?

   a) totally urban   d) mostly suburban
   b) mostly urban   e) totally rural
   c) totally suburban   f) mostly rural

g) mixed urban rural   i)   mixed urban suburban

h) mixed suburban rural

45. What is the last educational establishment you attended? (If respondent indicates that he attended university, ask 45a)

    a) What degree, if any, did you receive?

46. What was your age on your last birthday?

47. Do you presently have another occupation besides MP? If not, what was your previous occupation?

48. What is your religious denomination? (If respondent has a denomination, ask 48a)

    a) About how often do you attend the services at your church or synagogue?

        i)   often, at least once/wk.   iv) about once/year

        ii) once or twice/month   v) never

        iii) several times/year   vi) refused

49. How many terms in the legislature have you served, counting this term?

50. All together, how many years is that?

51. Party affiliation:

    a) Conservative   b) Labour   c) SDP/Liberal   d) Other

52. Sex: Male_____   Female_____

53. Name_____:

Thank you very much for your opinions and attention.

INTERVIEWER'S COMMENTS:

54. Were other people present or within earshot during the interview?

    a) yes, throughout

    b) yes, at times

    c) no

55. Estimate of respondent's frankness

    a) very frank

    b) frank

    c) not very frank

    d) very evasive

56. Estimate of respondent's cooperativeness

    a) very cooperative

    b) cooperative

    c) not very cooperative

    d) very uncooperative

OTHER COMMENTS:

Notes

1 This guiding phrase, which will be discussed in further detail, is taken
  from the Report of the Royal Commission on the Standards of Conduct in Public Life (The Salmon Commission).
2 Patterson, "Understanding the British Parliament," 449–62.
3 Searing, "Rules of the Game in Britain: Can the Politicians Be
  Trusted?" 256.
4 Johnston, "Social Conceptions of Right and Wrong in Britain," 13.
5 Nevitte and Gibbins, *New Elites in Old States*; Inglehart, *Culture Shift*.

CHAPTER ONE

1 Beard and Horn make similar observations about the American Congress. But since their book was published in 1975, there have been significant changes in congressional practice. See Atkinson and Mancuso,
  "Edicts and Etiquette," for a discussion of these changes.
2 For a discussion of these norms and conventions see especially Marshall, *Constitutional Conventions*.
3 In the early 1970s architect John Poulson built up an elaborate network of influence involving politicians, civil servants, and local councillors. In exchange for expensive gifts, payments, and hospitality, the
  officials provided preferential treatment to Poulson and his associates.
  This extensive influence-peddling was revealed only in the course of
  bankruptcy proceedings against Poulson. The resultant scandal was
  devastating, and ushered in a period of ethical introspection and scrutiny into the standards of conduct of politicians and officials. For a
  complete discussion of the Poulson case see Doig, *Corruption and Misconduct in Contemporary British Politics*.

4 These scandals include:

1) Westland Affair   Disputes over the tendering of helicopter contracts led to the resignation of two senior and prominent Conservative ministers, Michael Heseltine and Leon Brittan; the prime minister herself was accused of deliberately misleading the House (9 January 1986).

2) Jeffrey Archer, deputy chairman of the Conservative Party, resigned over a call-girl scandal (27 October 1986).

3) Conservative MP Patrick Thompson (Norwich North) was accused of selling access to ministers (6 November 1986).

4) Harvey Proctor, MP, was charged with four offences of indecency. The charges related to alleged spanking sessions with minors (March 1987).

5) Sir Jasper Hollom   His resignation was demanded after it was revealed that, as chairman of the Takeover Panel, he had sought to cover up a fraud investigation (27 March 1987).

6) British Telecom Shares   MPs Keith Best (C: Ynys Mon) and Eric Cockerman (C: Ludlow) were found to have made multiple applications for shares in the company, contrary to the rules of the privatisation campaign (2 April 1987).

7) Licensing Act   Three Tory MPs, Roger Gale (Thanet North), James Couchman (Gillingham), and Michael Colvin (Romsey & Waterside), members of the committee studying amendments to the Licensing Act, were found to have direct financial interests in concerns that would benefit from liberalization of licensing hours (8 April 1987).

8) MI5 accusations   Rumour and speculation about the activities of the Security Service. Allegations that rooms used by PM Harold Wilson had been bugged and that the Security Service tried to destabilize the Wilson government (April 1987).

9) The Select Committee on Member's Interests commences investigation into accusations that Sir Peter Emery, MP, and Sir Marcus Fox, MP, failed to disclose interests in accordance with parliamentary resolutions (February 1990).

10) John Browne, MP   Suspended without pay for twenty sitting days for failing to disclose all his relevant outside interests (March 1990).

11) The "Minister of Fun"   David Mellor, MP, resigned after tabloid publicity about his affair with an actress and the propriety of his paid vacations (1992).

12) Tim Yeo, MP, junior environment minister, resigned from cabinet following revelations that he fathered a child outside his marriage (December 1993).

13) Did he or didn't he? Prime Minister Major is further embarrassed by the bizarre marital discord between MP David Ashby and his wife. She claims that he left her for another man; he insists it was all an innocent vacation on the cheap (December 1993).

14) The Countess of Caithness kills herself in despair over rumours that her husband – junior transport minister Lord Caithness – was having an extramarital affair. Caithness immediately resigns (January 1994).

15) Senior party and government officials are implicated in schemes to manipulate council public housing sales in order to gerrymander London constituencies (January 1994).

5 A discussion of these issues under the heading "legislative ethics" may be found in Saxon, "The Scope of Legislative Ethics," 197.

6 Hastings Center, *The Ethics of Legislative Life*, 5–6.

7 Jennings and Callahan, *Representation and Responsibility*.

8 Hastings Center, *The Ethics of Legislative Life*, 13.

9 Hampshire, ed., *Public and Private Morality*, foreword.

10 Thompson, *Political Ethics and Public Office*, 118.

11 Hastings Center, *The Ethics of Legislative Life*, 10.

12 For a discussion of these higher standards see Thompson, *Political Ethics and Public Office*, 123–47.

13 Guttmann and Thompson, "A Theory of Legislative Ethics," 168.

14 Eulau, *Politics, Self, and Society*.

15 Saxon discusses this as a Platonic injunction in "The Scope of Legislative Ethics," 199.

16 Beard and Horn, *Congressional Ethics*, 45.

17 Jennings, "Legislative Ethics and Moral Minimalism," 149–66.

18 Hastings Center, *The Ethics of Legislative Life*, 14–15.

19 Williams, "Conflict of Interest," 137.

20 HMSO, *Questions of Procedure for Ministers*. Extracts from this formerly secret document had been published in *The New Statesman*, 14 February 1986.

21 Doig, *Corruption and Misconduct in Contemporary British Politics*, 222.

22 Mr. Powell appeared before the committee to express his views. See Select Committee on Members' Interests, *First Report*, Session 1986–7, 16 December 1986.

23 The case of John Browne, MP, discussed more fully in chapter 7, may indicate that parliamentary sentiment towards the register may be hardening after the removal of its most outspoken critic.

24 Select Committee on Members' Interests, *Third Report*, Session 1987–8, 1 March 1988, iv.

25 Atkinson and Mancuso, "Edicts and Etiquette," 1–18.

26 In Britain, a National Opinion Poll study showed that 61 per cent of those interviewed agreed that "MPs should demonstrate higher moral standards than the rest of the population." *Political Social Economic Review* 45 (December 1983): 21.

27 Williams, "Conflict of Interest," 135.

28 Radice, Vallance, and Willis, *Member of Parliament*, 33–7.

29 Richards, *Honourable Members*.

30 Clarke, *Regulating the City*, 4.

31 Atkinson and Mancuso, "Do We Need a Code of Conduct for Politicians?" 459–80.

32 Searing, "Rules of the Game in Britain," 256 n19.

33 For a complete listing of these inquiries see Butler and Butler, *British Political Facts*.

34 *The Corrupt and Illegal Practices Prevention Act* 1883; *The Public Bodies Corrupt Practices Act* 1889; *The Prevention of Corruption Act* 1906; *The Prevention of Corruption Act* 1916.

35 Harry Greenway, MP, was charged with a number of offences closely related to corruption in September 1991. The case made it to court a year later, but the judge dismissed it on the grounds of insufficient evidence. In his ruling, he made it clear that the case was not being excused on the grounds of parliamentary privilege. If there had been enough evidence to proceed, the case would have been the first time a member of parliament had been considered a public officer under common law.

36 Drewry, "Corruption: The Salmon Report," 87–91.

37 Zellick, "Bribery of Members of Parliament and the Criminal Law," 53.

38 Bolton, ed., *Erskine May's Parliamentary Practice*, 443.

39 Peters and Welch, "The Effects of Charges of Corruption."

40 Ibid., 697.

41 Gwyn, "The Nature and Decline of Corrupt Election Expenditure in 19th Century Britain," 391–403.

42 Brooks, "Apologies for Political Corruption," 391–403.

43 Peters and Welch, "The Effects of Charges of Corruption," 699.

44 Bolton, ed., *Erskine May's Parliamentary Practice*, 134.

45 Doig, "The Dynamics of Scandals in British Politics."

46 Adonis, *Parliament Today*, 60–3.

47 Jackson, *Rebels and Whips*, 42. One "dirt" that Jackson was shown stated that a Tory member, while drunk in the Members' Bar, called the Tory prime minister a "bloody fool."

48 Ibid., 43.

49 Beer, *Modern British Politics*, ch. 3.

50 Mitchell, "Consulting the Workers," 9–13. Surveying the British House of Commons, the author found that more MPs selected as their primary role "contribution to the national debate" than any of a number of other options, including "local ombudsman" and "constituency welfare officer."

51 Cain, Ferejohn, and Fiorina, *The Personal Vote*, 214.

52 For a discussion of these institutional constraints in a comparative context see Atkinson and Mancuso, "Conflict of Interest in Britain and the United States," 471–93.

53 Cain, Ferejohn, and Fiorina, *The Personal Vote*, 215.

54 Noel-Baker, "The Grey Zone," 88.

55 Hastings Center, *The Ethics of Legislative Life*, 32.

56 Thompson, *Political Ethics and Public Office*, 164.

57 Williams, "Conflict of Interest," 109.

58 Ibid., 110.

59 Doig, *Corruption and Misconduct in Contemporary British Politics*, 208.

60 Hastings Center, *The Ethics of Legislative Life*, 56–7.

CHAPTER TWO

1 Peters and Welch, "Attitudes of U.S. State Legislators toward Political Corruption," 451.

2 Mancuso, "Attitudes of Canadian Legislators toward Political Corruption."

3 The House of Lords is not within the scope of this study. While Lords are public office holders, they are neither elected nor representatives, and it is only to legislators who fill both roles that this discussion pertains.

4 Masculine pronouns have been used occasionally to refer to MPs of unspecified gender throughout this book because of the extreme rarity of female MPs. The reality is that such usage is almost never inaccurate (p < .05).

5 While the value '4' was not explicitly denoted as a neutral position on the Likert scales used in the interviews, the number of MPs who expressed uncertainty about a question by assigning it a 4 suggests that this interpretation was quite common.

6 Attitudinal studies that have made use of this format include Beard and Horn, *Congressional Ethics*; Peters and Welch, "Attitudes of U.S. State Legislators towards Political Corruption"; and Atkinson and Mancuso, "Do We Need a Code of Conduct for Politicians?"

7 In the discussion that follows, unless otherwise specified, the designation "corrupt" will be used to indicate a score of 1, 2, or 3; "not corrupt" indicates a score of 5, 6, or 7. The percentages reported are based on the total number of MPs who gave a score for the situation. In some cases, some members refused to reduce their answer to a numeric value; others objected to the very posing of the question, on the grounds that such activity was inconceivable, and thus refused even to consider the question.

8   Fenno, *Home Style*; Radice, Vallance, and Willis, *Member of Parliament*. Cain, Ferejohn, and Fiorina, *The Personal Vote*; Searing, *Westminster's World*.

9   Radice, Vallance, and Willis, *Member of Parliament*, 108.

10 The best-known case of this type involved Gordon Bagier and the Greek Junta in 1968.

11 The mean KNIGHT score given by Conservative respondents was 5.1; that of Labour members was 1.9. This difference was significant at $p < .001$. Cross-tabulation of party and KNIGHT yielded $\lambda = .68$, indicating that party affiliation alone was responsible for more than two-thirds of the variance on KNIGHT.

12 The median score for the scenarios could also be used to discriminate between high and low tolerance for each item. The median, however, suffers from several disadvantages: 1) respondents whose score equalled the median on an item cannot be clearly assigned a high or a low tolerance – this would tend to complicate further the construction of the typology by introducing neutral points; 2) because of the grouping of responses, and the tendency for respondents to use the extreme scores of 1 and 7 and the neutral 4 far more than the intermediate grades, the actual median of many of the items is at one extreme or the other, which hinders using it as a point of discrimination. Additionally, with respect to most of the scenarios, the median and mean are sufficiently close as to divide the respondents between low and high tolerance in the same way.

13 Factor analysis, which assumes that observed variables are linear combinations of some underlying factors, is an alternative procedure for aggregating variables. However, given that only nine variables were at issue in this case, additive scales based on conceptual distinctions and statistically significant correlations were considered preferable. This technique has been previously used in Atkinson and Mancuso, "Do We Need a Code of Conduct for Politicians?"

14 The use of orthogonal axes is not meant to suggest that CONFLICT and SERVICE are completely independent of one another (their Pearson correlation coefficient of .41 is significant at $p < .01$). In fact, this level of correlation is to be expected, given that both scales are measuring similar aggregate attitudes.

15 Others have made use of a typology to organize and report their findings. Most notable in the British context is Searing's *Westminster's World*. In his book, Searing uses a typology to illustrate the various roles MPs play in an attempt to understand their goals, careers, and impact on public policy.

CHAPTER THREE

1   Throughout this chapter (and the three that follow), unattributed quotations should, unless otherwise indicated, be understood to be drawn

from the interview comments offered by respondents who have been classified as Puritans (or as the respective types discussed subsequently).

2 Atkinson and Mancuso, "Do We Need a Code of Conduct for Politicians?" Peters and Welch, "Attitudes of U.S. State Legislators towards Political Corruption"; Beard and Horn, *Congressional Ethics.*

3 Atkinson and Mancuso, "Do We Need a Code of Conduct for Politicians?" The New Democratic Party (NDP) is in many ways the closest Canadian equivalent to the British Labour Party. While the NDP is clearly a third party, they share many socialist principles and identifications with Labour and have claimed for themselves the left end of the ideological spectrum, against Canada's right-wing Progressive Conservative Party and moderate Liberal Party.

4 The term "wet" was adopted by Margaret Thatcher as a pejorative description of those within in her own party who favoured a more patrician version of Toryism than her neo-Conservative ideology.

5 Atkinson and Mancuso, "Do We Need a Code of Conduct for Politicians?" Peters and Welch, "Attitudes of U.S. State Legislators towards Political Corruption."

6 Johnston, "The Cultural Rules of Politics," 24.

7 To examine this hypothesis, constituencies in the regions North, Northeast, Yorkshire & Humberside, Scotland, and Wales were considered to be 'northern,' while those in the regions Southwest, Southeast, East Anglia, and the East and West Midlands were considered to be 'southern.'

8 Constituencies were classified along a seven-point scale as Very Rural (1), Rural, Mainly Rural, Mixed, Mainly Urban, Very Urban, or Inner City (7). These categories were taken from the *British Journal of Political Science* constituency classifications.

9 One personal characteristic, which unfortunately cannot be analysed in depth, is gender. Peters and Welch's study of American legislators showed gender to be a significant indicator of attitudes towards political corruption: female legislators were less tolerant than their male colleagues. In the Canadian study by Atkinson and Mancuso, there were too few women in the sample to make any conclusive statements about tolerance differences between the sexes. This is a common problem for legislative studies that attempt to discern gender differences on various issues. With women such a rarity in the British House of Commons (only 4 per cent of all MPs at the time this study was undertaken), it remains virtually impossible to assess the effect of gender on political attitudes. What is of interest to this particular study is that, of the seven women interviewed, four fell into the Puritan category. This would have been a trend to investigate had more female MPs participated in the survey.

10 In an attempt to analyse the age distribution of the sample more closely, the respondents were divided into age cohorts of ten years (30–39,

40–49, etc.). The distribution of Puritans among the cohorts, however, was not significantly different from that of the sample.

11 Respondents who indicated adherence to an organized religion were asked to estimate how often they attended the services at their church or synagogue. Responses were grouped into four categories: frequently (about once per week), occasionally (about once per month), infrequently (about once to a few times per year), and never.

12 A comparative discussion of this issue may be found in Atkinson and Mancuso, "Managing Legislative Conflict of Interest in Britain and the United States."

13 British MPs are constitutionally precluded from voluntary resignation. In fact, except at the dissolution of Parliament, members may only vacate their seats if they die, are elevated to the peerage, are expelled from the House, or are legally disqualified from sitting in the House. The last method covers MPs who accept an "office of profit" from the Crown, such as a judgeship. Nevertheless, from time to time MPs do wish to quit between elections, and thus the chancellor of the exchequer has maintained two Crown sinecures (now only nominally "offices of profit" – neither entails any income or duties whatsoever) to permit what amounts to voluntary retirement. MPs seeking to leave do not resign, they apply for the position of Crown steward and bailiff of the three Chiltern Hundreds of Stoke, Desborough, and Burnham (or the same position for the Manor of Northstead). This appointment (no application has been refused since 1775) has no effect other than disqualifying the applicant from serving in the House, and thus ending membership. For a detailed history of this procedure see House of Commons Public Information Office, *Factsheet No. 34.*

14 Chapter 7 discusses this trend in detail.

15 As cited in the report of the Salmon Commission.

CHAPTER FIVE

1 Roth's 1972 book described the business and financial holding of MPs. It was considered to be a forerunner of the Register of Members' Interests.

CHAPTER SEVEN

1 Anthony King, "The Rise of the Career Politician in Britain."

2 Cain, "Constituency Service and Member Independence."

3 According to the 1990 Register of Member's Interests, 150 of the 650 MPs (23 per cent) describe themselves as parliamentary consultants or advisers to outside clients. A total of 460 corporate directorships are also declared in the register.

4 Jennings, "Legislative Ethics and Moral Minimalism," 197.
5 House of Commons, Select Committee on Members' Interests, Minutes of Evidence, Tuesday, 5 July 1988.
6 Ibid., 46.
7 The Ethics Reform Act, 1989.
8 King, "The Rise of the Career Politician."
9 Cain, "Constituency Service and Member Independence."
10 The current formula for establishing members' pay was adopted in July 1983. It provided for increases for the following four years to bring members' salaries to £18,500 in 1987, and enabled subsequent increases to be linked to future raises to civil servants of the same pay scale. These increases have been approved at the beginning of each new Parliament. Thus, as of January 1992, the salary for an MP was £30,854. For complete information see Review Body on Top Salaries, Report No. 32, July 1992.
11 Radice, Vallance, and Willis, *Member of Parliament*, 98.
12 Ibid., 99.
13 Mitchell, "Consulting the Workers," 9–13. Of the MPs surveyed, 77 per cent had a secretary in Westminster and 22 per cent had their own private secretary elsewhere, normally in a business, company, firm, or practice with which the MP was associated.
14 Members do, however, receive free stationery, telephone, and postage services for use in Westminster.
15 This allowance (£40,380, April 1993) is intended to cover such expenses as secretarial assistance, general office costs, and the employment of research assistants.
16 Mitchell, "Consulting the Workers," 12.
17 MPs whose constituencies were outside London could claim up to £10,958.
18 See also Select Committee on Members' Interests, Minutes of Evidence, Tuesday, 24 May 1988, 3. The Rt-Hon. Cranley Onslow suggested this abuse among various others of the pass system.
19 Ibid., Tuesday, 24 May 1988, 7.
20 Ibid., 9.
21 The group surveyed nearly 350 organizations drawn from a wide range of bodies, including the Royal Horticultural Society, Gay Liberation Front, Aims of Industry, Open Spaces Society, and other interest and cause groups. Comments from the various groups were compiled by Michael Rush, University of Exeter, in March 1987. The complete results of the study can be found in Michael Rush, ed., *Parliament and Pressure Politics*.
22 Only 7 per cent of the organizations admitted to paying an MP a direct retainer; another 11 per cent paid for some secretarial or research assistance for an MP. These figures, taken from a memorandum submitted

by Michael Rush et al. to the Select Committee on Members' Interests (Minutes of Evidence, Tuesday, 14 June 1988), seem somewhat low given the large number of MPS who have declared parliamentary consultancies in the Register of Members' Interests (171). Unfortunately, register declarations do not currently have to specify whether such consultancies are remunerated or voluntary, or the amount of remuneration.

23 C. Grantham offers a comprehensive look at parliamentary consultants in "Parliament and Political Consultants."

24 Although it was first alleged in May 1987 that Browne was not being complete in his declarations, it was not until two years later that the select committee began investigation of the matter.

25 In July 1994 two Conservative MPS, David Tredinnick and Graham Riddick, were accused by the *Sunday Times* of agreeing to put questions to Parliament in return for money. Prime Minister Major responded by suspending the two politicians from their duties as parliamentary private secretaries pending the results of an inquiry by House of Commons officials. This incident may prompt reconsideration of this reform proposal.

26 Select Committee on Members' Interests, *First Report*, Session 1991–2, 14.

27 For an excellent discussion of Canada's new lobbyist legislation see Stark, "'Political-Discourse' Analysis and the Debate over Canada's Lobbying Legislation."

28 House of Commons, Select Committee on Members' Interests, Minutes of Evidence, Tuesday, 5 July 1988, 47.

29 Select Committee of Members' Interests, *First Report*, Session 1990–1, xii.

30 Ibid., Tuesday, 29 November 1988, 126.

31 Ibid., Tuesday, 13 December 1988, 128–9.

32 A draft copy of the guide was provided by R.B. Sands, Registrar of Members' Interests, 2 September 1993.

33 Select Committee on Members' Interests, *First Report*, Session 1991–2, xxiv.

34 Ibid., xxiii.

35 Cited in Doig, "Self Discipline and the British House of Commons," 248–67.

CONCLUSION

1 D.N. Campbell-Savours, House of Commons, *Debates*, 17 December 1985.

Bibliography

Adonis, Andrew. *Parliament Today*, 2nd ed. Manchester: Manchester University Press 1993

Atkinson, Michael, and Maureen Mancuso. "Do We Need a Code of Conduct for Politicians: The Search for an Elite Political Culture of Corruption." *Canadian Journal of Political Science* 28, 3 (1985)

– "MP's Vice: Is a Code of Conduct Needed?" in Robert J. Jackson et al., eds., *Contemporary Canadian Politics*. Scarborough: Prentice-Hall 1987

– "Conflict of Interest in Britain and the United States: An Institutional Argument." *Legislative Studies Quarterly* 16 (November 1991)

– "Edicts and Etiquette: Regulating Conflict of Interest in Congress and the House of Commons." *Corruption and Reform* 7, 1 (1992)

Bailey, F. G. *Gifts and Poison: The Politics of Reputation*. Oxford: Blackwell 1971

Barber, James David. *The Lawmakers: Recruitment and Adaptation to Legislative Life*. New Haven: Yale University Press 1965

Barker, Anthony, and Michael Rush. *The MP and his Information*. London: Allen & Unwin 1970

Beard, Edmund, and Stephen Horn. *Congressional Ethics: The View from the House*. Washington: Brookings Institution 1975

Beer, Samuel. "The Representation of Interests in British Government: Historical Background." *American Political Science Review* 51 (1957), 613–50

– *Modern British Politics*. New York: Norton 1982

Bogdanor, Vernon, ed. *Representatives of the People? Parliamentarians and Constituents in Western Democracies*. Aldershot: Gower 1985

Boissevain, Jeremy. *Friends of Friends: Networks, Manipulators, and Coalitions*. Oxford: Blackwell 1974

Bolton, C.J., ed. *Erskine May's Parliamentary Practice*, 21st ed. London: Butterworths 1989

Bottomore, T.B. *Elites and Society*. New York: Basic Books 1965

Boulton, C.J. "The Conduct of Members." *The Table* 46 (1978)

Bourne, J. M. *Patronage and Society in Nineteenth-Century England*. London: Edward Arnold 1986

Brennan, Geoffrey, and James M. Buchanan. *The Reason of Rules: Constitutional Political Economy*. Cambridge: Cambridge University Press 1985

Bridge, Ann. *Permission to Resign*. London: Sidgwick and Jackson 1971

Brooks, Robert C. "Apologies for Political Corruption," in Arnold Heidenheimer, ed., *Political Corruption: Readings in Comparative Analysis*. New York: Holt, Rinehart and Winston 1970

Butler, David, and Gareth Butler. *British Political Facts*, 6th ed. London: Macmillan 1986

Cain, Bruce, John Ferejohn, and Morris Fiorina. "A House Is Not a Home: British MPs in Their Constituencies." *Legislative Studies Quarterly* 4 (1979)

– *The Personal Vote: Constituency Service and Electoral Independence*. Cambridge: Harvard University Press 1987

Cain, Bruce. "Constituency Service and Member Independence: An Anglo-American Comparison," in Harold D. Clarke and Moshe M. Czudnowski, eds., *Political Elites in Anglo-American Democracies*. Dekalb: Northern Illinois University Press 1987

Chibnall, Steven, and Peter Saunders. "Worlds Apart: Notes on the Social Reality of Corruption." *British Journal of Sociology* 28, 2 (June 1977)

Clapham, C., ed. *Private Patronage and Public Power: Political Clientelism in the Modern State*. London: Frances Pinter 1982

Clarke, Harold, and Moshe M. Czudnowski, eds. *Political Elties in Anglo-American Democracies*. DeKalb: Northern Illinois University Press 1987

Clarke, Michael. *Fallen Idols: Elites and the Search for the Acceptable Face of Capitalism*. London: Junction Books 1981

– *Regulating the City: Competition, Scandal and Reform*. Milton Keynes: Open University Press 1986

–, ed. *Corruption: Causes, Consequence and Control*. London: Frances Pinter 1983

Cullen, Tom. *Maundy Gregory, Purveyor of Honours*. London: Bodley Head 1974

Dahl, Robert. *Who Governs*. New Haven: Yale University Press 1961

Davies, Malcolm. *Politics of Pressure: The Art of Lobbying*. London: BBC 1985

Dexter, Lewis Anthony. *Elite and Specialized Interviewing*. Evanston: Northwestern University Press 1970

Doig, Alan. "Self-Discipline and the British House of Commons: The Poulson Affair in a Parliamentary Perspective." *Parliamentary Affairs* 32 (1979)

– "Watergate, Poulson and the Reform of Standards of Conduct." *Parliamentary Affairs* 36 (1983)

– *Corruption and Misconduct in Contemporary British Politics*. Harmondsworth: Penguin 1984

– "The Political Culture of Corruption: A Case Study of Two Regions." Paper presented to the International Political Science Association, Paris, 1985

- "The Dynamics of Scandals in British Politics." Paper delivered to the Political Science Association, Plymouth, April 1988

Douglas, Jack D., and John M. Johnson. *Official Deviance: Readings in Malfeasance, Misfeasance, and other Forms of Corruption.* Philadelphia: J.B. Lippincott 1987

Douglas, Paul. *Ethics in Government.* Cambridge: Harvard University Press 1952

Drewry, Gavin. "Corruption: The Salmon Report." *Political Quarterly* 48 (1977)

Edinger, Lewis J., and Donald Searing. "Social Background in Elite Analysis." *American Political Science Review* (1967)

Eisenstadt, A.S., A. Hoogenboom, and H.L. Trefousse, eds. *Before Watergate: Problems of Corruption in American Society.* New York: Brooklyn College Press 1978

Eulau, Heinz. *Politics, Self, and Society.* Cambridge: Harvard University Press 1986

- et al. "The Role of the Representative: Some Empirical Observations on the Theory of Edmund Burke." *American Political Science Review* (1959)

- and John C. Wahlke. *The Politics of Representation.* Beverly Hills: Sage Publications 1978

Fenno, Richard F. *Home Style.* Glenview, Ill.: Scott Foresman 1978

Finer, Samuel E. "Patronage and the Public Service: Jeffersonian Bureaucracy and the British Tradition." *Public Administration* 30 (1952)

- *Anonymous Empire: A Study of the Lobby in Great Britain.* London: Pall Mall Press 1969

Fishbein, Martin, ed. *Readings in Attitudes: Theory and Measurement.* New York: Wiley 1967

Fitzwalter, Ray, and David Taylor. *Web of Corruption.* London: Granada 1981

Fleishman, Joel L., Lance Liebman, and Mark Moore, eds. *Public Duties: The Moral Obligations of Government Officials.* Cambridge: Harvard University Press 1981

Friedrick, Carl. "Political Pathology." *Political Quarterly* 37 (Jan.–March 1966)

- *The Pathology of Politics: Violence, Betrayal, Corruption, Secrecy and Propaganda.* New York: Harper and Row 1972

Getz, Robert. *The Conflict of Interest Issue.* Princeton: Van Nostrand 1966

Grantham, C. "Parliament and Political Consultants." *Parliamentary Affairs* 42 (Oct. 1989)

Greenstein, Fred. *Personality and Politics.* Chicago: Markham 1969

Guttmann, Amy, and Dennis Thompson. "A Theory of Legislative Ethics," in Bruce Jennings and Daniel Callahan, eds. *Representation and Responsibility.* New York: Plenum Press 1985

Gwyn, William B. "The Nature and Decline of Corrupt Election Expenditures in 19th Century Britain," in Arnold Heidenheimer, ed., *Political Corruption: Readings in Comparative Analysis.* New York: Holt, Rinehart and Winston 1970

Hamilton, Willie. "Members and Outside Interests." *The Parliamentarian* 56–7 (1975–6)

Hampshire, Stuart, ed. *Public and Private Morality*. Cambridge: Cambridge University Press 1978

Hastings Center, The. *The Ethics of Legislative Life*. New York: The Hastings Center: Institute of Society, Ethics and the Life Sciences 1985

Heidenheimer, Arnold J. *Political Corruption: Readings in Comparative Analysis*. New York: Holt, Rinehart and Winston 1970

– Michael Johnston, and Victor LeVine. *Political Corruption: A Handbook*. New Brunswick, NJ: Transaction Publishers 1989

Helmore, Leonard Mervyn. *Corrupt and Illegal Practices*. London: Routledge & Kegan Paul 1967

Houghton, Rt. Hon. Douglas. "The Financial Interests of Members of Parliament." *The Parliamentarian* 55 (1974)

House of Commons Public Information Office. *Factsheet No. 34: The Chiltern Hundreds*. 1987

Hurstfield, Joel. "Political Corruption in Modern England: The Historian's Problem." *History* 52 (Feb. 1967)

Inglis, Brian. *Private Conscience – Public Morality*. London: André Deutsch 1964

Inglehart, Ronald. *Culture Shift*. Princeton, NJ: Princeton University Press 1990

Jackson, Robert J. *Rebels and Whips*. Toronto: Macmillan 1968

Jennings, Bruce. "Legislative Ethics and Moral Minimalism," in Bruce Jennings and Daniel Callahan, eds., *Representation and Responsibility*. New York: Plenum Press 1985

– and Daniel Callahan, eds. *Representation and Responsibility: Exploring Legislative Ethics*. New York: Plenum Press 1985

Johnston, Michael. *Political Corruption and Public Policy in America*. Monterey, Cal.: Brooks-Cole 1982

– "Social Conceptions of Right and Wrong in Britain: Exploring Subjective Definitions of Corruption." Paper prepared for the XII World Congress of the International Political Science Association, Paris (July 1985)

– "The Political Consequences of Corruption: A Reassessment." *Comparative Politics* 18 4 (July 1986)

– "Right and Wrong in British Politics: Fits of Morality in Comparative Perspective." *Polity* (Fall 1991)

– and Douglas Wood. "Right and Wrong in Public and Private Life," in Roger Jewell and Sharon Witherspoon, eds. *British Social Attitudes: The 1985 Report*. London: Gower 1985

– "The Cultural Rules of Politics: Right and Wrong in Great Britain." Unpublished paper, fall 1988

Jones, G.W. "Corruption and the Public Interest." *New Society* 20 (Sept. 1973)

Judge, David. "British Representation Theories and Parliamentary Specialization." *Parliamentary Affairs*. 33 (1980)

Kavanagh, Dennis. "The Deferential English: A Comparative Critique." *Government and Opposition* 6, 3 (1971)

King, Anthony. "The Rise of the Career Politician in Britain and Its Conse-
quences." *British Journal of Political Science* 2 (1981)
– "Sex, Money and Power: Political Scandals in Great Britain and the United
States." *Essex Papers in Politics and Government* 14 (June 1984)
Linklater, Magnus, and David Leigh. *Not with Honour: The Inside Story of the
Westland Scandal*. London: Sphere Books 1986
Mancuso, Maureen. "Attitudes of Canadian Legislators toward Political Cor-
ruption: An Empirical Analysis." MA thesis, Carleton University 1984
Marshall, Geoffrey. *Constitutional Conventions: The Rules and Forms of Political
Accountability*. Oxford: Clarendon Press 1984
Martin, James Stewart. *All Honourable Men*. New York: Little Brown 1950
Matthews, Donald. *The Social Backgrounds of Political Decision-Makers*. New York:
Doubleday 1954
McCabe, Joseph. *The Taint in Politics: A Study in the Evolution of Parliamentary
Corruption*. London: Grant Richards 1920
McGill, Barry. "Conflicts of Interests: The English Experience 1782–1914."
Western Political Quarterly 12 (1959)
Mitchell, Austin. "Consulting the Workers on Their Job." *The Parliamentarian*
no. 66 (Jan. 1985)
Moodie, Graeme C. "On Political Scandals and Corruption." *Government and
Opposition* 15, 2 (1980)
Mueller, William. *The Kept Men*. Harvester Press 1977
Nevitte, Neil, and Roger Gibbins. *New Elites in Old States: Ideologies in the Anglo-
American Democracies*. Toronto: Oxford University Press 1990
Newman, Frank. "Reflections on Money and Party Politics in Britain." *Parlia-
mentary Affairs* 10 (1956–7)
Noel-Baker, Francis. "The Grey Zone." *Parliamentary Affairs* 15 (1961)
Noonan, John T. Jr. *Bribes*. New York: Macmillan 1984
O'Leary, Cornelius. *Elimination of Corrupt Practices in British Elections 1868–
1911*. Oxford: Oxford University Press 1962
Parry, Geraint. *Political Elites*. New York: Frederick A. Praeger 1969
Patterson, Samuel. "The British House of Commons as a Focus for Political
Research." *British Journal of Political Science* 3 (1973–4)
– "Understanding the British Parliament." *Political Studies*. 37 (1989)
Peters. John G., and Susan Welch. "Attitudes of U.S. State Legislators towards
Political Corruption: Some Preliminary Findings." *Legislative Studies Quar-
terly* 2, 4 (Nov. 1977)
– "Political Corruption in America: The Search for Definitions and a Theory:
If Political Corruption Is in the Mainstream of American Politics, Why Is it
Not in the Mainstream of Political Research?" *American Political Science Review*
72 (1978)
– "The Effects of Charges of Corruption on Voting Behavior in Congressional
Elections." *American Political Science Review* 74 (1980)

Pinto-Duschinsky, Michael. "The Survival of Political Corruption in Advanced Democracies." Paper delivered at 10th World Congress of the International Political Science Association, Edinburgh (August 1976)
– "Corruption in Britain: The Royal Commission on Standards of Conduct in Public Life." *Political Studies.* 25, 2 (1977)
– "Political Corruption in Britain." Paper prepared for the European Consortium for Political Research, Workshops on Political Corruption, Freiburg (March 1983)
Pitkin, Hanna. *The Concept of Representation.* Berkeley: University of California Press 1967
Platt, D.C.M. "The Commercial and Industrial Interests of Ministers of the Crown." *Political Studies* 11 (1961)
Putnam, Robert D. *The Beliefs of Politicians.* New Haven: Yale University Press 1973
– *The Comparative Study of Political Elites.* Englewood Cliffs, NJ: Prentice-Hall 1976
Questions of Procedure for Ministers. London: HMSD 1992
Radice, Lisanne, Elizabeth Vallance, and Virginia Willis. *Member of Parliament: The Job of a Backbencher.* London: Macmillan 1987
Register of Members' Interests on 12th January 1987. HC 155. London: HMSO 1987
Register of Members' Interests on 1st December 1992. HC 325. London: HMSO 1992
Review Body on Top Salaries. *Report No. 32: Review of the House of Commons Office Costs Allowance.* Cm 1943. London: HMSO 1992
Richards, P. G. *Honourable Members: A Study of the British Backbenchers.* London: Faber and Faber 1959
Rockman, Bert A. *Studying Elite Political Culture: Problems in Design and Interpretation.* Pittsburgh: University Centre for International Studies 1976
Roth, Andrew. *The Business Background of MPs.* London: Parliamentary Profile Services 1972
Royal Commission on the Standards of Conduct in Public Life. London: HMSD 1976
Rundiquest, Barry, Gerald Storm, and John G. Peters. "Corrupt Politicians and Their Electoral Support – Some Experiment Observations." *American Political Science Review* 71 (Sept. 1980)
Rush, Michael, ed. *Parliament and Pressure Politics.* Oxford: Clarendon Press 1990
Saxon, John. "The Scope of Legislative Ethics," in Bruce Jennings and Daniel Callahan, eds., *Representation and Responsibility.* New York: Plenum Press 1985
Schwartz, Nancy L. *The Blue Guitar: Political Representation and Community.* Chicago: University of Chicago Press 1980
Searing, Donald D. "The Comparative Study of Elite Socialization." *Comparative Political Studies* 1 (1969)
– "Measuring Politician's Values: Administration and Assessment of a Rating Technique in the British House of Commons." *American Political Science Review* 72 (March 1978)

– "Rules of the Game in Britain: Can the Politicians Be Trusted?" *American Political Science Review* 76 (June 1982)
– "The Role of the Good Constituency Member and the Practice of Representation in Great Britain." *Journal of Politics* 47 (Feb. 1985)
– *Westminster's World: Understanding Political Roles.* Cambridge: Harvard University Press 1994
Searle, G.R. *Corruption in British Politics, 1895–1930.* Oxford: Oxford Univeristy Press 1987
Select Committee on Members' Interests. *First Report,* HC 135, Session 1989–90. London: HMSO 1990
– *Second Report,* HC 506, Session 1989–90. London: HMSO 1990
– *Third Report,* HC 561, Session 1989–90. London: HMSO 1990
– *Minutes of Evidence: Parliamentary Lobbying,* HC 389–i, Session 1989–90. London: HMSO 1990
– *First Report,* HC 108, Session 1990–1. London: HMSO 1991
– *Third Report: Parliamentary Lobbying,* HC 586, Session 1990–1. London: HMSO 1991
– *First Report: Registration and Declaration of Members' Financial Interests,* HC 326, Session 1991–2. London: HMSO 1992
– *First Report,* HC 383, Session 1992–3. London: HMSO 1993
– *Second Report,* HC 469, Session 1992–3. London: HMSO 1993
Small, Joseph. "Political Ethics: A View of the Leadership." *American Behavioral Scientist* 19, 5 (1976)
Stark, Andrew. "Political-Discourse" Analysis and the Debate over Canada's Lobbying Legislation." *Canadian Journal of Political Science* 35, 3 (1992)
Thompson, Dennis F. *Political Ethics and Public Office.* Cambridge: Harvard University Press 1987
Tompkinson, Martin, and Michael Gillard. *Nothing to Declare.* London: John Calder 1980
Vose, Clement. "Conflict of Interest." *International Encyclopedia of the Social Sciences,* vol. 3, 242
Wakefield, Susan. "Ethics and the Public Service: A Case for Individual Responsibility." *Public Administration Review* 6 (Nov./Dec. 1976)
Walker, John. *The Queen Has Been Pleased: The British Honours System at Work.* London: Seclar and Warburg 1986
Willey, F.H. "The Declaration and Registration of Members Interests." *The Parliamentarian* 56–7 (1975–6)
Williams, Sandra. "The Conflict of Interest Issue and the British House of Commons: A Practical Problem and a Conceptual Conundrum." PhD thesis, University of London 1982
– "Conflict of Interest: The Experience of the American Congress." *The Parliamentarian* 64, 3 (1983)
– "Observations on Conflict of Interest: A View through the Parliamentary Telescope." *Public Administration Bulletin* no. 44 (April 1984)

– *Conflict of Interest: The Ethical Dilemma in Politics.* London: Gower Publishing 1985

Wilson, Colin, and Donald Seaman. *Scandal: An Encyclopedia.* London: Weidenfeld and Nicolson 1986

Wilson, James. "Corruption Is Not Always Scandalous." *New York Times Magazine* (April 1968)

Winnifrith, C.B. "Members' Interests." *The Table* 43 (1975)

Wolfinger, Raymond. "Why Political Machines Have Not Withered Away and Other Revisionist Thoughts." *Journal of Politics* 34 (May 1972)

Young, Wayland. *The Profumo Affair: Aspects of Conservatism.* Harmondsworth: Penguin 1963

Zellick, Graham. "The Imprisonment of Members of Parliament." *Public Law* (1977)

– "The Conduct of Members of Parliament." *Public Law* (1978)

– "Bribery of Members of Parliament and the Criminal Law." *Public Law* (1979)

Index

DATE DUE
